Peppermint Twist

Also by John Johnson, Jr.

Blood Brothers:
The Inside Story of the Menendez Murders
(with Ron Soble)

Also by Joel Selvin

Ricky Nelson: Idol for a Generation
Monterey Pop (with Jim Marshall)
Summer of Love
Photopass: The Rock Photography of Randy Bachman
San Francisco: The Musical History Tour
For the Record: Sly and the Family Stone
Treasures of the Hard Rock Café (with Paul Grushkin)
Smart Ass: The Music Journalism of Joel Selvin
Red: My Uncensored Life in Rock (with Sammy Hagar)

The Mob, the Music, and the Most Famous Dance Club of the '60s

Thomas Dunne Books
St. Martin's Press
New York

Peppermint Twist

John Johnson, Jr.
and Joel Selvin
with Dick Cami

THOMAS DUNNE BOOKS.

An imprint of St. Martin's Press.

PEPPERMINT TWIST: THE MOB, THE MUSIC, AND THE MOST FAMOUS
DANCE CLUB OF THE '60S. Copyright © 2012 by John Johnson, Jr.,
and Joel Selvin. All rights reserved. Printed in the United
States of America. For information, address St. Martin's
Press, 175 Fifth Avenue, New York, N.Y. 10010.

www.thomasdunnebooks.com

www.stmartins.com

Design by Kathryn Parise

ISBN 978-0-312-58178-7 (hardcover)

ISNB 978-1-250-01353-8 (e-book)

First Edition: November 2012

10 9 8 7 6 5 4 3 2 1

Authors' Note

This is a true story, though a handful names have been changed.

Contents

A two-toned Cadillac purred to a stop on a sleazy block of Manhattan's West 45th Street. Out climbed a distinguished-looking, gray-haired man. He negotiated the litter-strewn sidewalk, threaded his way through a scattering of post-teen wenches in black leather jackets and boys with duck-tailed haircuts. For a moment, he stared dubiously at a hole-in-the-wall honky-tonk called the Peppermint Lounge, then rushed back to the waiting limousine burbling, "This is the place!" Quickly, the socialites, two men and three women got out and gingerly followed their scout past the long, noisy bar into the back room. Through the low-level light, furred over by cigarette smoke, they could make out a few guitar-slapping, foot-waggling singers, all yelling unintelligible words against the driving, torrential blast of rock 'n' roll music. On the dance floor, a tight tangle of people shuddered and shook through a series of hip-tossing, pelvis-thrusting, arm-swinging gyrations that go by the name of "The Twist." Everything Moves. The Peppermint Lounge is the latest shrine for Manhattan's pleasure-sated café society. Scattered in the swarm of habitués, like rhinestones in a bowl of raisins, the interlopers watch with delighted approval as the dancers squirm and wrench.

—*Time* magazine, Friday, October 20, 1961

Peppermint Twist

Ground Zero

Dick Cami was lounging by the pool at the Fontainebleau Hotel in Miami Beach mid-October 1961 when he got the call from New York. Something about celebrities, socialites, and other A-listers crowding into the off-Broadway dive that his father-in-law and his boys owned on West 45th Street.

The teen dance club didn't have a phone. The boys were smart enough not to have one because that way it couldn't be tapped. When Dick called back, he had to dial a pay phone that rang in the Knickerbocker Hotel lobby, which was right outside the club's back door. He was not surprised to hear a flirtatious woman's voice come on the line. The Knickerbocker these days rented as many rooms by the hour as they did to the luckless out-of-towners, the unemployed, and those only a week away from living on the streets.

"Hi, honey," Cami said. "Do me a favor and stick your head in the door behind you, the one to the Peppermint Lounge, and ask for Louie or Sam."

The girl hesitated. "There's a big guy blocking the door."

"Tell him to come to the phone—please."

A moment later, the gruff voice of the Terrible Turk came on the line.

"Who is it?"

"Turk, it's me, Dick."

"Dickie, holy shit, you can't believe what's happening here."

The Turk was a former professional wrestler with a shaved head and a body that looked like it'd been stamped out on a truck assembly line. In a tuxedo, he looked official, and officially dangerous.

"It's fucking unbelievable, I tell you. They put me on the back door because we got so many people trying to sneak in through the fucking hotel lobby. You guys coming up or what?"

"Soon," Dick said. "Get me Louie, will you?"

"Sure, hold on. He's on the other side, giving an interview to a newspaper guy."

Holy shit, Cami thought. *Louie Lombardi giving an interview? About what? Breaking arms? Making book? Buying swag? Jesus, that's all we need.*

Finally, Louie's voice came on the phone. "You guys don't want to listen to me? I'm telling you, this joint's exploding. You know who I was just looking at?"

"Who?"

"Greta Garbo. That broad that wants to be left alone."

This was too much for Cami, who laughed and said, "Greta Garbo? She doesn't go anywhere; it must be a look-alike."

"Look-alike my ass," Louie said. "This broad is Greta-fucking-Garbo, I'm telling you. And she's here tonight. You guys are the only ones that ain't here."

Dick looked up to see his father-in-law coming into the beach cabana. Dressed immaculately in a black silk shirt, custom ivory trousers, alligator belt, and matching shoes, Johnny Biello created a barely noticeable ripple of excitement among the pool boys and sunbathers. They couldn't know that he was a high-ranking mafioso, *caporegime* of the Genovese crime family, at one time considered the most likely heir to Frank Costello's unofficial title of prime minister of the Mob.

But they did know, by the way he carried himself, that he was somebody you stepped out of the way for.

"It's Louie again, I think we better go up," Cami said.

Johnny nodded. "Okay. Get the tickets," he said.

After Dick and Johnny landed at LaGuardia and grabbed their bags, Dick hailed a cab. When he leaned forward to give directions, Johnny put his hand on his shoulder and cut him off.

"Take us to the Peppermint Lounge," he said.

Dick shot him a look of disbelief. *What airport cabbie was going to know the Peppermint?*

"You kidding me?" the driver said. "We won't get within blocks of that place."

After deciding to take the cab into Manhattan and abandon it on the East Side, the two men made their way across 45th Street. Traffic was stopped dead between Fifth Avenue and Broadway. Long before they got to the Peppermint, they could see what looked like a street riot up ahead. Floodlights cut the night sky and the sounds of the noisy crowd bounced off the skyscrapers.

Cops had erected barricades and a small battalion of mounted police tried to steady their spooked horses while driving back an exuberant, barely controllable mob onto the sidewalk. At the entrance, a parade of limos dispensed women in gowns and men in tuxes.

The line waiting outside the candy-striped awning was a full sidewalk wide. It stretched all the way down to Broadway and beyond. The din of rock-and-roll music grew louder and became more distinct as the line approached the Peppermint's entrance.

Johnny led the way to the front door, where they were met by Lenny Montana, a six-foot-six flesh monolith known as "the Bull" during his time as a professional wrestler. Years later, he would be better known as the murderous Luca Brasi, Marlon Brando's bodyguard in *The Godfather*. Montana flashed a big grin and cracked open the door, leaving the waiting throngs buzzing with curiosity over the identities of the two men. Politicians? Movie moguls? High rollers?

Inside, the dim light made it hard to see. They made their way along the rope separating the long mahogany bar in the front. Three bartenders worked as fast as they could, shouting themselves hoarse and opening bottles of Chivas every few minutes. Customers were too thrilled to have made it inside to notice the acrid taste of the cheap booze Scatsy had substituted for the Chivas—a practice from his bootlegging days in the twenties, when he and his brother Johnny worked for the Dutch Schultz mob.

At the end of the rope was the back of the club, where Joey Dee and the Starliters were blasting "The Twist" from a raised bandstand. The dance floor, just eight by twenty feet, was packed with shuddering, shimmying bodies. Mirrored walls bounced their images to infinity, jammed together, asses to elbows, moving to deafening rock-and-roll music. No two dancers moved the same way, but all were doing a version of the Twist.

As Dick's eyes adjusted, he could see that Louie was not imagining things. Sitting at the edge of the dance floor with several handsome young hangers-on was Ava Gardner, one of Hollywood's leading screen queens. Gardner got up and nearly shook the bolts out of her chassis. Dick decided she'd had too much to drink. At the next table was Shirley MacLaine, one of the day's best young actresses. MacLaine laid claim to the dance floor, shaking and twisting like a pro. Spotting her, Joey Dee jumped down from the bandstand and wriggled alongside her.

If the Peppermint burns down tonight, Dick thought, only half of New York society will go with it. The other half was still waiting on line outside.

Johnny had connections to numerous businesses. Some he had on the arm, which meant the owners paid him to keep anyone else from doing to them what he was doing to them. Some he owned, often registering a legitimate partner's name on the license. Some he used as fronts, holding strategic meetings and conducting his illegal activities in the back rooms. The Peppermint Lounge he owned and used as a front. When the club became the most-asked-about New York City attraction at the Times Square information booth, the attention was neither expected nor welcomed. Drawing squads of cops, hordes of teens mixed with society types, and noted celebrities to this club or any of his business connections was never in his plans. Johnny Biello lived quietly, respectably, and always in the background.

The reason he had moved to Miami three years earlier, uprooting not only his family but also son-in-law Dick's was to distance himself from day-to-day life in gangland New York. After Frank Costello was shot, Johnny knew things in the Mob would never be the same for him and he wanted to retire. He had a great business opportunity in Florida and, while not entirely legit yet, that was the dream.

At age fifty-five, he had survived a lifetime of Mob wars, FBI investigations, and criminal prosecutions. He wanted out, but extricating oneself from the highest levels of organized crime in the Five Families of New York was no simple matter. Having the entire Western world's eye trained on the teenage rock-and-roll dance club he owned on 45th Street was not going to help. Johnny decided that it would be better to play it safe and stopped any illegal activities out of the Peppermint. But Johnny was no fool, either. Sensing an opportunity after witnessing firsthand the nightly madness that followed the club's meteoric rise, he decided to return to Miami Beach and open a second, all-new and completely legitimate Peppermint Lounge as quickly as possible.

Chapter 2

October 1961

The new president and his glamorous wife had not been installed in the White House ten months yet and the Cold War was heating up to a brisk boil. Soviet troop buildups in Berlin were reported. As tensions grew between the two former allies, New York governor Nelson Rockefeller called for fallout shelters to be built in public schools.

President Kennedy dispatched General Maxwell Taylor to a small Asian country called South Vietnam to study means to assist the country's struggle against communism, although the general hinted on the eve of his departure that he would be reluctant to commit U.S. troops.

October began with New York Yankees outfielder Roger Maris breaking Babe Ruth's home run record on the last day of the season. The Yanks went on to defeat the Cincinnati Reds in the World Series, with ace Whitey Ford pitching fourteen shutout innings. Downtown, New York City mayor Robert Wagner and attorney general Louis J. Lefkowitz were locked in a bitter election brawl, each claiming the other was not qualified to run the city.

The 1962 automobile models were in the showrooms. The new Rambler Ambassador V-8 Custom Cross-Country offered optional Lounge-Tilt driver's chairs. The 1962 Chrysler Newport featured torsion-bar suspension and unibody construction for $2,964. The age of jet air travel was dawning; Pan Am asked $350 for round-trip air fare to Europe.

Old-timer Rudy Vallee was making a comeback attempt with a new musical opening that month on Broadway, *How to Succeed in Business Without Really Trying*. British playwright Harold Pinter was opening his play *The Caretaker* at the Lyceum with a cast that included Donald Pleasence, Robert Shaw, and Alan Bates.

The film version of *West Side Story* starring Natalie Wood was opening at the Rivoli. *Breakfast at Tiffany's* with Audrey Hepburn was already a big hit at Radio City Music Hall. *Devil at 4 O'Clock* was the new Spencer Tracy–Frank Sinatra movie. *Bonanza*, starting its third season that September, was the most popular show on television, but it would soon be challenged by newcomers *The Dick Van Dyke Show* and *Ben Casey*, a series about a young hospital intern, starring Elvis Presley look-alike Vince Edwards.

Harper Lee's *To Kill a Mockingbird* topped bestseller lists, along with Irving Stone's fictionalized life of Michelangelo, *The Agony and the Ecstasy*. Hot nonfiction tomes included Theodore White's *The Making of the President 1960* and William Shirer's *The Rise and Fall of the Third Reich*.

But a fever gripped New York in October 1961. The most important pop music event between the emergence of rock and roll and the arrival of the Beatles—a new dance called the Twist—hit Manhattan that fall. In a matter of weeks, the craze altered the social landscape. Everybody—adults, kids, politicians, and garbage collectors—was suddenly doing the Twist.

A deceptively simple dance consisting of swiveling hips and shifting feet, the Twist was the real beginning of the sixties. The seeds to the black power movement, student protest, psychedelics, draft card burnings, Woodstock—everything that became the sixties—can be seen in the coming of the Twist, and the breaking-the-mold freedom it promised.

Dance crazes had come and gone before, almost always greeted with some measure of controversy. Fifty years earlier, the Turkey Trot was an obsession with youth of the gilded age. The editor of *Ladies Home Journal* was reported to have fired fifteen young ladies for Turkey Trotting during their lunch hour. The Tango was denounced when it appeared in 1914. Vernon and Irene Castle, a popular brother-sister dance team, introduced the Castle Walk, in part to stem the orgy of Turkey Trotting.

The Charleston, from a song by pianist James P. Johnson in the 1923 Broadway musical *Runnin' Wild*, became the dance craze of the Jazz Age, a raucous fling with lustful abandon to a ragtime beat. The Lindy Hop burst out of Harlem in the thirties, incorporating some of the swivels and steps of the Charleston, but strictly within the context of Lindy Hopping, which was a hallmark of swing-era dance floors.

None of them generated the combination of frenzied excitement and moral outrage with which the nation greeted this new dance. Black Panther Party firebrand Eldridge Cleaver credited the Twist with teaching white America to shake their asses. Canadian sociologist Marshall McLuhan, not averse to doing the Twist himself, pronounced the dance "very cool, very casual, like a gestural conversation without words."

By changing the way people danced with each other, the Twist had ramifications beyond the dance floor. Because each dancer was an independent contractor, women were liberated from having to follow their partners and, in that way, the dance cracked open the door ever so slightly to the women's movement and sexual liberation yet to come.

The Twist was sexy. At a time when coyly posed topless models in *Playboy* magazine were racy fare indeed, the sight of a woman churning her hips and spreading her legs in public was something new to polite American dance floors. The dance's proponents loudly and unconvincingly proclaimed innocence—describing the dance as good exercise and wholesome fun—but its erotic content was not the least of its secret appeals and maybe the most. It was not open rebellion—not yet—but the Twist represented the stiffest challenge to the established order and the rules governing public behavior since the end of the Second World War.

The list of detractors was long and vocal. "Not for me," said Fred Astaire, America's foremost dancer, whose nationwide chain of dance studios soon enough began offering Twist lessons. Television's Jackie Gleason called it "a silly jiggle for amateurs that will last about as long as chlorophyll." Nat King Cole sang "I Won't Twist" on the Dinah Shore TV variety show. The dance was not allowed at society events.

"The Twist is not a social dance and we won't permit it," said Mrs. Douglas Williams of the Grosvenor Ball.

Lou Brecker, proprietor of Midtown's Roseland Ballroom, also banned it. "It is not, in our opinion, a ballroom dance," he said. "It is lacking in true grace and since we have previously outlawed rock-and-roll as a feature at Roseland, we likewise will not permit the Twist to be danced." The education writer of *The New York Times* fumed, "Instead of youth growing up, adults are sliding down."

Critics went so far as to declare the Twist a health hazard. The Chiropractic Research Council noted that forty-nine cases of "Twisters back" were reported in a single week in New York. "The dance puts unusual stress on the soft tissues of the lower spine just below the pelvis and can cause serious damage," said Dr. Thure Peterson of the Chiropractic Institute of New York. "Twisters are leaving themselves open to charley-horse-like pains and spinal spasms."

The issue was debated in side-by side columns in *The New York Times Magazine*. "The Twist? I'm sitting this one out," wrote Trinidad-born dancer Geoffrey Holder. "It's dishonest. It's not a dance and it has become dirty. Not because it has to do with sex. Everything does. But it's not what it's packaged. It's synthetic sex turned into a spectator sport. Not because it's vulgar. Real vulgarity is divine. But when people break their backs to act vulgar, it's embarrassing."

"In defense to the charge that the Twist is lewd and 'dirty,' I can only say that any movement can be made to appear suggestive, depending on the dancer himself," responded Chubby Checker, whose recording of "The Twist" was rocketing up the charts that winter. "I have often watched couples Waltzing or doing a Fox-Trot and have been more embarrassed than when viewing the most uninhibited Twisters."

Besides being a signal event in the history of American popular dance, the Twist was a landmark in the history of popular music. It arrived at a time when the rock-and-roll movement, which had struck so forcefully five years earlier, was losing momentum, pandering to a strictly teenage market in ever more venal, insipid ways. The fierce warriors of rock-and-roll's initial assault—Elvis, Little Richard, Fats Domino, Jerry Lee Lewis, Buddy Holly, the Everly Brothers, Gene Vincent, Eddie Cochran, and the others—had largely fallen by the wayside. In their place, freshly scrubbed, homogenous white males with sculpted hair were paraded before an eager public tuned to television's *American Bandstand*, a three-hour after-school broadcast from Philadelphia hosted by an equally clean-cut, clear-eyed disc jockey named Dick Clark.

Old-time, blue-chip music publishers couldn't get arrested and kids barely old enough to drink were writing hit after hit. The power shifted from the old guard at the Brill Building, where big bands from Duke Ellington to Tommy Dorsey kept their offices alongside music publishers of the era, to 1650 Broadway, an office building two blocks away that housed the budding rock-and-roll empires like Aldon Music, a firm that signed young songwriters such as Neil Sedaka and Howard Greenfield, along with Gerry Goffin and Carole King, scarcely older than the teens who bought the records. The firm had more than one hundred songs recorded in 1961.

Independent record labels had largely captured the hit parade from staid majors such as Columbia or RCA Victor, but rock and roll, the independent label's specialty, was losing vitality, showing signs of waning. Typical of the show business mentality that pervaded was Bobby Darin. He ditched rock and roll for big-room swing and "Mack the Knife" as soon as he could, telling interviewers that rock and roll was only for teenagers and he was an all-round entertainer. With the music business almost entirely centered in New York, conservative forces worked to marginalize this new, uncontrollable music. Under their noses, the Twist would finally demolish those barriers to rock and roll. The Twist gave rock and roll its first adult constituency.

The Twist hit like an atomic bomb, and the Peppermint Lounge was ground zero.

Grown-ups in fur coats waited in line alongside gum-chewing teen-agers. Newspapers and magazines stumbled over one another covering the phenomenon. No less an authority than *Newsweek* reported that the Twist "a rock 'n' roll comedy of Eros, has suddenly turned the Peppermint Lounge, a run-of-the-ginmill, into a melting pot for socialites, sailors, and salesmen."

The Manhattan swinging set abandoned cobwebbed, old outposts such as El Morocco, Toots Shor's, the Stork Club, and the Harwyn Club for the Peppermint Lounge. The simplicity of the dance was greatly in its favor when the adults joined in. Anyone could learn it. The Stork Club instituted Twist dancing. "I love to watch them dance," said owner Sherman Billingsley. But the El Morocco banished actress Janet Leigh, fresh off her shocking shower murder scene in *Psycho*, for Twisting in her stocking feet.

One regular visitor to the Pep—as it was called—was man-about-town Ahmet Ertegun, the son of the Turkish ambassador to the United States and the founder of Atlantic Records. Ertegun rented a bus ev-ery night to ferry around his wealthy friends and hangers-on. They started with dinner at the El Morocco and invariably wound up at the Peppermint Lounge. Always a trend-setting playboy, Ertegun started frequenting the club in July 1961, ranking him among the first trickle of swells slumming with the rock and rollers. Almost overnight that fall, the little Theater District bar was turning away a thousand customers a night.

Other clubs were twisting, but the center of the Twist universe was the Peppermint Lounge, where six NYPD patrol cars were parked nightly, trying to control the crowds and cars. Fire marshals were permanently assigned. The street was so packed, crosstown traffic stopped at Broadway. Bob Hope, hosting a black tie dinner at the Waldorf=Astoria, looked over the audience that included President Kennedy, General Douglas MacArthur, and Cardinal Spellman and joked, "I have never seen so many cop cars or limousines outside. What is this—the Peppermint Lounge?"

Night after night, celebrities and socialites in furs and jewels crammed together with the teenagers in leather jackets and bouffant hairdos. The kids were a varied group, from suburban girls with their hair teased and blown to motorcycle toughs like Big Daddy, who parked his bike right in front of the club. He later owned a junkyard in Jersey where it was suspected for a time that Jimmy Hoffa was buried.

The club retained its rough-hewn style. The ham-fisted Peppermint Lounge doormen recognized and ushered in some of the celebrities—Marilyn Monroe, Judy Garland, Greta Garbo. Others they didn't recognize and denied entrance—Ethel Merman, Tennessee Williams, even Chubby Checker. When the *New Yorker* reporter visited, he found *American Bandstand* host Dick Clark standing next to dance instructor Arthur Murray and his wife, Kathryn.

There was no surer sign of the Twist's acceptance by the broader society than the presence of Arthur Murray, the patriarch of American dance and proprietor of a nationwide chain of dance studios. "Any new dance craze will stimulate all kinds of new business," said Kathryn Murray.

The two hosted a television program that catered to the white-gloves cotillion set, but they soon started haunting the Peppermint Lounge. "We wanted to observe the dance in its native habitat," Murray said. "After a while even we felt the urge come across to us. And so, we got up and Twisted along with the others."

Still, Murray didn't think much of the Twist as dance. "No steps, pure swivel," he sniffed. But that didn't stop him from sitting next to the dance floor, studying every move. Within a week, the Arthur Murray Dance Studios took out a large newspaper advertisement. "Quite frankly, the Twist is not our favorite dance," began the ad. "But, if you're young at heart, you just have to dance it these days. It's all the rage, and you can become a Twist expert in six easy lessons . . ."

When the sixty-six-year-old fuddy-duddy started coming in, Louie Lombardi was alarmed. "He looks like he's going to drop dead any minute," Louie said. "I told Captain Lou (one of the bouncers) to take him outside if he starts to go. I don't want anyone dying in here."

It was maitre d' Joe Dana who told Louie who Murray was. "He's here to learn all the new dances for his studios."

"You're kidding, right?" Louie said. "These kids dance so far from their partners, you need a search party to find them when the song's over." Around the Peppermint Lounge, Murray was known as a lousy tipper.

If the Murrays represented one end of the spectrum of popular American dance, Killer Joe Piro was at the other end and he, too, took up residence at the Peppermint Lounge. A former champion Jitterbugger, the athletic Piro was the master of ceremonies at the Palladium and presided over New York's Mambo craze through the fifties. He taught New York bluebloods to dance in his West 55th Street studio, where he quickly started giving Twist lessons. Unlike Murray, Piro was an enthusiastic Twister.

Broadway, just around the corner, was not immune. Actor Phil Silvers, starring in the musical *Do Re Mi* at the St. James Theatre, came by the club one night and immediately whisked the Twist into the production. Three dancers did the Twist to a jukebox in the show. Hal March, star of the Broadway play *Come Blow Your Horn*, swapped out the Cha-Cha-Cha in one scene in the show for the Twist after a visit to the club.

Life magazine shot photos of Senator Jacob Javits with Jean Smith, President Kennedy's sister, and Tennessee Williams, tie loosened, fingers cradling a cocktail glass.

Joey Dee and the Starliters, the house band, had been the hottest band in northern New Jersey when they landed the Peppermint Lounge job a year before and had honed the band's act razor sharp.

Dee's band was the hit of the society season in New York. Earl Blackwell, publisher of the *Celebrity Register* and a Peppermint Lounge habitué, booked the band to play a Girls Town benefit at the Four Seasons restaurant that was hosted by Eleanor Roosevelt in November. They appeared the next night at the victory celebration for Mayor Robert Wagner, played the Bourbon Ball at the Plaza Hotel and a $100-a-plate Party of the Year fund-raiser at the Metropolitan Museum of Art. The Met's director, James J. Rorimer, fumed when he saw "photographers hastening to photograph the guests doing the Twist at the shrine of Rembrandt and Cezanne," wrote Gay Talese in *The New York Times.*

"I did not invite them," he said. "I was not aware of this." His wife was in the other room, getting Twist lessons.

In playing midwife to the Twist and the adult liberation of rock and roll, the Peppermint Lounge laid the blueprint for all future rock nightclubs. It may not have been the first rock-and-roll club, but it was the first famous one, the fountainhead of every rock-and-roll nightclub that would follow. The club employed its own set of dancers, the Peppermint Twisters. The waitresses danced when they weren't serving drinks (and sometimes when they were). In a sense, Go-Go dancing was invented at the Peppermint Lounge. One of the cute, young waitresses who offered impromptu demonstrations and casual lessons, in between carrying trays of drinks from the bar, was Janet Huffsmith, an underage girl from Pittston, Pennsylvania, who was known as Granny Peppermint because she'd used her older sister's ID to land the job. She was an inspired Twister. "If you couldn't shake your fanny you weren't hired," she explained decades later. In a moment of abandon one night, Huffsmith leaped up on the chrome railing that surrounded the dance floor and inadvertently invented rail dancing, almost immediately adopted as a signature trademark of the raucous scene. Later on, she couldn't recall what inspired her. "I just got up there and did it," she said.

That was really the beginning of a new kind of professional dancing—untrained, acrobatic, rock-and-roll dancing. The power of the Twist was such that Huffsmith became a celebrity herself, doing the Twist on *The Ed Sullivan Show*, at Carnegie Hall, and then on a tour of South America.

Within a few years, the Peppermint's rail dancers would be transformed at French discotheques into the prototypical sixties Go-Go dancers, clad in thigh-high white boots, ponytails flying, suspended high above club stages in cages.

As the elite of New York society flocked to the dingy dive, sending out shock waves that reverberated around the world—London, Paris, Tokyo—few of the patrons of the Peppermint Lounge gave much thought to the management of the club. Ralph Saggese, a former NYPD lieutenant, thirteen years off the force, acted as the owner. His name was on the records. He was there every night and usually did the talking when the reporters came around. In his midnight blue suit and white tie, Saggese radiated the kind of genial authority expected of a nightclub owner. Only he wasn't really the owner.

The world-famous Twisters and high-society dilettantes who converged on the West 45th Street rock-and-roll bar would have been surprised to know that the club was actually owned by a powerful figure in New York's criminal underworld, a *capo* in the Genovese family, Johnny Biello. Few knew that the Peppermint Lounge had been the headquarters and hangout for Biello and his men, who operated loan sharking and gambling rackets out of the back room. Waitresses like Huffsmith never knew, either, although there was a lot of whispering when they saw "these big men" come in and huddle with Sam Kornweisser, Johnny's man on the scene, in the back room.

Mob associations with New York nightclubs was hardly big news. Birdland, the top jazz spot on 52nd Street, was owned by Morris

Levy, who also ran the Roulette Records label, fingered by the FBI as the front man for the syndicate in the record business. He and Joe (The Wop) Cataldo, another known crime figure, also operated the Roundtable, where the risque Jewish comedienne Belle Barth was playing when they decided to convert to a Twist program. They brought in a rock-and-roll band from Memphis, Bill Black's Combo, whose latest hit was "Twist-Her." Keyboardist Earl Grant, booked to follow Barth into the club, suddenly found himself with a hole in his schedule.

The Peppermint was not really a major part of Biello's business. After moving to Miami to free himself from his Mob entanglements, he had invested in a carpet plant with the hope of lying low and easing into a mellow retirement, forgetting and forgotten.

Never a murderous criminal, Biello's fate lay balanced between shifting powers and shaky loyalties, none of which was what it seemed. He wanted to slip away quietly. Easier said than done. The son of Italian immigrants, Biello had spent his entire life on the other side of the law, having grown up with the founders of the modern Mafia, Frank Costello and Charles (Lucky) Luciano. The life was something Biello was practically born into.

Chapter 3

Mad Dogs and Irishmen

A large picture of Pope Pius X looked over the living room in the two-bed, no-bath walkup at 149th Street and Morris Avenue where Johnny Biello was born and raised. It was the only touch of the divine in the Biellos' miserable South Bronx home. Born May 3, 1906, Johnny was the third of five children of Giuseppe and Conchetta Biello. A devout, diligent couple, they slept in one of the beds. The children—oldest brother Raf, Mary, Johnny, Mandy, and baby Albert, later known as Scatsy—shared the other. The toilet was in the hall outside. Bathing was done in the kitchen sink.

Poppa Biello was honest and hardworking, but getting steady construction work was a challenge. And when he did, it barely paid enough to keep food on the table, even with Conchetta's near miraculous ability to stretch the little they had with peppers, onions, salt, and bread crumbs. Dinner was too often scraps of bread sprinkled with sugar. The drink of choice was a small glass of heavily diluted wine. To earn a little extra money, Momma collected discarded flour sacks, washed them over and over by hand to soften the stiff cloth, and cut them into diapers that she sold to neighbors. In her teeming community, there were always babies.

Despite the privation, Johnny and Scatsy both remembered their mother's meals as the standard against which all future cooking would be measured. In Italian families, food was the oil that greased the machine. Meals were where relationships were solidified, suitors were scrutinized, jobs bestowed, and fates sealed.

By the time he rose to be the boss of 149th Street under Lucky Luciano, Johnny regularly conducted business over dinner. When the FBI started tracking his movements, they found all they had to do was wait outside one of Johnny's favorite restaurants, Laurentano's, or the Stage Deli. Remarkable for his calm demeanor and cool head, the one thing that was sure to make his Italian blood boil was anyone cooking with tomato paste.

Raf, the eldest, was the family ne'er-do-well, leaving it to Johnny to do something about the family's dismal fortunes. He slipped easily into the role of family protector and provider. Not tall, about five-foot-eight fully grown, and not much more than a hundred and fifty pounds, he had the natural poise of a born leader. But he was also tough and fearless, with good sense and a charismatic likeability. Towing little Scatsy, whose legs were stunted by a childhood disease and never grew taller than an inch or two above five feet, Johnny worked his way up Morris Avenue and down 149th Street.

They appeared to be two runty kids threading their way carelessly through the choked streets of the South Bronx. But they knew all the grocery stores, produce stands, bakeries, and street vendors who sold Pellegrino and Fiuggi water straight from Italy. A cousin of Poppa's had a stand selling goat's heads, known as *caputsel*, a delicacy among the old-timers, for thirty-five cents. Years later, Scatsy would remember the dish fondly. "Ooooh, I love the eyes," he said.

As the boys skittered by, the shopkeepers kept a wary eye on them. If the bread man left his truck idling while he had a quick espresso at the club on the corner where the local toughs hung out, Johnny vaulted inside, grabbed as many loaves as he could, and tossed them down to Scatsy. Then they were off and running. When he presented his bounty to his mother, she looked him straight in the eyes, smacked her wooden spoon down on the kitchen table, and said he'd better not be stealing. But to feed her family, how could she refuse any gift?

One time, a trolley car collided with a horse-drawn carriage, and the confused, dazed passengers spilled into the street. Looking to help, a water salesman left his cart unguarded long enough for Johnny to grab a case of Pellegrino and disappear around the corner. Out of sight, he stopped and put a bottle to his mouth, the sharp bite of the mineral water making his mouth burn with a delicious fire. He took the rest home to his mother, who was bent over her sewing.

"Let me guess," she said. "It fell off a wagon."

Johnny's first brush with big-time gangstering occurred when he was shining shoes at a local espresso club to make some extra money. The club was one of those places during Prohibition where bad men sat around smoking, playing cards, and drinking bootleg hooch they kept behind the counter. Johnny was fascinated by the fact that none of the men seemed to work. Yet they all had the trappings of wealth: gaudy rings, shiny shoes, and new suits.

One afternoon, in walked Dutch Schultz (real name, Arthur Flegenheimer). Johnny's neighborhood was Dutch's territory. The Dutchman was a sadistic gang leader who once blinded a rival by tying him up and taping rags filled with pus to his eyes. With Prohibition, he made his fortune. According to Scatsy, on this day Schultz, who had just bought himself a big, chrome-plated Roadmaster, came in raging.

Somebody had stolen the tires from his new car. As he stomped around, spewing curses and threats, Johnny looked up from his work. "Your car the blue Buick?" he said.

"Who said that?" said Dutch.

When Johnny stood up, Schultz saw he was just a kid.

"Did you steal my tires?"

"Yes, I did," Johnny said. "But who knew it was yours?"

Everyone held their breath until Schultz threw his head back and burst into laughter.

Word of the incident spread quickly through the neighborhood. One of the men at the club, a walking whale called Benny the Blimp, said maybe the kid needed a job. "We could use some help cleaning up," he said.

"What does it pay?" Johnny said.

"Look at this *Meemo*. What do you care? You'll make more in tips than salary, I'll tell you that. That's if you can learn to keep your wise-ass mouth shut."

Johnny's parents saw their son growing beyond their control and fought it like parents in every generation. "Do you have a lucky saint?" his father asked him one morning at breakfast.

"I guess we all get lucky once in a while," Johnny said carelessly.

"Everybody has a lucky saint," Giuseppe said. "You don't know where he is, but he's got his eye on you."

Johnny had given up trusting anything to luck or fate or invisible saints floating by in the sky. By this time, he'd become a skilled thief. Down at the espresso club, he saw plenty of evidence that crime did indeed pay. He got up to leave. "Sit down, Johnny," his mother said. "And *mangiare*."

When it became law of the land in 1920, Prohibition was perhaps the nation's grandest social experiment. While it proved inefficient at imposing sobriety on a nation on a bender, it was remarkably successful at unleashing the greatest expansion of criminal activity in American history. In just one year, Lucky Luciano made $12 million from bootlegging.

But it was Dutch Schultz who first recognized the great opportunity in making illegal booze. The math was hard to dispute. A barrel of beer cost five dollars to produce but could be sold to a speakeasy for $36.

Soon after Prohibition began, Schultz and his boys installed "alley cookers" in sheds, basements, and the back rooms of stores all over the Bronx. They also got interested in stronger spirits. The process of making bathtub gin was a simple one. Sugar and yeast were poured into a mixing tank. The mixture was covered with warm water and stirred with an agitator. The mix was allowed to ferment for forty-eight hours, then pumped into a copper kettle, in which the whole thing was cooked down to 190-proof alcohol. When sugar was unavailable, one of the boys, who was something of a self-taught chemist, figured out a way to convert witch hazel into decent-enough 170-proof drinking alcohol. "What the hell," Scatsy would say. "We ain't making twelve-year-old scotch or nothing."

There was one problem with manufacturing illegal booze in a dense urban area. Occasionally gases built up as the yeast and sugar broke down. To keep it from stinking up the neighborhood around their basement operation, Scatsy plugged the manhole covers with corks. Sometimes the equipment malfunctioned and released a big ball of pent-up gas all at once, basically creating an industrial-scale gas attack.

When that happened, plugs on the street started popping. Scatsy would scramble down the street, replacing the corks. The sight of the stumpy Biello kid running from manhole cover to manhole cover amused the neighbors. "Look at that kid scatting all over the street," they said. That's how Scatsy got his nickname. Much later, after the Miami Beach Peppermint became successful and the family opened a fine dining rooftop restaurant in Hollywood, Florida, Johnny decided his brother needed a new, more respectable name. He called him Scotty. Calling the little pit bull of an Italian who tortured the English language "Scotty" became a family joke. Scatsy remained Scatsy to friends and family.

There were two different stories about how Johnny got his nickname, Johnny Futto. One story held that when Johnny was working as a bookmaker at the racetrack, which was legal then, he collected a debt from a guy who called him a "dirty Jew." When Johnny proceeded to tap dance all over the deadbeat's head, people started calling him Johnny the Foot, or "Futto."

But Scatsy always said that the nickname was conferred after Johnny had a deadly encounter with a member of a secret Italian criminal organization called the Black Hand.

The Black Hands predated the Mafia, less organized but every bit as vicious. The name came from their practice of sending threatening letters to shopkeepers demanding tribute. The letters were signed with the imprint of a hand dipped in black ink. For an extra touch of the macabre, members dressed all in black.

A particular Black Hand had been preying on a local grocer on 149th Street, where Johnny's mother shopped. Johnny and Scatsy stole from the same grocer, but that was different. They were from the neighborhood. The Black Hand was an outsider.

Conchetta came home one day in tears. She said the grocer was planning to close up shop because he couldn't afford the payoffs anymore. That set Johnny off. Why should a guy who gives beatings and kills innocent people be rewarded? And why prey on their own?

When the Black Hand came back, fourteen-year-old Johnny confronted him, according to Scatsy, in hopes of changing his mind.

"Shut up, kid, this is not you business," the Black Hand said. Seeing little threat in the mouthy teenager, the older man punctuated his warning with a firm slap across Johnny's face.

Johnny had never been struck before. His father was a peaceable man who never used violence. The boy's blood froze as he reached into his shirt for the large butcher knife he had brought just in case. He thrust the knife into the older man's stomach. The force of it threw the Black Hand off his feet and onto his back, where he lay squirming and kicking,

"You son of a bitch, I'm going to kill you," he said.

The Black Hand grappled with the knife, finally managing to pull it free. But before he could get to his feet, Johnny rushed in and began kicking him in the head. A crowd gathered and cheered the kid on as he planted his foot into the man's face again and again. As the man lay dying from his wounds, the crowd finally pulled Johnny off.

The Black Hand was deeply hated in the neighborhood. A familiar sight, he'd preyed on merchants up and down the street. Maybe some of the crowd helped Johnny. Scatsy only ever said, "When the fight was over, the Black Hand was dead and neighbors rushed Johnny away."

Nobody identified Johnny to the police. The bystanders had their own scores to settle with the Black Hand, and the street code of silence prevailed. Peter Clemente, the FBI agent who tailed Johnny for years, said he never heard of any killings directly attributed to Johnny. Of course, by the time Clemente was on the trail, Johnny was a *capo* who would have ordered killings, not carried them out. According to Clemente, when Johnny got in, there was only one way to become a member of the Mafia: killing someone.

Johnny and Scatsy graduated from bootlegging to more serious crimes. While they were still kids, Scatsy started running the neighborhood with Vincent Coll, a wild Irish psycho. They made a bizarre couple, Mutt-and-Jeff pals with mayhem on their minds.

One hobby Coll indulged in when he got the money for his first car was to cruise the black neighborhoods of Harlem. While Scatsy drove, craning to look over the steering wheel, Coll took aim at pedestrians with an air gun. To Coll, shooting at black people was nothing more than target practice.

One afternoon, after they returned to the Bronx and were walking by an open-air coffee shop, Coll saw a man sitting at the counter drinking a cup of coffee and took out his air gun.

"What are you doing now?" Scatsy said.

"You'll see," Coll said, and took aim, shooting the cup of coffee out of his hand.

"Pretty good shot," Scatsy said.

"Bullshit," Coll said. "I was trying to hit him in the fucking head."

Coll rose through the ranks quickly. After being kicked out of Catholic reform schools, he went to work for Dutch Schultz as a guard on his delivery trucks. A tall, good-looking kid with a pencil-thin mustache and an explosive temper, Coll was charged in 1927 with killing the owner of a speakeasy who refused to sell Schultz's product. After being acquitted, Coll demanded to be made a partner in the beer baron's empire. When Schultz refused, Coll, a diagnosed schizophrenic, went into one of his rages and quit Schultz's gang. He took with him a dozen gangsters, including his brother Peter. Not all were willing, but a tough guy named Er was one of the first to join Coll. Er's name was derived from his original nickname, Crazy. After some bizarre feats his name became Crazier and, over time, that somehow was shortened to Er. Coll wanted more recruits, so he took Er with him and went to Schultz mob member Vito Zingara's house. When Coll knocked on the door, Zingara was having dinner with his family. When he opened the door, Coll flat out told him he had to join up with him against the Dutchman. When Zingara refused, Coll shot him dead in the doorway of his home.

After the Zingara incident everyone wanted Coll's head. Even Scatsy knew it was hopeless—his pal had stepped over the line. War between Schultz and Coll followed, leading to the destruction of several of Schultz's beer trucks and the murder of Coll's brother. Because of the war, Coll could no longer make a living in illegal booze, so he resorted to a new business: kidnapping and holding wealthy people for ransom.

Prior to the kidnapping of trans-Atlantic flier Charles Lindbergh's eighteen-month-old son in March 1932, the crime was not a federal offense. More than a few thugs made a good living snatching celebrities off the streets. Coll went for the best. He kidnapped singer Rudy Vallee, the man with the velvet megaphone, and earned $100,000 for it. For Stork Club owner Sherman Billingsley, he got a more modest $25,000.

When Coll attempted to kidnap Joey Rao, a pal of Johnny's from Harlem who was also working for Schultz, the botched attempt resulted in a gunfight on the streets of New York City in July 1931, which left several children injured and one dead. That earned Coll the nickname he carried to his grave, Mad Dog. After being arrested, he escaped punishment through the legal legerdemain of his defense attorney, Samuel Leibowitz, the Clarence Darrow of New York.

Vince Coll's one-man crime wave didn't come to an end until after Dutch Schultz and Lucky Luciano put a $50,000 bounty on his head. Schultz was so desperate to be rid of him that he supposedly walked into a Bronx police station and offered a house in Westchester to any cop who took him down. Finally, on February 8, 1932, Coll used a pay phone in a drugstore to call Owney Madden, the smooth-as-silk owner of the Cotton Club, from whom Coll was demanding $50,000 in exchange for not kidnapping Madden's brother. Madden kept him on the phone long enough to have someone inside the phone company trace the call. Shooters were dispatched, who hit Coll with eighteen submachine-gun bullets while he was still standing in the phone booth. All that was some years in the future when Coll and Scatsy began running together.

In the mid-twenties, Johnny joined a gang of Bronx ruffians who knocked over jewelry stores. It seemed like a good racket. The stores were easy targets and getting away was not difficult unless you were unlucky enough to run into a police car. New York wouldn't put two-way radios in its police cars until 1933.

The first few robberies were snaps. But on January 4, 1927, Johnny got popped for assault and robbery. It was only his second arrest. Three years earlier, according to FBI records, he'd spent two weeks in jail after being arrested for felonious assault. He was never convicted of that crime, and it looked as if he might slide again after the jewelry heist. New York police files show he was released after being held a week, during which police applied pressure to get him to admit his guilt. At that time, cops had plenty of freedom to obtain confessions practically any way they could. But Johnny could take a pounding.

Two months after his release, he was arrested again. A witness recovered her memory. This time they had him. He was sent to Sing Sing prison for seven and a half to fifteen years.

By the time Johnny arrived, Sing Sing had a well-earned reputation for state-sanctioned cruelty that had already left an indelible mark on the English language. If you were sent up the river, you were going to prison; the river being the Hudson and the prison being Sing Sing.

A few months after Johnny's arrival, there was considerable excitement surrounding the execution of Ruth Snyder, the first woman to get the electric chair at Sing Sing. On the night of her execution, three thousand protesters and rubberneckers milled around outside the prison walls. "This was a very exciting night," the executioner, Robert G. Elliott, wrote in his diary, "second only to the Sacco and Vanzetti night." Sacco and Vanzetti, the famous anarchists, had been executed the previous August.

Sing Sing, at the time, was pretty much a recruiting office for the Mafia. Among the inmates Johnny got to know on the yard was a young Joe Valachi, the man who would become famous many years later for revealing to the world the existence of the Mafia. Johnny's most significant contact, however, was Charlie Noto, a good friend of Lucky Luciano and Francesco Castiglia, aka Frank Costello. Scatsy liked to say that if the horse he'd bet on had Charlie's nose, he would have been a winner.

On the prison yard, there was a gorgeous garden, flowers everywhere, and even a big birdhouse. The kind of birdhouse you could walk into and watch the birds jumping from branch to branch. This thing of beauty, plunked down in the middle of this unlikely place, was the creation of newspaper editor Charles Chapin, serving twenty years for killing his wife.

Johnny and Noto spent all the time they could around that garden with Futto learning the ways of the Mob and figuring out how he might fit in. One time, an inmate who got on the wrong side of the Italians was knifed right in front of Johnny. The victim bled to death on the floor. Questioned about it, Johnny said he didn't see anything. The bulls knew he was lying and kept him off the yard for a few months to jar his memory. Johnny never budged. When they let him back, Johnny had a reputation as a guy who knew how to keep his mouth shut.

Chapter 4

War and a Piece
of the Action

I f there was any upside to Johnny being stuck in Sing Sing, it was
that all-out war was breaking out in the streets of New York. Being
in prison might have been the safest place for the impetuous Futto.
Estimates of the dead ranged into the hundreds. But even by conservative law enforcement numbers, sixty—not counting innocent bystanders—died in the Castellammarese War that led to the birth of
La Cosa Nostra, better known as the Mafia.

In the twenties, there were two major Italian criminal gangs in
New York. The leader of one faction was Joe "the Boss" Masseria,
known as Joe the Glutton for his terrible table manners. Masseria
was part of the barely Americanized generation of mobsters fresh
from Italy derided as Mustache Petes by more Americanized gangsters. When he wanted someone to disappear he would bluster, "Take
that stone from my shoe." A crude barbarian, Masseria's one virtue
was an ability to spot talent, as defined by the Mob. Charles "Lucky"
Luciano, who got his nickname by surviving being sliced up by razor
blades and hung by his thumbs from a tree on Staten Island by rival
gangsters, was the leader of the Masseria young Turks, which included

Vito Genovese, Frank Costello, Albert Anastasia, and Carlo Gambino. Each would rise to a pinnacle of power and influence in *La Cosa Nostra*.

Where Masseria was a vulgar philistine, Salvatore Maranzano fancied himself an heir to a tradition far more ancient and honorable. He lectured his minions on classical literature and the writings of Julius Caesar while traveling around town in an armored Cadillac, sharing the backseat with a machine gun. His principals included Joe Profaci and Tommy Lucchese, known as Three-Finger Brown because he had lost two fingers in an industrial accident during a brief, unhappy period when he tried working for a living. Rivalry between the two factions broke into the open in 1930, when Masseria anointed himself boss of all bosses (*capo di tutti capi*) and demanded $10,000 tribute from Maranzano. When Maranzano refused, war was inevitable.

Prior to this, Lucky Luciano had become a power in the bootlegging business with his childhood pal Meyer Lansky, first as protectors of the extremely lucrative distribution business headed by Arnold Rothstein, then assuming the business when Rothstein died. From this power base Luciano was now the number two man in Masseria's mob. But he had come to believe that it was time for a new order and that both Masseria and Maranzano had to be eliminated. Masseria was murdered first, Maranzano followed, and with Luciano in the lead the new syndicate came into being.

Luciano divided New York into five families. Each family was to be ruled by a boss who commanded several *capos* in the field. The *capos* in turn commanded their own battalion of street-level soldiers. Each family was to have a *consigliere*, or counselor, who could help mediate disputes between families. Problems that could not be handled by the *consiglieri* would be referred to a seven-member commission that would serve as a kind of judicial body of last appeal. Finally, he ruled that the bloody title, boss of all bosses, would be retired along with its previous aspirants.

All this occurred while Johnny Futto served out his sentence.

When he was released, he was introduced to the man who would become his boss and role model—Luciano's top lieutenant, Frank Costello.

After serving time on a concealed weapons charge as a youth, Costello vowed he would never again carry a gun. Instead he made his way with his brains. He was so successful that he would rarely again see the inside of a jail cell, despite rising to the very top ranks of the Mob and earning a living equal to any of his neighbors on Central Park West. The very image of the modern-day American mobster, Costello, like millions of ordinary Americans worn down by the stress of the fast-paced urban life, even visited a psychiatrist.

"Frank was a peaceful guy, a diplomat," was how Joe Valachi described him.

For Johnny, who was repelled by the instinctive viciousness of so many of the men he was surrounded by, Costello was a revelation. Here was a man who could walk into court and have the judge extend his hand. He was friendly with congressmen. About the only powerful man Costello couldn't influence was New York mayor Fiorello LaGuardia, who in 1934 confiscated thousands of Costello's slot machines. Costello got an order from a friendly judge to stop LaGuardia, but the mayor, ignoring the order, loaded the machines on a barge and dumped them in the East River.

Watching Costello up close, Johnny decided that he was a man to emulate and wore the same kind of tailored suits and adopted the same attitude toward Mob business—conciliation over violence, mercantilism over murder.

Johnny Futto's look was more Madison Avenue than Mafia. His complexion was fair. His wide-set almond eyes could sparkle. In later years, few would guess that Johnny Biello was a man other men feared. Never flashy. Never called attention to himself. A simple man of business was how he described himself when the FBI came calling.

Fresh out of Sing Sing in 1932, Johnny and Scatsy went back to bootlegging, this time in the employ of Luciano and his *consigliere*, Costello. When the operation outgrew the Bronx, they set up a still in a barn up in Mount Vernon, which was at that time farming country in Westchester County.

The still had six big fermentation vats. To avoid detection, they tapped the gas, rigged the electricity, and siphoned off the water from the main pipe. When sugar became difficult to obtain, they stole it. When the booze was ready, it was delivered to New York in a Lincoln sedan with a secret compartment under the seat where Johnny stored six five-gallon cans, three on each side. One five-gallon can of pure alcohol made eleven or twelve cans of booze.

Johnny and Scatsy dealt with stolen goods as well, but illegal alcohol was the cash cow that lasted well beyond the end of Prohibition in 1933.

Repeal didn't snuff out the criminal gangs that Prohibition unleashed. The gangs simply turned to other criminal activities: extortion, gambling, loan-sharking, drugs, prostitution, and muscling in on the trash collection, garment, construction, and fishing trades. Johnny was always adamant about not getting involved in drugs or prostitution, and his attitude about most of the things that made him money was that people wanted what he offered. Why should the government get in the way?

The government wasn't as broad-minded. With bodies piling up on the streets of New York and compromised judges and prosecutors afraid to do anything about it, the situation demanded a heroic figure brave enough to take a stand alongside LaGuardia. That hero was Thomas E. Dewey, the son of a Michigan newspaper editor and a devout churchgoer with a baritone so moving that he considered a singing career. Instead, he became a lawyer and, in 1935, was appointed a special federal prosecutor with a single mandate: Get organized crime.

Dewey's first target was Johnny's old boss, Dutch Schultz, whom he hauled in on the same tax evasion charges that brought down Al Capone in Chicago in 1931. Though he beat the case with the help of a sympathetic jury, the Dutchman knew Dewey wouldn't stop. He started agitating to hit Dewey.

"All the Dutchman can talk about is Tom Dewey this and Tom

Dewey that," Luciano told friends one afternoon after having lunch with Schultz.

Fearing that Schultz would try to hit Dewey and unleash a crackdown that would put them all out of business, Charley Lucky decided Schultz had to go. Schultz was shot dead October 23, 1935 in a Newark, New Jersey, bar and grill. In his death throes, he ranted so crazily that the detective taking it all down ordered him to be quiet. His last sentence was worthy of a dethroned king: "Let them leave me alone."

Saving the crusading prosecutor's life didn't help Luciano when Dewey turned his dogs loose on him. For a long time, Luciano's nickname held. As head of his own family, he lived year-round in suite 36C of the Waldorf=Astoria, paying a princely sum for the privilege. He was so well connected politically that he and Costello accompanied New York's Tammany Hall delegation to the 1932 Democratic convention in Chicago.

The lucky streak ran out when Dewey's men raided eighty bordellos and rounded up dozens of prostitutes, only a trifle compared to the estimated two thousand women working for Luciano's combine at the time. Dewey spared the women long jail terms in return for testifying that Luciano was head of what may have been the largest prostitution ring in U.S. history. He was convicted and sentenced to thirty to fifty years in prison. Everyone in the Mob believed that Luciano was framed. Charley Lucky was no pimp, they said. It didn't matter. On his way to the can, he named Costello as acting family head.

Having risen to a position of influence under Costello, Johnny was then in his middle twenties, rather late for an immigrant male of his generation still to be single. As a top button man in New York he had access to plenty of women, but none moved him until he met a young woman who had only recently left the orphanage that raised her after her parents were killed in a trolley car accident.

Millicent Costelli was lovely, reserved, and respectful, the very image of a good Italian wife. And she could cook; she learned everything at the apron of Johnny's mother and came to outshine her in the years when every Sunday called for a feast. Her childhood abandonment

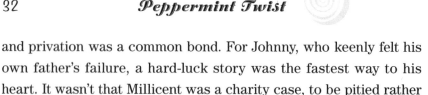

and privation was a common bond. For Johnny, who keenly felt his own father's failure, a hard-luck story was the fastest way to his heart. It wasn't that Millicent was a charity case, to be pitied rather than loved. It was simply that, whatever her other gifts, her vulnerability gave her, in Johnny's mind, an insight and depth beyond the grasp of other girls.

Even so, the idea of marrying purely for love would have struck Johnny as a strange, indulgent conceit. Where he was from, people married for lots of reasons, most of them practical. The idea that one must be smitten, and remain smitten the rest of one's life, would have seemed pointless. To Johnny, Millicent's victimization was simply another crime perpetrated by a callous society, more ammunition for his belief that in America, one had to battle for one's bread every day. In Italy, Johnny believed, a child who lost her parents would have been taken in by her extended family. In America, Millicent was confined to an institution until she reached an age when the state sent her on her way, to whatever fate awaited.

"They sell you a bill of goods here," Johnny would often say over the years. "They tell you anybody can get ahead. But I'll tell you something, it ain't so. This place is all about money. If you got it, you can do anything. If you don't, you're nothing." Johnny didn't intend to be nothing.

Once he met Millicent, he made a lifetime commitment. His private behavior notwithstanding, his side of the bargain was that he would protect and provide for her every need, a promise he never broke or showed any signs of regretting throughout their long marriage.

Her part of the bargain was that she would not interfere with his business. She was not some naïf. She knew, at least generally, what he did with his time. It wasn't that she made a deal with the devil for a life of security and ease. The deal she cut was with Johnny Biello. Nor was it that a strong man manipulated her. She fell in love and reasoned that if such a man as this did things of which society disapproved, then perhaps it was society that was wrong.

To Johnny, there were hard and unyielding rules about how you handled your family obligations, just as there were for how you handled your working life. "You know how I know a guy is full of shit?" Johnny once said to Dick. "It's when he takes his girlfriend to the same joint he takes his wife and kids to. That ain't right."

Johnny always referred to Frank Sinatra, known to be an intimate of mobsters, as a degenerate. He disliked Frank not because he had affairs, but because he made them public and for the way he abandoned his family to marry Ava Gardner.

By the mid-thirties, with his first daughter, Beverly, in diapers and two more soon to come, Futto was chosen by Costello to succeed Schultz as the big man in the Bronx. Johnny was one of an estimated three hundred soldiers at Costello's command, but he steadily grew so close to Frank that the FBI considered him the likely successor to run the family after Costello stepped down years later after a botched assassination attempt.

Bootlegging continued to be a good cash business after repeal, but Johnny developed other rackets as well. For years, he ran a big dice game in Harlem. He got into shylocking but found it distasteful. He didn't mind so much when somebody could not afford to pay his debts. It was running out on the debt that was the big sin to Johnny. He went to one guy's home and burst in, intending to get his money or else, but was brought up short by what he saw. The family was at dinner. There were all these kids and nothing on the plates. Johnny pulled out a hundred and threw it on the table.

"Next time, don't duck me," he said.

"To be a shylock, you've got to be without mercy and no regrets, no matter what," Johnny frequently told Dick.

As soon as Johnny had acquired enough money from gambling and bookmaking, he started shying the shylocks, loaning money to other moneylenders. It was a good business and it allowed him to avoid having to deal with the poor wage slaves at the bottom of the pile.

By World War II, the boys had branched out into other businesses. Labor racketeering was a good, steady source of income. Charley Lucky had the waterfront unions locked up. Even though Luciano was in prison, the feds asked him for help keeping peace on the docks during the war. The navy was losing a lot of ships to Nazi submarines, and the War Department believed German spies working the docks were responsible. Sandi Lansky Lombardo, Meyer's daughter and a close friend of Dick's, said her father came up with the idea of offering to ferret out the spies in return for Luciano's freedom. After initially hesitating, the navy approved Operation B3.

Luciano summoned every important wiseguy connected to the docks to his cell, ordering them to spread the word that if anyone was seen with a German sympathizer, the penalty was death. To enforce the order, a mobster walked up to a group of men on the crowded docks and asked for a German dockworker. Pointed to him, the mobster asked, "Excuse me, but are you Otto Meinvogel?"

"Yes," the man said.

Leaning in closer, the gangster said, "Are you sure?"

"Vat do you mean am I sure? Of course I'm sure who I am."

Meinvogel was shot dead on the spot. The gangster held up his hand and shouted, "Listen to me, all you cocksuckers. This guy was a German spy. If we hear that you're talking to pricks like this, you'll end up just like this guy here."

Operation B3 was a success, and Luciano got his freedom. Unfortunately for the success of Lansky's plan, Luciano was not allowed to return to America; he was deported to Italy.

In the late thirties, with the world on the brink of war and the wrath of Dewey still lingering, Costello, like any good businessman, began to seek opportunities outside his home territory. His slot machines didn't look to be rising out of the river anytime soon, so Frank and Lansky began looking south and west.

Reno was the hot spot in Nevada, but big things were beginning to happen in Las Vegas, which had been little more than a water stop on the train from Salt Lake City to the coast. Boulder Dam, later renamed

Hoover Dam, was being built in the rocky desert of Black Canyon. Thousands of dam workers were drawing good pay with no place to go and little to spend it on. the air Force was about to take over the Western Air Express airfield—basically a shack, a water tower, and a few dilapidated planes—and turn it into the 12,000-acre Nellis Air Force Base. More men with time and money on their hands.

In 1931, the Nevada legislature legalized gambling. Three years later, Lansky sent Benjamin "Bugsy" Siegel—who, according to Sandi Lansky, was like a brother to her father—to scout Vegas for possible operations. But Siegel hated the place and fled back to his Hollywood haunts and movie-star friends as soon as he could.

Costello turned to his trusted lieutenant, Johnny Futto, to assess the opportunities for a casino operation. With Johnny's experience running no-limit card games and floating crap games around the Bronx and Manhattan, it was a natural choice.

"Have you ever been to the Southwest?" Frank asked Johnny one day.

"No. I like Miami," Johnny said. In fact, he was already buying up businesses down there.

"It's beautiful out there, purple mountains everywhere and the desert has a beauty all its own," Costello said. Before he started sounding any more like a Realtor, Johnny cut him off.

"Where we going with this, Frank?" Johnny said. "You didn't get me up here to give me the mutuals on desert life, did you?"

The mutuals, in Mob lingo, meant information, as in, "Give me the mutuals on that guy." Originally it was picked up from the track, referring to the daily totals on any illegal enterprise, but over the years, it came to mean the bottom line on any subject.

"I'd like you to go out there and look around. Take your family for a vacation," Costello said. Frank always liked Millicent. His name, after he changed it, was close to her maiden name, Costelli. He was always kidding Johnny, "How's my niece doing?"

Frank continued, "Meyer Lansky thinks there's a potential for big things to be happening out there."

Johnny pointed out that as a felon he would have a hard time doing business in Nevada. In a well-intentioned, but ultimately useless attempt to keep crooks away, the legislature required all felons doing business in Nevada to register with the police. Johnny had no intention of doing that, so Frank suggested he locate to Tucson.

"We've got a friendly sheriff there," Costello said. "Maybe you can rent a house."

"No problem," Johnny said. "That's in Arizona, right?"

Costello told Johnny that Meyer was the only one who knew what Johnny would be up to. "Keep a lid on this. Just tell everyone you're going to Arizona for the winter."

By this time, Futto was a package deal. He and Millicent had three small daughters. From the moment Johnny stepped off the plane, he knew Arizona was for them. As he descended the ramp, he was surprised to feel the difference between the heat of Miami and the lack of humidity in the Southwest. He knew this would please Millicent. Within a week, he had rented a house and made arrangements for the family to come out by train. The family loved it in Tucson. The people seemed nicer and more down-to-earth. The girls had the freedom to run and play in the sand and scrub. Mostly, Millicent was thrilled that her husband had escaped gangland New York. From the outside, their lives looked as normal as anyone's. The biggest problem was finding the Italian food products Millicent needed for cooking.

The desert would prove to be a boon to their oldest daughter, Beverly, who suffered from a rheumatic heart. Middle daughter Joanie loved the outdoors, nature, and animals, and it was all there in abundance. But, Connie, the baby, developed *polioencephalitis*, which left her permanently brain-damaged. Although the couple was advised to put her in a home for the severely mentally retarded, Millicent wouldn't consider it and Johnny backed her up.

This simple kindness was one of the things that would first impress Dick about his future father-in-law years later. Dick had a friend who kept his retarded brother in the attic, but Johnny and Millicent sat Connie right at the table. Over the years, Johnny organized numerous charity functions at the famed Copacabana, headlining acts such as Jimmy Durante and singer Billy Daniels, with all the proceeds going to benefit retarded children. He was also a regular benefactor of the Montanari Clinical School in Hialeah, Florida, for children with extreme mental, behavior, and emotional challenges.

Connie had a ferocious appetite and watching her diet was a twenty-four-hour challenge. "Come on, Pop-Pop," she'd say. "Can I have another piece of bread?"

When he refused, she'd beg. "Just a pusher, please, just a pusher."

A pusher was a piece of bread you held in your off-hand to push bits of food onto the fork. By the time the meal was done, the pusher had sopped up all the wonderful juices of Millicent's cooking. It was the best and last thing to eat before the cannoli. Connie always got her pusher.

"Fat, fat, the water rat," Johnny would say to her. "Fifty bullets in your hat."

Johnny was gone a lot, running a big gambling operation out on Nogales Highway. True to Frank's word, the friendly sheriff left Johnny alone . . . for a certain consideration. Johnny wasn't there long before other wiseguys heard about the desert and followed him. One of them was Joe Bonanno, the founder of one of the Five Families. In 1942, Johnny sold Bonanno his house in Tucson. The Bonanno family still owns the house.

After selling his house, Johnny built his family another place. The games that Johnny set up went well. Even the gamblers were a different breed out west. Things he had to contend with in New York were nonexistent. People stood by their word. If they promised something, they did it. Costello called it Western hospitality.

After a while, Costello sent word that it was time to take a look at Vegas. He heard about a hotel that was looking for casino people. They didn't know how to make the place over themselves, so Johnny went in to take a look.

"It's supposed to be a small joint downtown," Costello said.

Johnny rolled into town early one afternoon, figuring to take his time and get the lay of the land. On Fremont Street, every other place was a saloon or a hotel with a casino. Music and the clink of glasses mingled with the rattle of chips at the gaming tables. It was almost too much to believe, people gambling openly, all day and all night, unafraid of the law. On every sunbaked block there were a hundred ways to lose money. Johnny realized the potential right away.

The Apache Hotel was an old building on the corner of Fremont and Second streets. It didn't look like much. The owner knew he couldn't make a go of it alone and gave Johnny a good price. We'll renovate the place and put in a sweet little casino, Johnny told him. In return, the owner would get 5 percent off the top. It sounded good and he offered his hand to seal the deal.

"Just one thing," Johnny said. "You got to get the casino license in your name. You understand?"

The man said he didn't mind one bit.

The conversion costs were not unreasonable. It was the gaming equipment that would be expensive. For that, Johnny called on a friend, Al Miniaci. Miniaci was one of the founders of the coin machine industry and a great character who would play a key role in the Peppermint Lounge. Nobody had seen slot machines like the ones Al got for Johnny. The renovated Apache Hotel, with its ground-floor casino, opened quietly in the winter of 1939.

The front was perfect and the Mob had one of its first footholds in Las Vegas. In 1945, Billy Wilkerson, owner of *The Hollywood Reporter* and several popular nightclubs on the Sunset Strip in Los Angeles, dreamed of building a luxurious hotel on the strip a mile south of the Last Frontier. Benny "Bugsy" Siegel was put in charge because the boys believed he could bring in the Hollywood swells and celebrities to make it famous. The Flamingo Hotel was named for Siegel's girlfriend, Virginia Hill, an actress known as the Flamingo.

It's long been said that Benny was killed by the Mob because he spent so lavishly on the hotel. True enough, he ran up the bill on such things as providing each of the ninety-three rooms with its own sewer system. He bought the finest building materials when the country was still suffering wartime shortages. Maybe Benny's wild spending was the last straw.

But there were other reasons, according to Cami and others with knowledge about the situation. Once, Charley Lucky called a big meet in Cuba. He was sick of exile in Italy and wanted to find a way to get back in the States to take back his rightful position as head of his family. Siegel arrived late to the meeting, a big no-no with Luciano, who believed in military promptness. Maybe he thought Lucky was past his prime and it didn't matter. In any event, it was only Meyer's friendship with Luciano that saved Benny that day.

But the protection went only so far. Siegel's carelessness and lack of attention to detail on the Flamingo project sealed his fate. On June 20, 1947, Siegel was shot in the head while reading the *Los Angeles Times* in the living room of Virginia Hill's Beverly Hills mansion. The crime was never solved.

Years later, a very dangerous gangster Dick got to know well called Tony Plate told Dick there were two shooters outside Virginia Hill's house that day. Plate identified one as Frankie Carbo, a close friend of Johnny's and long considered a chief suspect in the assassination by the LAPD. The other gunman with Carbo at the Hill estate, Plate said, was Johnny Futto.

Plate was probably the last man on Earth to want to polish Johnny's reputation, which is what giving him a role in the Siegel hit would amount to. He hated Johnny, carrying a grudge for years, he told Dick, because Johnny voted against him when he was made. Dick went to Scatsy with Plate's version. Could it be true? he asked.

"I don't know nothing," Scatsy said.

Usually, when Scatsy said that, he did know something.

A year after Siegel's murder, Johnny returned to New York to reclaim his position as Costello's right-hand man. Johnny got into the garbage-hauling business, partnering with Nicholas Ratteni, with whom he'd been arrested for the jewelry heist twenty years earlier. Together, they formed Westchester Carting Company, which, according to the feds, went about wrapping up business by destroying the

equipment of its rivals and that of shopkeepers who declined to sign with them. In 1952, according to the FBI, an upstart garbage hauler in New Rochelle was told to see Johnny if he wanted the contract. When the two met, Johnny told the aspiring garbage man that if he wanted to solve his problem he should make Johnny a partner. In the end, according to the FBI, the man decided against it. Nothing happened to him as a result.

Many times in the coming years, whenever things got hot, whenever his rackets got pinched, Johnny would reminisce about Tucson and talk about moving back and reclaiming the simple desert life he'd known.

Meanwhile, most guys left the Mob the same way—feet first. That included Tony Plate. He disappeared not long after telling Dick Cami the Bugsy Siegel story. John Gotti, the so-called Dapper Don, had him killed over some stupid beef. Showing how feared Plate was, he'd been missing six months when Dick ran into his girlfriend. She was a pretty little thing, but she looked bad. Dick asked how she was doing. She was lonely, she said. He told her a nice-looking gal like her should get out and circulate.

"I'd like to," she said, "but if Tony came back, he'd kill me."

Chapter 5

You Do Now, Son

The Camillucci family's apartment on the top floor of a five-story walkup on 165th Street was no more than a mile in distance from where Johnny and Scatsy grew up. But it was a thousand miles from the poverties and indignities suffered by the Biellos.

Dick's paternal grandfather came from Faenza, a small mountain town south of Bologna, in the 1890s, not as a scuffling, threadbare immigrant like Johnny's father. Frank Camillucci was brought over to work as a chef at the Waldorf=Astoria. He was not a shy man.

"Italy is the garden spot of the world and the best garden in Italy is Faenza," he said. "And, of course, I am the most beautiful flower in that garden."

The Camilluccis were not just big talkers. They were big people. Dick's Italian great-grandfather was a giant of a man who could fight bare-fisted for hours. He had to. A born troublemaker, his temper finally got him in so much hot water that he had to take it on the lam. He lit out for Turkey and was never seen again.

Dick loved to spend weekends with his grandfather. Master chef

Frank Camillucci was already retired, but kept his hand in by making sauces for some of the best restaurants and pizzerias in the upper Bronx. He also made sausages for Mercurio's, the finest Italian food market in Mount Vernon, the same town where Johnny and Scatsy moved their bootlegging operation after it outgrew the vaults and tunnels in the Bronx.

"I must have pricked the skin of a million sausages," Dick said. "Miles and miles of them."

His grandfather also had him grate the cheese.

"Dickie," he would call from the kitchen, "make sure you whistle when you grate the cheese."

When Dick asked why, he would respond, "So I know you no eat the cheese."

There wasn't a day that went by that his grandfather didn't have an argument with Dick's grandmother. He had the louder voice, but she was more cunning. If they had a fight and he stomped out to have a few drinks, she'd rearrange the furniture. When he returned, tipsy, he stumbled into the repositioned chairs and tables, cursing them all the while as if they had moved into his path of their own volition.

During summers, Dick was shipped off to New London, Connecticut, where his mother grew up near the shores of the Thames River. The kids he ran with used to razz him. "Dickie's going up the country with the hayseeds." They had no concept of the world outside New York.

Dick didn't mind the teasing. He loved the visits, particularly the grand outdoor Sunday feasts where the extended Camillucci family came together at his uncle Sam and aunt Sue's house.

"It always started the same way. On Sunday, about one o'clock in the morning, Uncle Sam would come into my cousin Buddy's bedroom and wake us up by blowing a trumpet. That got our blood pumping, to say the least. Then we'd put on our crabbing gear: bathing suits, sneakers, heavy coat, and flashlights hanging around our necks because it was still dark. We carried nets to scoop up blue crabs and jigs to spear eels that swam by or flounders that lay on the river bottom. The occasional striped bass was a real treat."

They returned home just as the sun was breaching over Fishers Island. The men separated and cleaned the catch while the women began working up the special dishes: pasta in blue crab sauce, baked stuffed blue crabs, grilled and breaded filet of flounder, grilled fresh lobster, eels in tomato sauce, plus endless varieties of fresh vegetables and salads from Dick's grandfather's garden.

Dick and his cousin Buddy, after dumping their first load, climbed on their bikes and went clamming down at Ocean Beach. When they had filled two bushel baskets, they pedaled home. By mid-morning, their work was done. Then, Dick could wander down to the basement kitchen to watch the women, captained by his grandmother, Emilia, baking and chopping, roasting and peeling, preparing everything they'd brought. By two o'clock in the afternoon, the feast was under way.

"I learned everything about food watching my grandmother in Connecticut and my grandfather back in the Bronx," Dick said. "Their cooking styles were very different. When I got married, my mother-in-law introduced me to a third kind of cooking, the Neapolitan kitchen. Her skill in the kitchen was equally unbelievable; she had a natural talent for mixing ingredients. So my knowledge of cooking comes from all of Italy, the north, the middle, and finally the south. All different styles, all Italian, all delightful."

Dick's parents met by a strange convergence of family connections. His uncle Emilio, his father's brother, was a salesman for Italian waters, Fiuggi, Pellegrino and the like—the same waters that Johnny liked to pinch off the street peddlers. The distributor was based in Little Italy in lower Manhattan, and Emilio's territory was the tri-state area.

Whenever he visited a new town, Emilio had a habit of looking in the phone book for the family name. "For Italians, there can never be too much family," Dick said.

In New London, he struck gold with the family of Alba Camillucci, a lovely young woman with an operatic soprano voice. So far as anyone knows, neither family shared blood. Cami's mother's family came from Fano, north of central Italy on the Adriatic Sea.

Alba had graduated from the prestigious Rossini Conservatory in Pesaro, Italy. Her parents expected her to make a career on the stage at the Met, not to marry a struggling musician like Dick's father, Richard.

"I have pictures of her singing with USO tours in World War II and an image of her on a poster advertising a concert in Italy with Beniamino Gigli, the most beloved tenor of his generation," Dick said.

Her marriage to Richard Camillucci Senior short-circuited all that. Getting married was one thing, but having children would be more than an impediment to a singing career. Alba was so afraid to face her father with the news that she was pregnant that she kept the baby's existence in New York a secret for three years after Dick's birth.

"My grandmother was another story," Dick said. "When she found out, I was like a new toy."

Everyone wanted to see Alba's baby, and Dick Junior gloried in the attention.

Alba was a fine musician but, to his son, Richard Senior "stood in no one's shadow."

The senior Camillucci gained a reputation as one of the top teachers of singing in New York. He worked with Eartha Kitt, Billy Dee Williams, and the child movie star Gloria Jean. When Shirley Jones was cast as Laurey in the movie adaptation of the Rodgers and Hammerstein musical *Oklahoma!*, Richard Camillucci spent six months working with her to bring her register down to match her voice to her co-star, Gordon MacRae.

One time, a businessman went to see Mr. Camillucci because he wanted to entertain his friends at a big party he was throwing in advance of a serious operation. He had lost the ability to urinate properly; the surgery to clear the blockage was delicate and chancy. After a few weeks of vocal exercising, he came into the studio shouting, "It's a miracle."

With tears streaming down his face, he told the voice teacher he no longer needed the operation. "Because of you, I can piss," he said.

Camillucci was blasé. "What miracle? The exercises must have loosened your abdominal muscles."

This was typical of the elder Camillucci. Direct and uncomplicated, his attitudes were not filtered by prejudice or class consciousness. To Richard Camillucci, his famous students were no more important than the neighborhood kids who showed up at his studio in the Apollo Theater building on 125th Street in Harlem. A friend remembers a maxim Dick's dad typically used when one of his students came up short at the close of the session. "That's all right, you can pay me when you're a star," he would say.

Despite his lax attention to the bottom line, Dick Senior's business took off. He opened new studios and took two of the leading African-American impresarios in New York, Buster Newman and Luther Henderson, as partners. Every time Buster met Richard's kid, he would thunder, "Hey, Dickie, whattya got?" His whole body shook with laughter.

Luther was more serious. He was never less than friendly and courteous when Richard's kid dropped in. But it was clear he had things on his mind, important things to do for important people. Luther was Lena Horne's accompanist for years. He did arrangements for Duke Ellington and scored countless Broadway musicals such as Rodgers and Hammerstein's *Flower Drum Song*. He was all business.

When he was just nine years old, Dick began sneaking down the stairs from his father's studio to stand backstage at the Apollo. From the edge of the curtain, blending in to the ropes, props, and women in skimpy clothes, the white kid watched the greatest black acts of the day perform for some of the toughest crowds any entertainer ever faced. At the Apollo, you couldn't just stand still and sing your song; you had to entertain. Dick's favorite was Bill "Bojangles" Robinson, the greatest dancer he'd ever seen.

Dick didn't think it odd that his father worked with African Americans. The most race-based comment Dick ever heard his father

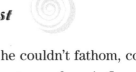

make was to say that, for some reason that he couldn't fathom, colored folks could go to the place where that vast sea of music flowed pure and untroubled a lot easier than white people. He'd seen it over and over. They had the first, and best, swing bands. And, of course, they invented rhythm and blues, jazz, and rock and roll.

Dick's dad received invitations to house parties all over Manhattan where there were always racially mixed couples. He took his son one time. Young Dick met Warren Berry, part of the great dancing team, the Berry Brothers. The high point of their act came at the end, when Warren would jump off the balcony onto the stage and into the splits. It was a gag-inducing triumph that left every man in the house clutching his privates, which is why they kept it in the act. There was nobody, not Bill Robinson, Fred Astaire, or anybody else who could top that. One time, while filming a scene for *The Ed Sullivan Show*, Warren did the big jump but failed to land it. He broke his hip and never danced again. In an effort to rebuild his career, he took singing lessons from Richard Camillucci.

At the party, someone sat down at the piano and tried to coax Berry into singing. He refused, claiming he wasn't ready. The rest wouldn't have it, so he limped over to the piano, bent, and whispered in the ear of the pianist.

Berry turned and, his face a mask of deep sadness and resignation, began to sing: "I won't dance, don't ask me. I won't dance, don't ask me. I won't dance, madam, with you. My heart won't let my feet do things that they should do."

Around the room, women dabbed at their eyes and men tried, and failed, to remain stoic. Dick felt like an intruder. He was witnessing something far too private. The man's open wound was there for everyone to see. But he was so completely devoid of self-pity that there was no pathos in it. If tragedy could be beautiful, that was it. That was the day Dick discovered the meaning of soul.

His first brush with show business came when he was still a teenager in high school. He heard that Mike Todd, the famous film producer and one of Elizabeth Taylor's husbands, was staging *A Night in Venice*, complete with floating gondolas. With the innate chutzpah that would later allow him to move so easily between the straight world and the world of wiseguys, Dick talked a friend into going out with him to the newly constructed Jones Beach Theater on Long Island.

"I'd heard there were jobs as extras," Dick said. "When we showed up, a member of the staff told us we weren't needed."

Ninety-nine out of a hundred would have gone away. There must be some mistake, the boy said. He'd been told to come. The guy shrugged and jerked his thumb over his shoulder. "Talk to him," he said.

The guy he pointed to was Mike Todd, who turned an icy glare on the two boys slouching nervously in front of him. Dick bluffed his way through a brief, tense interview with Todd and got the job. He and his pal, Ralph Grasso, earned six dollars a day for the run of the show.

While Dick was standing around on a Jones Beach stage pretending to be "stupid as an oyster," he was also running the streets of the Bronx. He wasn't a bad kid, but he could be reckless. In 1948, his freshman year of high school, the same year his sister Maria was born, and, coincidentally, the same year Johnny returned from Arizona, the family decided it was time to move to the suburbs. They settled in Freeport, on Long Island.

Tragedy struck when, shortly after the move, Dick's mother developed terminal ovarian cancer. It took a long, painful three years for her to succumb to the disease.

Compared to the Bronx, Freeport was like stepping into an old Frank Capra movie. The streets were uncluttered and the shopkeepers knew your name. Classes at Taft High in the Bronx had housed seventy kids, but in Freeport they held only twenty. Dick was still learning his way around the campus when one of the teachers walked up.

"You play football?" he said. By this time, Dick was full-grown, over six feet tall, broad-shouldered, long-armed, wide-hipped.

"No," Dick said.

"You do now, son."

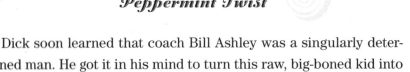

Dick soon learned that coach Bill Ashley was a singularly determined man. He got it in his mind to turn this raw, big-boned kid into a real football player. On the very first down he ever played, Dick was told to block a varsity player, Tommy Malinowski.

"I looked over at Tommy and I could tell I had fifty pounds on him," Dick said. "My first thoughts were, I don't want to hurt this guy."

When the ball was hiked, Malinowski flew at the new recruit. A forearm sent Dick tumbling. The blow opened a gash on his chin and blood spurted everywhere. He still has the scar.

After that, he worked hard to make sure no one ever got a jump on him again. Eventually Dick Camillucci was selected as a first-string center on the *Newsday* All-Scholastic team, where he was photographed standing next to future pro-football immortal Jim Brown. Even better for his prospects in college, he was chosen first-string on the prestigious *Herald-Tribune* All-Metropolitan team, which included every high school in the area, including New Jersey. The Associated Press also awarded him honorable mention on the High School All-American team.

On graduation, among the many scholarship offers, his first choice was the number one–rated college football team in the country at the time, the University of Tennessee. But after being told by a coach that they didn't like Italians there, he signed on with Kansas State University, where a new coach, Bill Meek, was determined to reverse the school's dismal football fortunes. Meek didn't recruit solely among the prairie farm crowd. He cast his net widely, scooping up not only Camillucci, but some of the finest recruits in the country.

At Penn Station, as Dick waited for the train west, a two-hundred-fifty-pound foundation stone of a man walked up and stuck out his hand. "Lou Albano," he said.

The trip to Manhattan, Kansas, lasted three days. Three battle-filled days. Dick and Albano never exchanged a cross word. The dozen fights were between Albano and every other passenger in a scrapping mood.

At K-State, Albano and Camillucci got off to a bad start. On the first day, they were walking across campus on the way to class when a tall student approached. He was a member of the basketball team, a first-rate program that competed for the national championship the year Dick arrived. When the boy walked up, Dick thought he was going to welcome the new kids to campus. He'd heard about Midwestern hospitality. Instead, the guy wanted to know where their beanies were. "All freshmen must wear a beanie when they're on campus," he said.

A meaty hand shot out and grabbed the basketball player by the shirt, lifting him off his feet, all seventy-seven inches of him, and pinned him against a wall. "Listen, asshole," Albano said, "the next time I see you, you better be wearing a fucking beanie."

From his elevated position, feet dangling, the basketball player began to protest. "I can't wear a beanie. I'm a junior."

"Who gives a fuck?" Albano said. They were called to the dean's office later that day and both written up for bad conduct. That was just the first of their run-ins with authority.

The one that ended their Kansas college adventure occurred when a group of players—all the athletes lived together in rooms attached to the stadium—decided to go to the movies one night. Accompanying Dick and Albano as they walked down the hall to invite others to come along was their roommate, Vinnie Aulisi, who was wearing a new shirt he'd just received in the mail from his mother in New Jersey. The trio encountered Ronnie Clair, who was wearing a sour expression.

"What's up with the face?" Dick asked.

"You know what's up," Clair said. He pulled out his wallet and opened it to reveal the crime. Someone had stolen his money. When he found out who—and from the look on his face it was clear who his top suspects were; he was known to hate the Easterners—he was going to the police. Dick asked how much was taken. Six dollars, he said.

Dick started laughing. "That's quite a heist," he said. "They're probably going to call in the FBI."

Everyone laughed except Clair. A full-scale brawl was soon

under way. Aulisi and Clair went at it. This time, Albano was a peace-maker. Just when it looked like everything was over, Aulisi looked in the mirror. His beautiful new shirt was spotted with blood. He went off all over again, and shot out of the room after Clair. Dick and Albano followed but this time there was no stopping him. Ironically, Albano, who had no part in starting it had everything to do with finishing it, mistakenly broke a mirror over Dick's head during the fight he was supposedly trying to break up.

When the fight was over, every window, every door, and every piece of furniture was broken. The police were called and took Dick, Aulisi, and Albano into custody until the school decided what to do.

The decision was simple, really, given their record as troublemakers. A coach gave them fifty dollars each and told them they were dismissed. The sheriff took the three to the edge of town and, like some B western, told them to never return.

The incident made the wire services. By the time they hitchhiked home, they found their families worried stiff. A few months later, Coach Meek sent Dick a letter acknowledging that he hadn't done anything other than try to stop the fight. He urged him to return, but by that time, young Camillucci was already enrolled at the University of South Carolina. He managed to log two years at one of the Southern football powerhouses before he ran into a new set of problems.

Dick was asked to come to campus early and the team made arrangements for another ballplayer to show him around. Ned Brown was from Moncks Corner, South Carolina. Dick had trouble understanding him when he spoke. "You want to put the potato on the other side of your mouth," Dick kidded him.

In the South, Dick was stunned by rules requiring blacks to sit in the back of the bus, drink from separate fountains, and use separate restrooms, entrances to the movies, and even occupy blacks-only cabs.

Brown was always talking about "niggers." The topic seemed to fascinate him. One day they were walking downtown on State Street and Brown said to Dick, "Let me show you how we treat niggers here in the South."

An elderly black lady was walking toward them, barely shuffling along, bent over with her head down. Brown stood with his arms crossed, blocking her path. When she came up to where he was standing, she stopped and looked up. Then she put her head back down and calmly walked around him. "That's the way we treat niggers here in Carolina," he said.

Dick knew he would be in for a rough ride. He knew there weren't any black ballplayers on Carolina's team, but was surprised to learn that South Carolina would not even play a team with blacks on the roster.

He never expected to see the blunt stupidity of it in class until one of his professors mentioned that there was a move afoot to integrate the campus. "If they let any into my classroom, I'm going to give him a tom-tom and let him beat it in the back of the room for music appreciation," he said.

Dick couldn't believe what he was hearing, from a college professor no less. There was a student in class who had some experience in the matter, the professor said. "Would you get up and explain to the class what it's like to go to school with niggers, Mr. Camillucci?"

Sitting behind him was another ballplayer, Eddie Fields, who was from South Boston. "Give it to him, Cam," he said.

"Where I'm from everybody goes to school with colored people. Nobody thinks anything about it," Dick said.

"You mean to tell the class that you didn't come down here to get away from all the niggers?"

Dick was disgusted. "The only reason I came here was this school offered me the biggest scholarship. That's it."

Despite his revulsion at the overt racism that Southern blacks faced every day, the event wasn't the cause of his still premature, but by then expected, departure from South Carolina. A halfback from Brooklyn, Ralphie "Blackie" Fasano, was playing with his rifle one day in the dorm and decided to fire it. Luckily, the bullet went down the hall and lodged in the metal door without encountering any flesh on the way.

Nevertheless, the police were called. After some sleuthing, they found the rifle where Ralphie had hidden it—in the trunk of Dick's car. They were both given the usual option: Leave school or we'll prosecute. On the drive back to New York, Ralphie apologized a hundred times.

"I finally told him enough already," said Dick.

A few months later, Dick got his letter from Uncle Sam, extending him a hearty welcome to the nation's military. At the induction physical, he was asked to list any injuries. He wrote: broken leg, dislocated shoulder, broken nose (four times), broken fingers, and a cracked spine. All but the last were suffered playing football. Dick figured that would keep him out of the draft.

He was wrong. He was classified 4-E. It was the lowest rating you could get without being disqualified, but it was no exemption. He was shipped off to Camp Gordon in Georgia for basic training. By the end of basic, when he was awarded Best in Battalion, Dick was recruited by a bunkmate to join the Screaming Eagles paratrooper unit. His classification prevented that. After basic, Dick was assigned to Fort Belvoir in Virginia where, in spite of his classification, they vigorously recruited him for the football team. However, after one game Dick decided he'd had enough of broken bones and was content to spend his two-year hitch behind a desk as a finance clerk. The person he replaced told him that he had landed the best job in the army. "If anyone fucks with you, just tell them you'll ship their pay records to Alaska," he said.

Chapter 6

Rock and Roll Is
Here to Stay

Dick was home on leave from the army over Christmas 1956 when a friend from high school invited him to a New Year's Eve party. The friend wanted him to meet a girl who was down in the dumps over a failed relationship.

Dick was unenthusiastic. Nursing a girl's wounded heart was not his idea of a good time, especially on New Year's Eve. But he eventually agreed to go. At the party, the introduction proved to be one of those life-altering moments that, at first, seemed anything but. Dick didn't have the sense of taking one road and leaving another, of making some fateful choice.

Petite with short brown hair, high cheekbones, and hazel eyes, Joanie Biello bore a casual resemblance to Jackie Kennedy. Even more notably, the very thing that most charmed Dick was the thing that would eventually cause trouble in their relationship—her feisty personality. Coming from an Italian family, where emotions were expressed with enthusiasm, Dick liked the way she parried his teasing with her wry sense of humor.

Joan, growing up pampered, attending private schools, and

associating with other pampered Mafia daughters, had no shortage of suitors who were just as thrilled with themselves as Dick was. High-spirited, smart, and with a privileged appreciation for her gifts, she wore the title of Italian princess as a badge of honor. She had left each of her previous suitors behind and that was likely to be Dick's fate as well.

That night, Dick got his New Year's kiss, the standard exchange of holiday bonhomie between the sexes. It did not promise anything more. Joan thought Dick was very handsome. They got along well from the start. But she reserved judgment on this new guy, whom she tended to dismiss as a "clam digger from Freeport."

Maybe so, but this particular clam digger had ambitions. While serving desk duty in the army, Camillucci promoted shows around the Washington, D.C., and New York areas. He hired the groups, found the venue, charged an admission fee at the door, and gave the club the food and drink money. The practice was called "four-walling." He also booked several of his father's professional students into the lounge of the Mayflower Hotel in Washington. After he left the army, he thought, he might give the music business a try, not yet having any concept of the dirty business it could be.

By the time Dick mustered out in March 1957, he and Joanie were dating more or less exclusively. The first time he picked her up at her house in Atlantic Beach, New York, he was impressed. Only a half block from the ocean, with a big kitchen and sprawling dining room that could—and did—seat a dozen heavy eaters, it was a grand home fit for a captain of industry. Frank Erickson, the biggest bookmaker in America, lived across the street. Anthony Carfano, known as Little Augie Pisano, a *capo* himself and a close associate of Johnny's, lived around the corner. Another *capo*, Big John Ormento, a Lucchese man and a major crime figure in East Harlem since he was old enough to count twenties, was down the block, as well as Genovese associate Frank Livorsi.

By this time, Johnny had even adopted a new last name, Biele, for use in public, whether in the hope of shedding his scuffling criminal

past or his ragged origins he never said. Officially, to the census tak-
ers and Social Security agents, he would always be Biello. But he
eventually came to regard himself so closely with the new character
he created that even in family gatherings he became John Biele, well-
to-do businessman and investor.

This appearance of affluent normalcy was in keeping with the
policy consciously adopted by the Mob in the modern era. Join the
PTA, Frank Costello urged. Have barbecues in the backyard. Learn
to play hearts and bridge instead of stud poker. You might even try
walking around in Bermuda shorts on weekends and patrolling the
front yard with a hose in your hand.

Dick knew nothing of the neighbors. The place was luxurious and
quiet, the kind of well-manicured suburbia that seemed to represent
the best of what America could offer.

Dick had no idea what Joan's father did for a living, although it
was beginning to dawn on him that his girlfriend did not have your
average American family. She was coy on the subject, just as she had
learned to be when her teachers asked about her father's work. "He
makes books," she said.

"You mean, like a publisher?" Dick said.

"Something like that," she said.

Dick was no dummy. He knew she was teasing, but he decided to
leave the subject alone for the time being.

On one of their early dates, Dick arrived late, well past nine o'clock.
He'd been held up at the base. He'd tried calling, but the phone was
always busy. She'd said she would leave the door open and when he
walked in he found her in her nightgown. He laughed and made a motion with his hands like he was taking a picture.

She covered up and yelled, "Get out." She was in a rage. "I've been
waiting half the night. Did you forget we had a date?"

He explained, launching into a song to lighten the mood. "Kiss me
once, kiss me twice. Kiss me once again. It's been a long, long time."

"I'm glad *you're* in a good mood," she said angrily. "I was worried
to death. You could have called."

"I tried. Your phone was busy all night."

Joanie looked at the phone, which was partly off the hook. She brightened. "I've decided to forgive you," she said. "This time."

Dick slipped his hand inside her nightgown and drew her in. A muffled noise from the garage interrupted them. Joanie pushed him away.

"Uncle Albert?" she said as she scampered away. "Is that you?"

"Yeah it's me, *babalousch*," Scatsy said, coming inside.

"Say hello to Dick," Joanie called from her bedroom. Dick was sitting in the living room, trying to wipe the smile from his face.

"We're going out," Joanie called. "I'll be down in a sec."

Scatsy came through the hallway into the kitchen, carrying bags of groceries nearly as big as he was. He looked like a fireplug that had been dressed up, badly, with a crew cut on top.

"You know anything about dogs?" he said to Dick.

"Dogs?" Dick said. "Not much."

"I'm gonna take care of this fucking dog next door that keeps the old man up all night. We warned the rat bastard a million times." Scatsy said, in case the kid had scruples about harming neighborhood pets. As Joanie and Dick were leaving, Scatsy poured the contents of a paper bag over a steak in the sink. It smelled like rotten eggs.

In the car, Joan asked what the smell was. "I think your uncle is going to poison the dog in the corner house," Dick said.

"You've got a bizarre sense of humor."

"Me?" Dick said. "The last time I saw anything like your uncle Albert was in the movie *Arsenic and Old Lace*," he said, referring to an old chestnut about two spinsters who poisoned old men and buried them in the cellar.

When they met, Johnny barely acknowledged Dick's existence. They shook hands, Johnny's eyes dusting Dick like a fine mist before shifting away.

"I don't think he even got my name," Dick said later to Joan. "Is he always like that?"

Her father, Joan said years later, was self-conscious about his accent and questionable grammar, which could make him appear standoffish to strangers. Dealing with dangerous men never seemed to worry him all that much, but when Joanie's older sister was chosen May Queen in school, Johnny became a nervous wreck upon learning he would have to give a speech. He labored over it like a kid studying for an exam. Luckily, for him, Beverly broke her leg, relieving him of the burden.

Joanie reassured her new beau. "Don't worry about him," she said. "He knows everything about you."

"I never did anything," Dick said. "What's to know?"

"That's what he likes about you—you're a nobody and you're not with anyone," she said.

"With anyone? What does that mean?"

"You'll find out," Joan said. "Right now you're with me and you're my nobody and it better stay that way."

What Dick didn't know was that Joanie had a very specific résumé in mind for the man she planned to spend her life with. Certainly, he had to treat her well and support her when she had children, all the usual requirements of a young, pretty woman of her generation. On top of these things, she had an extra requirement, which she expressed to her older sister when the two talked about their dream matches.

"For sure, no wiseguy like daddy," she always said.

She had seen the effects of her father's career choice on her mother. Even though Millicent didn't know—and didn't want to know—the details of Johnny's work, she knew it was dangerous. She'd overheard enough of Johnny and Scatsy's conversations to know her husband was an important man in the Mafia. She knew that important men were even more likely than unimportant ones to die in the service of the life.

Joan's father was gone a lot when she was growing up and she didn't get to know him well until he got older, when, she said, he became "a very kind man. I remember my father being good to every-body." But, at first, Dick had trouble feeling comfortable around him. "I don't think he likes me," he said.

"Who cares anyhow," Joan said. "We won't be seeing much of him except for Sundays. He's never around."

As Joan overcame her initial doubts, she opened up to Dick a little more. She told Dick that when teachers asked how her father earned a living, she was tempted to answer that he was a specialist in break-ing knees, that he invented the Breaka the Knees Club, but she didn't think that would go over well.

Around the same time, in the spring of 1957, Dick used a $20,000 gift from his dad to start a bootstrap record company, Cambria Records. He also took on a partner, Vinny Marchese, a smart, talented bundle of energy who had been a professional dancer. Cambria's office was in the same building as one of Dick's father's studios, at 44th and Broadway. Outside the window was the famous smoking Camel sign that puffed out real smoke rings. Dick couldn't have been blamed for seeing the smoke rings as a metaphor for his chances of making it in a very tough business. But he wasn't the sort to nurture doubts. He was sure they would storm the fortress of the music industry.

The trouble was he was looking for the sort of Italian crooners, stand-up nightclub singers, he grew up listening to in his musical home. When he got the chance to handle some promising recordings of rock-and-roll music he didn't yet understand its significance.

His first missed opportunity came when a sanitation worker by the name of Ricardo Weeks gave him a demo of a song he'd written that was recorded by a kid named Dion DiMucci, a member of a local gang called the Fordham Daggers. The song, "I Wonder Why," was a harmony-laden rocker filled with the kinds of vocal histrionics and guttural flourishes popular with the young vocal groups. The song was good, Dick thought. It just wasn't what Cambria Records was looking for. Dick suggested that Weeks take it to another label he knew about that was looking for that kind of thing. Laurie Records had been started by a couple of guys also seeking their first big break. When they released the song in the spring of 1958, it became the first of a string of hits for Dion and the Belmonts.

Next, a doctor from Boston sent along a recording by a group with the unlikely name of the Tune Weavers. The song was called "Happy, Happy Birthday Baby." It wasn't a jump tune like "I Wonder Why," but it was also nothing like the buttery pop sound Dick wanted. There was nothing happy about it. Neither did it sound like something that would go over onstage, which is where Dick and Vinny thought the money was. Once again, Dick said thanks but no thanks. Once again, the song shot up the charts, this time on a small label named Casa Grande Records.

Hunkered down behind the Camel man, Dick and Vinny focused their efforts on two of Dick's father's most promising students. One was an Italian kid from Brooklyn, Gino Telli, a tall, handsome baritone who sang old-fashioned love songs with all the sincerity and emotionalism necessary for stardom, at least in Dick's mind. All they thought he needed was the right song.

In those days Dick was ignorant about a lot of things in the music business, but his and Vinny's biggest mistake was in thinking the act was the important thing when the song was really the thing. An artist gets old and loses his voice; the song is forever young, always shows up, and never complains. It took a while before Dick learned the hard way the profane wisdom of Syd Nathan, whose King Records would soon release "The Twist" and change music history: "Fuck the artist, take the song."

Dick took a demo of Telli to Gene Goodman, Benny's brother, who ran Irving Berlin's music publishing. Impressed with Gino's performance, Goodman said Berlin had a new song. At Berlin's age, Goodman thought this might be his last new song. "You Can't Lose the Blues with Colors" was not destined to join the ranks of Berlin's many hits, but Telli gave it all he had.

The other Camillucci voice student was Naomi Caryl, who Dick was certain had a commercial voice and, with the right piece of music, would take off. Caryl's full name was Naomi Caryl Hirshhorn; her father, Joseph H. Hirshhorn, made a fortune in the mining business, where he was known as the Uranium King. In 1955, he described his attitude toward money for *Time* magazine: "After the first million, unless a man loves money, it's all meaningless."

Dick and Vinny harbored hopes that the millionaire investor might shower them with some uro-bucks, but that never happened. Nevertheless, the partners were so convinced Naomi had what it took to be successful, even without a cash infusion from her father, that they paid for her to record Berlin's all-time blockbuster hit, "Alexander's Ragtime Band," at the same session where Gino Telli recorded the other Berlin song.

That summer, Dick and Vinny hit the road with their records, visiting every radio station they could find between New York and Chicago. In Chicago, a distributor set them up to be patsies for one of the city's top deejays, Marty Faye.

Faye, whose sister was the noted cabaret singer Frances Faye, was one of radio's first shock jocks. With a well-earned reputation for insolence and meanness when most radio personalities were fawning sycophants, Marty Faye exploded out of radio and onto the little screen. His television show, *Marty's Morgue*, was, he said, "where I bury people I don't like."

Faye thought the best route to success was making people hate him. He called Elvis Presley "a bouncing orangutan, a musical degenerate," and said Eddie Fisher sang like "a dead fish."

At a charity event at Soldier Field attended by 62,500 people, his fans gleefully pelted him with coins, ice cream cones, and paper cups. Faye grabbed the microphone. "Whatever you think of me, I think of you," he shouted.

Faye's radio show broadcasted from a large room with two sets of bleachers filled with his fans, all the better to savor the public roasting of the hapless and sincere. As Dick and Vinny sat nervously awaiting their turn, Faye finished up with Frank Parker, the featured tenor on Arthur Godfrey's popular radio show. That made Parker no small potatoes. Faye demanded to know why he thought he could make a record.

"I've had requests to do it for a while," Parker said.

"Why? You stink," Faye said.

Dick looked at Vinny, wondering what they'd gotten themselves into. When it was their turn, Faye nearly squealed with pleasure.

"You should see what's coming my way," he said, "two gangsters from New York."

Maybe it was his look. Dick's size and competitive instinct had won him honors in football. Now it caused Faye to go into rapturous hysterics.

"Put down the gun, fellas, I'll play your record," Faye said.

Dick had a quick tongue himself. He played along. Faye signaled his engineer to play the Gino Telli record. After eight bars he cut in. "Geez, take that off. That's the worst song I ever heard in my life. Who the hell wrote that stinker?" Faye said.

Dick pounced. "Irving Berlin."

"That shows what you know," Vinny said.

Faye was unfazed. "He's old and should get out of the business," he said.

After some more of this alley fighting that passed for an interview Faye said the pair should consider new career choices. Dick thanked him for the advice and invited him to New York, where they could reciprocate.

"But be careful when you're in New York not to stand up in a crowd, Marty—they might pick you off," Vinny said.

When they came off the set they were met by, of all people, Jesse Owens, the star of the 1936 Berlin Olympics and a personal hero of Dick's. He had a radio show at the same station. "Don't let Marty get to you fellows," he said. "It's just an act."

Despite Dick and Vinny's best, road-weary efforts, neither of

Cambria Records' releases went anywhere. The guys wouldn't have lasted more than a few weeks in the music business if it weren't for the jukebox king, Al Miniaci.

Miniaci owned Paramount Vending, the biggest independent jukebox operator in America. An underappreciated visionary of the modern music business, Miniaci funded the start-up of *Cashbox* magazine, was a Knight of Malta, helped start Boys' Town of Italy and, out every night, fit the role of Mr. New York. Tall, elegant, and warm—"If he wasn't happily married, he could have had any twenty-year-old woman he wanted," Vinny said—Miniaci took a fancy to the two young producers. Dick later found out it was Johnny who had given Miniaci his start in the business, introducing him years earlier to Frank Costello.

Costello and Miniaci did good business together. Costello bought hundreds of Miniaci's slots, the same ones that ended up at the bottom of the river, thanks to Mayor La Guardia. Think of a jukebox as a slot machine that takes your quarter but never has to pay off, and you can see why Costello would be interested in those, too. Al never forgot Johnny's favor. He loved Johnny, but Dick didn't know any of that on the day he walked into Paramount Vending.

Miniaci happened to be in the front of the office when young Camillucci came calling. They hit it off and he told his buyer to take a few records from the kid. Over the years, Miniaci became a huge ally who would help Dick and Vinny out when acts they managed had records. But the order he gave Dick for the Cambria titles couldn't save the label. Watching the smoke rings waft past his office window, Dick understood at last. Rock and roll was here to stay.

Chapter 7

No Simple Bookmaker

When Dick got the inevitable invite to Sunday dinner at the Bi-ello house, he knew what that meant. He was Italian. It would be his formal introduction to the family, as well as a declaration that he and Joanie were a serious couple, something short of an engagement but more than an exclusive dating relationship.

Even with his memories of summering at New London fresh in his mind, Dick was unprepared for the magnificence of the unending feast that was Sunday dinner at Joanie's house. Millicent had studied at the altar of Johnny's mother, learning how to combine simple ingredients into exotic dishes.

Dick never had Sunday dinner when there weren't ten to twelve people there. Millicent set a table that could have fed many more. Ornate platters overflowed with antipasto: *caponata*, a warm eggplant and olive salad consisting of cubes of browned eggplant mixed with onions, pickles, capers, celery leaves, and chopped olives, with pine nuts; prosciutto with toasted bread slices to pile everything on; and an assortment of raw vegetables that included fennel, whole radishes, and sliced zucchini, which Scatsy called "ca-goots." There was often a cold seafood salad of Maine lobster and Louisiana shrimp, baked calamari, stuffed mushrooms, and spicy Italian sausage with roasted fresh peppers.

The pasta course was fusilli swimming in *filetto di pomodoro* sauce or, on other occasions, fresh-made tagliatelli drenched in an *larrabbiata* sauce, made by blackening garlic cloves and hot peppers in a pan of olive oil. The baby lambs with bones so supple you could chew them came from the Rockefeller estate and were a high point of the meal. Prepared by marinating the lamb in an oil and lemon dressing with garlic and fresh vegetables, the dish was started three days in advance.

On the table there were always baskets of Zito's bread. The best in New York, Johnny and Scatsy believed it was the coal-fired ovens that conferred the special crunch. Johnny warned everyone, "Don't eat the bread. It'll fill you up. Just use it as a pusher."

Around four o'clock, the aroma coming from the kitchen was so intense that Dick could hardly restrain himself. Nobody could top Al, though, who was married to Millicent's sister, Rose. Al was a major-league eater. Johnny joked that Al ate like he was going to the chair. Johnny told Al, "When you come to the hard part, that's the plate."

Dick made a point of contributing something special to the meals, a nice bottle of wine or a rare Italian cordial. Johnny always insisted he shouldn't bother. Belying his lack of pretension, Johnny's liquor cabinet was stocked with very serious wines, vintage French premier crus. But Dick could see Johnny was pleased when he turned up with something exotic.

Table etiquette was of paramount importance to Johnny. He wouldn't abide bad language at the table, even from the mobsters who occasionally dined with the family. "I remember someone cursing and my father sending him away from the table," Joan said. The image of a gangster being upbraided like a mouthy kid might seem difficult to picture, but with Johnny, there were rules to everything and there was no deviation. That first dinner, Dick was seated next to Johnny, who was dressed in casual attire, an open-collared shirt and slacks, with shined shoes and dark socks, the fashion approach of a businessman expecting to be on the golf course soon. Dick was nervous, needlessly. The men fell into easy conversation, the start of a relationship that would grow over the years.

When the meal was over, Dick knew he'd passed inspection. Soon after, he and Joanie realized that the natural thing for them to do was to get married. Dick never recalled asking for Joanie's hand or anything formal like that. They just began talking about the future with the assumption that any plan they made would include both of them.

Joan wanted a lavish, storybook wedding, like her sister Beverly had gotten—the church filled with more flowers than a mobster's funeral, the reception overflowing with food, carts stuffed with booze, a big band with an Italian singer belting out "Cella Luna." Dick couldn't have cared less, but he knew it was important to Joanie, so he went along. Johnny resisted.

He confided to Millicent that the timing was bad. "I'm going through hell right now."

"Please, Johnny," Millicent said. "How's Joanie going to feel when her sister had more than every girl's dream wedding and she has to go to the courthouse?"

Johnny still didn't like it. "It's so hot right now a lot of my people won't be coming. No envelopes."

It was a Mob tradition for the boys to bestow envelopes bulging with cash on the happy couple.

Millicent was surprised by her husband's resistance. "Would it be better if they just eloped?" she said.

"That would be perfect," Johnny said.

Realizing Johnny was serious, Millicent dropped her opposition. Things must indeed have been bad if Johnny was willing to let his daughter run off to get hitched. This was the fifties. The only girls who ran off to get married were already pregnant.

"All right," she said. "But before you tell Joanie, you better talk to Dick. I asked him for a list of his relatives. He thinks it's going to be a big wedding."

Johnny's temper flared. "Who does he think he is?"

"Don't blame him," Millicent said. "He doesn't know about your problems."

The next time Dick was over, Joanie told him her father wanted to talk to him. Johnny had never before asked to speak to him privately. Dick went into the living room and sat down to wait, nervously anticipating the meeting. When Johnny came in the front door, he took off his gray fedora and dark blue cashmere overcoat, hung them up and, seeing Dick seated on the French provincial chair, ambled over. He sat down, looking troubled.

"I want to ask you something," Johnny said. "Do you care whether there's a big wedding or not? What if you just went off somewhere and got married and I give you thirty or forty G's or something."

Dick was floored by the offer. *How much money is this guy worth?* he wondered.

"Would you care?" Johnny said. He looked away, waiting for a reply.

"I don't mind at all," Dick said. "I'd rather have it that way. I was never one for those big, fancy weddings and, as far as the money goes, whatever you want to give us will be fine."

Johnny, looking mildly surprised, took off his glasses and rubbed the bridge of his nose. He stood and put his hand on Dick's shoulder.

"Good, fine," he said, turning away.

The cause of Johnny's anxiety, Dick discovered much later, was the attempted assassination of his boss and role model, Frank Costello. Returning to his penthouse apartment after dinner on May 2, 1957, Costello heard someone shout, "This is for you, Frank."

It wasn't meant as a warning—more like a victory cry—but it gave Costello the time he needed to shrug away from the bullet. Fired by Vito Genovese's handpicked gunman, Vincent "the Chin" Gigante, the shot creased Costello's head. To the great disappointment of Genovese, Costello survived with only a minor wound and returned home from the hospital that same night.

The shooting provoked the greatest crisis that the five Mafia families in New York had faced since the Castellammarese War thirty years earlier. Genovese saw himself as the legitimate heir to Lucky Luciano's crime family, which Costello had been managing as a steward in Luciano's enforced absence. Genovese had grown up with Lucky Luciano in the slums of New York, and felt his claim should have superseded Costello's. Genovese, innately violent and deceitful even with those closest to him—he once had one of his own lieutenants murdered so he could marry the man's wife—didn't care that under Costello the Mob had enjoyed unrivaled peace and prosperity. His ambition blinded him to everything outside his own desire. Johnny's favorite term for Genovese was "fucking animal."

When Costello was shot, many of his loyal soldiers itched for a showdown with the greedy Genovese. Costello commanded a lot of loyalty and, although Genovese was a powerful *capo*, he was not much liked.

Costello realized he had to retire, and he let Genovese know that he was willing to let him take over. In return, all Costello wanted was to be allowed to live out his years at his Sands Point estate, puttering in his garden, without having to look over his shoulder.

Genovese agreed, but to secure his position, ordered the killings of some of Costello's top lieutenants. One was Johnny's neighbor, Little Augie. He and Johnny were so close that when Augie decided to unload his big, roomy '57 Ford Fairlane, Johnny took it off his hands. Augie was shot to death by his good friend Anthony "Tony Bender" Strollo. Dick drove the Ford for years after Augie's death.

By the narrowest of margins, and with the support of some powerful allies, principally Tommy "Three-Finger Brown" Lucchese, who headed his own family, Johnny avoided the assassin's bullet. In the wake of Costello's retirement, however, Johnny was required to swear allegiance to Genovese.

Among those most spoiling for war with Genovese after Costello's shooting was Albert Anastasia. Known as the Mad Hatter, Anastasia led a specially chosen assassination squad, Murder Inc., which was responsible for at least a hundred killings in and around New York. Anastasia and Johnny Biello were friends, though Johnny privately despised the man's bloodthirsty nature. When the Mad Hatter took his family on vacation to Miami, he stayed at Johnny's Bel Aire Hotel.

Anastasia had plenty of resources to throw into the fight, but Costello continued to insist that he was not interested in revenge. According to Dick, who gleaned the information from Johnny and Scatsy over the years, neither Johnny nor Costello believed Anastasia's display of rage at Genovese. They were convinced Vito would never have had the balls to take on Costello without Anastasia's approval.

Costello withdrew from public view, ostensibly to recuperate at his estate and begin his placid life in retirement. Privately, he began plotting his revenge with Johnny and a handful of other trusted *capos*. One thing was clear: Any plan he made against Genovese had to take Anastasia into account.

Dick was sitting in the living room of Johnny's house reading the *Daily News* one morning in October, shortly before the wedding, when Johnny walked in, seeming lighthearted, almost jovial. As Johnny walked by, he tapped the front page.

"That's gonna cost you five grand," he said.

When Dick turned the page, he saw a picture of a body lying under a sheet in the barbershop of the Sheraton Hotel. The caption identified the deceased as Albert Anastasia.

"He was coming to the wedding," Johnny said. "Now he can't make it."

That was the moment Dick realized his future father-in-law was no simple bookmaker. At the time, Dick couldn't make out why Johnny seemed so happy about losing a wedding guest to murder.

Mob historians have asserted that Anastasia was murdered at the behest of Genovese because the Mad Hatter had been so public in his threats of retaliation. According to Vincent Teresa, a made man who wrote a book later in life, Anastasia's murder was carried out for Genovese by a gang of ambitious young toughs led by Lawrence and Joey Gallo, reliable Brooklyn assassins.

Knowing they would never get within sight of Anastasia without being recognized, the Gallos looked for someone Anastasia didn't know. Because most New York hit men were understandably scared of Anastasia, the Gallos sought the help of Boston Mob family leader Raymond Patriarca, for whom Teresa served as a lieutenant. Patriarca, Teresa wrote, provided two cold-blooded outsiders to do the job on Anastasia, one known only as "the Syrian."

From conversations with Johnny and Scatsy, Dick came to believe the supposedly retired Costello orchestrated the Anastasia killing. In fact, according to Dick, it was Johnny's idea to recruit the Syrian, using Patriarca, who was a good friend of Johnny's. Years before when Raymond Patriarca had to go on the lam, Luciano advised him to go to the Bronx, where Johnny Futto would make all the arrangements and take care of him. For three months, Patriarca lived in secret in a luxury apartment Johnny provided off Fordham Road. Johnny assigned Albert Facchiano, known as Chinky, and Scatsy to take care of his every need. Patriarca never went anywhere except to the movies at the Paradise Theater and, occasionally, to a baseball game at Yankee Stadium when the Red Sox played.

Johnny's reaction to his supposed friend's death was right in line with that of a man who had advance knowledge of the assassination of Anastasia, as well as no love for him.

The next part of Costello's plan to take down Genovese, Dick said, now went into action. Knowing there was a lot of confusion in the families, Costello recommended that Genovese hold a big meeting, inviting bosses all over the country for an air-clearing sit-down at which Genovese would be officially crowned *Capo di Tutti Capi*. Genovese agreed and the date was set at Joseph Barbara's house in Apalachin. According to Cami, Costello leaked word of the meeting to the authorities, who raided the Mafia conference, sending made men scampering through the fields. The whole degrading experience ruined any chance of Genovese realizing his ambition.

The final installment of Costello's plan was to set up Genovese on charges of distributing heroin. Convicted, Genovese went to prison in 1959, where he died ten years later.

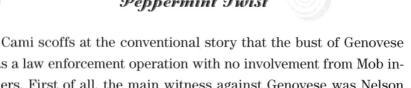

Cami scoffs at the conventional story that the bust of Genovese was a law enforcement operation with no involvement from Mob insiders. First of all, the main witness against Genovese was Nelson Cantellops, a low-level street thug who would never have gotten close enough to a powerful man like Genovese to have anything on him.

"I'll say this, too. Cantellops would never have dared testify against Genovese on the say-so of the authorities," Cami said. "He'd know they would never be able to protect him."

The Mob had shown its ability to get to anybody. One witness being guarded full-time by New York detectives mysteriously jumped out a hotel window to his death before taking the stand. To Dick, getting Cantellops on the stand would have taken a lot of convincing, meaning big stacks of money, from someone like Costello, who had ways of getting people in and out of the country without being detected.

With Anastasia dead and the plan to get Genovese under way, Joanie got her big wedding after all. The reception was held at the Jackson Hotel in Long Beach, a fine old matron of an establishment. It was a luxurious affair and there were plenty of envelopes.

One guest was very interested in their honeymoon plans.

"Where's you going?" said Lou Black in a high-pitched rasp. Black was a favorite of Lucky Luciano's, a very tough gangster who was once defended by Clarence Darrow on a murder rap. Black got off. Darrow refused his fee, so Luciano paid him with a sumptuous spaghetti dinner at Vesuvio.

"Bermuda," Dick said. "I've never been out of the country, so I'm looking forward to seeing what it's like."

"Forget about it," Black said. "You should go to Italy. Naples, now that's where it's nice."

Dick laughed. Who had heard of going to Europe on a honeymoon? This was only twelve years after the end of World War II. Europe was still on its knees, particularly Italy, having rashly cast its lot with the Nazis.

Black was insistent. "There's beautiful joints there to stay in and the food? The best."

The mobster moved closer and tilted his head conspiratorially. "Don't forget, that's where Charley is. You can say hello for us."

Seeing his new son-in-law in a huddle with the formidable Black, Johnny hustled over. He wanted to know what was going on.

"Nothing, Johnny," Black said. "I was just telling Sonny here that if he went to Naples he—"

"Forget it," Johnny said, and led Dick away.

Dick found out later that "Charley" was Lucky Luciano. Frustrated by life in exile, he was scheming to find a way to get back in the United States and reassert his control over the Five Families. The plans never came to fruition. Luciano never got out of Italy.

This was the first time Johnny steered Dick away from Mafia business, but hardly the last. He certainly never even intimated that Dick should become involved in Mob business. That was never discussed. He clearly wanted Dick to stay clean. Besides, by this time, Johnny was thinking of getting out himself.

The FBI always remained suspicious of the relationship, doubting Dick's civilian status. As for the boys, over time, Dick got to know them all and occasionally got embroiled in some of their shenanigans. But Johnny was scrupulous about keeping him just outside the glow of the campfire, where he might see some of what was going on but avoid getting burned.

Christmas 1957 found Dick and his new wife heading off to Florida to join Johnny and Millicent at the Biellos' sprawling house on Alton Road in Miami Beach.

Johnny asked Dick to pick up some of Zito's bread on the way down, along with some *bacala*—codfish that is usually filleted and dried. Cold or hot, it's a delicacy. But before serving, you had to soak it for three days while frequently changing the water. When it thawed it stank like the bodies of the damned.

The night before he was to leave, Dick picked up the bread and headed to the Wagon Wheel, a club that Johnny operated near Times Square, for the *bacala*. Al Prisco, a pal from the neighborhood whom Johnny put in to run the place, tried to get Dick to sit down and have some veal and peppers. Regretfully, Dick said no. He was too busy. Al helped him pack the *bacala* in a cardboard box and put it in the car's trunk. When Dick got home, he decided to leave the fish in the car that night. It was as cold as any walk-in freezer.

At the airport the next morning, Joanie warned him not to check the bread or the *bacala*. God forbid the airline should lose them. There would be hell to pay with Johnny. While waiting on line, Dick looked down and saw a puddle of water under the box of *bacala*.

Holy shit, he thought. Instead of the dried cod Dick was expecting, Al had given him fresh fish packed in ice. Now it was thawing. His mind raced, but the line moved so swiftly, all he could do was board the plane with his leaking box of fish.

On the plane, Dick grabbed a stewardess. "Unless there's a refrigerator on board that we can put this box in we're in for the most miserable, stinking flight this airline has ever seen," he said.

In the age before jets, the flight to Miami took almost six hours. Even with the fish packed away in the plane's small refrigerator, Dick sweated out the whole flight. When Johnny met them at the airport, his first words were, "Where's the *bacala*?"

One day near Christmas, Johnny invited Frankie Carbo to lunch. Besides being a chief suspect in the Bugsy Siegel killing, Carbo was a Lucchese family member and a well-known contract killer for Murder Inc. He also fixed boxing matches; the word among Mob colleagues was that he had something to do with the strange outcome of the first heavyweight championship fight between Cassius Clay and Sonny Liston, in which Liston suddenly quit after the sixth round, claiming he'd suffered a shoulder injury.

The house on Alton Road looked beautiful, all decorated with a big tree and Bing Crosby on the hi-fi filling the place with soft, good cheer. This was another Mafia neighborhood. Just down the street was "Trigger Mike" Coppola. He was the top man in Miami and a good friend and associate of Johnny's. He was also a major sourpuss who didn't look like he ever got a moment's pleasure out of his wealth and position. One time, Dick went with a friend to deliver a message to

Coppola. When no one answered the front door, they went out back. When Trigger Mike saw Dick's friend in his backyard, his face froze as a bolt of fear tore through his body. He thought the jig was up. It was a lesson in the realities of the gangster life that Dick never forgot.

Something similar happened at the lunch with Carbo. Since Dick was new to the family, Frankie was introduced as Mr. Maguire, Carbo's *nom de guerre.*

Also at the table was a priest. As Millicent laid out the steaks, she realized what she had done. It was Friday and the priest couldn't eat meat. She quickly whipped up a tuna salad for the father and Carbo joined him in the meatless meal.

As they were digging in, a Miami Beach motorcycle cop roared into the driveway and loudly backed down his motorcycle. Having no desire to confront the authorities, Christmastime or not, Frankie scrambled up the stairs to hide.

"You'd have thought the SWAT team was out there with dogs, the way Mr. Maguire jumped up from the table," Dick said.

The cop, Bobby Johnson, was a friend of Johnny's. He'd come for his Christmas gift—an envelope of money. After the cop rumbled away, Johnny went to the foot of the stairs. "You can come down now, Frankie. All's clear."

Back at the table, Joanie turned to Dick. "Interesting lunch," she said.

Chapter 8

Going Legit

A few months later, Dick learned firsthand the cruel facts about the life his father-in-law had chosen. Joanie announced one morning that they were going to her uncle's funeral. At first Dick was alarmed, thinking she meant Scatsy. But this was Mandy, Johnny's hotheaded younger brother.

Mandy had never been around. Dick had never met him and knew nothing about him. He found out later that Johnny had turned Mandy down when he asked his brother to sponsor him into the Mob. Even though no one was tougher than Mandy, Johnny had no interest in becoming Mandy's angel. That caused hard feelings between the brothers, but Johnny was right. Mandy was too volatile. He enjoyed beating people who didn't come across with the money on time— even the collectors who worked for Johnny, which Scatsy told him was really stupid.

"They're going to buzz it all over town what you're doing," Scatsy said. "These guys work for us. Sometimes the customer comes up short. You got to try to work it out."

Mandy wouldn't hear it. "That's what I'm doing, working it out," he said. "When I'm collecting money from the cocksuckers, I don't want to hear nothing from nobody. Tell it to the marines. Just come up with the fucking money."

Eventually, Mandy found someone else to sponsor him and he got made. Then the inevitable happened and Mandy ended up with a bullet in his head. The coroner ruled it an accidental shooting. He said Mandy was cleaning his gun when it went off.

Scatsy, who'd met Dick only a few times at that point, cornered him at the funeral and started talking like an old friend.

"I can't sleep," he said, going into a long-winded story. Surprised by his openness, all Dick could do was listen and give an occasional nod. Scatsy took this as encouragement, opening up about his fallen brother.

Scatsy was one of the first to see Mandy's body. Responding to a call from Mandy's wife, he could hear Vickie's screams even before he got to the front door of their house. After Scatsy went inside and calmed her down, he saw the police had roped everything off. In the basement, Mandy's body was on its back, arms askew, one leg bent under the body. A red smear ran down the side of the dead man's neck. A gun-cleaning kit lay open on the floor next to him, the reason police believed Mandy had accidentally shot himself.

Accident? Scatsy didn't buy that for a second. There was no way that a mobster as familiar with guns as Mandy was would fail to unload the weapon before cleaning it. It was clear to Scatsy that Mandy got whacked.

"You mean to tell me he was cleaning his gun and it went around the room ten times and hits him in the back of the head?" Scatsy said. "Who they bullshitting?"

Johnny had expected something like this. Still, no matter how badly Mandy had behaved, he was his brother. At the funeral, Johnny took the news quietly, saying little, just whistling softly through his teeth, his standard way of expressing disapproval and anger.

It was a big funeral, with scores of mourners. Across the street, an FBI truck filmed the whole thing.

Everyone was dressed in black and the old women were crying and fingering their rosary beads. In Italian families, the funeral is more than an occasion for mourning. There is a show business aspect to it. Sometimes, if the family is afraid there won't be enough mourners to make it look like the deceased was well loved, it was a custom to hire professional mourners. Older women who showed up with shawls over their heads were favored.

One such type was sobbing. "It's Dio's way, you no suffer no more," she said.

"Yeah, it's God's way," Scatsy told Dick. "He's going to heaven with a fucking bullet hole in his head."

"Poor Giuseppe," the woman said. *"Jesu Christo mio."*

A woman next to her interrupted. "This is not Giuseppe," she said. "This is Mandy."

"Oh, scusi," the woman said, getting up. "I'm in the wrong room."

A photographer from the neighborhood came to the funeral to take some family pictures. He arrived too late and apologized to Johnny.

"Don't worry about it," Johnny said. "Next time."

"Next time?" the photographer said. "What next time?"

"There'll always be a next time," Johnny replied.

By now, Johnny Biello had acquired not just the look but also the income and obligations of a successful businessman. In the Bronx, he owned an apartment building on 169th Street and a bowling alley. In Manhattan, he had the Vogue Room on East 57th Street, a fashionable bar and restaurant where jazz pianist Art Tatum built his reputation in postwar New York, plus a couple of lots near Yankee Stadium in partnership with the boxer Jake LaMotta.

Johnny also had contacts in Hollywood. A photograph taken from the Vogue Room days shows Johnny, bareheaded, tie cinched Adam's apple tight, flanked by Betty Grable, the GI's premier pinup girl, whose perfect gams were insured for a million dollars by Lloyd's of London. Actress June Haver is on the other side of Johnny, making the snapshot likely taken on the set of the 1945 movie *The Dolly Sisters*, the only film featuring both Haver and Grable. Johnny's wife, Millicent, and their two older daughters are also in the picture. Grable was married at the time to trumpeter Harry James, but theirs was a tumultuous pairing marked by infidelity and alcoholism. Whatever there might have been between Grable and Johnny, only the photograph remains.

In Florida, where Johnny was spending increasing amounts of time, he partnered up with Tony Ricci, alias Tony Goebels, one of the guys who was once involved in an attempt by the Chicago Mob to annex the New York families. Johnny and Ricci owned a three-hundred-room hotel, the Bel Aire, on the ocean in Miami Beach.

It never surprised Dick to find out from casual remarks dropped by Johnny and others that his father-in-law had money in one place or another. One day, late in the winter of 1957, Joe Scandore, who managed Totie Fields and owned a nightclub called the Elegante in Brooklyn, came to Johnny with an idea. He wanted to headline a club Johnny owned down in Miami Beach with a new comic he managed named Don Rickles.

According to Scandore, Rickles was about to appear on the Jack Paar TV show. Scandore was convinced the appearance would catapult Rickles to fame after he insulted the host on national TV. Scandore and Johnny would cash in when people heard Rickles was playing the club.

Knowing Dick's interest in the entertainment business, Johnny invited him to be there when Scandore and Rickles came over to the house at Atlantic Beach to make the deal. Dick had never heard of the guy.

"He's supposed to be a new hotshot comic who insults everyone," Johnny said.

When they arrived, Johnny and Scandore went into the den while Dick sat in the living room with the comic. Rickles said he'd just made a movie with Clark Gable and Burt Lancaster. (The movie, *Run Silent, Run Deep*, was the only film to pair Lancaster and Gable, two of the biggest stars in Hollywood at the time. About submariners in World War II, it would be a big hit.) Dick thought Rickles had to be kidding, like a routine. He didn't look like an actor. Dick laughed, thinking there had to be a punch line in there somewhere. When Rickles didn't offer even a smile, he realized he was serious.

After a time, Johnny and Scandore returned. "We'll call it the Riot Room," Scandore announced.

Things did not go as planned when Rickles got his shot on the Jack Paar show, the first version of television's *Tonight Show*. Paar's producer had the comic come onstage dressed as a cabdriver without informing Paar of the setup. The producer figured Rickles's ad libs and Paar's retorts would make great television. Unfortunately, it didn't.

Rickles, according to his autobiography, came out with his cap pulled down over his ears. "Who are you?" Paar said.

"Maxie the cabbie," Rickles said.

According to Rickles, Paar figured this was a bit, but didn't feel like playing along. "Wh-wh-where you going with this?" said Paar, who had overcome his childhood stutter except under stress.

"Jack," Rickles said, going into his act. "I'm a friend. Do yourself a favor and look for other work."

Paar turned to his producer and whispered, "Who is this guy? Get him out of here."

Nothing could save the bit. It didn't help the Riot Room, either. When the club opened, it laid an egg. A few weeks later Johnny said, "Put a lock on the door."

Nightclubs were a very hit-and-miss proposition. Johnny continued to invest but he knew that a club could drain your pocketbook quickly. His motto was, if things were going bad, close it down. One thing the clubs had going for them, however, was that even if they made no money, they were good fronts for the gambling and shylocking operations that were the main moneymaking operations for Johnny and his crew. It didn't much matter if the front room was empty if business was good in back. Not all of Johnny's businesses were fronts. The

Vogue Room operated clean, as did the Riot Room, which is one reason he shut it down when the customers failed to show.

B. S. Pully, a sometime actor and comic, was the houseman at one of Johnny's clubs. Pully had been around for years. His bulk and a voice that sounded like it had been dragged over a gravel road made him perfect for roles as a mobster. Most famously, he played Big Jule in the Broadway musical (and later the movie) *Guys and Dolls*.

Pully was into Johnny for so much money that he lost on the horses that he worked off his debt running the club. He also served as chief stand-up comic, working the blue end of the spectrum.

Johnny's crew knew Pully had the right initials in his name because he always had a bullshit story when things went wrong, as they always did when he was around. When Dick first met Pully, Johnny warned, "Don't lend this character a quarter. He'll come at you from more angles than a triangle. Remember, not a quarter."

One time Pully went to Johnny with a recommendation for a new singer. "He's the best singer I ever worked in front of," Pully said. "I mean, this kid's great."

Johnny agreed to put the kid onstage and business picked up. Just when things were looking good, trouble began. The kid singer had a major drinking problem. And when he was drunk he lost interest in showing up for work.

Johnny told Pully that he was responsible for the kid and to solve the problem. "If you think I'm going to have Johnny Futto dump my ass in some swamp over in Jersey because of you, you got another think coming," Pully told the singer.

Realizing that no matter how many promises the kid made, he was totally unreliable, Pully did the only thing he could think of. He took the singer down to the basement of the club and chained him to the water heater. The only times the kid got free was to go to the bathroom and go onstage. He ate chained up.

That worked for a while. Then one night Johnny stopped in to find the stage empty and the singer gone. "Where's the hot shot?" Johnny said.

"Everything was going good, Johnny, I swear. Then he up and did it," Pully said.

"Up and did what?" Johnny asked.

"He escaped."

A while later, Pully went out to Hollywood to make a movie. The studio rented Fredric March's house for him. March was a two-time Academy Award–winning actor who had been a leading man in an earlier era and was still working steadily. He considered Connecticut his primary residence, so his Los Angeles home was available, for a price. Even though Pully was making good money and living in a beautiful place, no amount of money was enough when you spent all your free time at the track in Santa Anita.

To make good on his losses, he sold off March's furniture. Pully was back in New York when the studio called about the missing goods.

Pully went into his Big Jule act. "You mean they robbed the house? In my life, in my heart, I never heard of such a thing. Everything was there when I left. Such beautiful things, too. I didn't even like to sit on that couch." It was a coincidence they called, he said. "I was just going to call you and ask you to go to the house because I left my Audemars Piguet behind. That's a $10,000 watch. My mudder gave it to me. I hope you guys got insurance."

Dick, by this time, knew his father-in-law was much more than a bookmaker. He saw how other very dangerous men tended to treat him. And, he'd already met Mr. Maguire. But Johnny wasn't the type to walk around boasting about his relationship with Frank Costello or how he grew up under Lucky Luciano. One day, Johnny invited Dick to lunch at Laurentano's Restaurant, which was virtually Johnny's office. "Be there at one," he said.

Arriving at the restaurant, he spotted Johnny seated at his customary table, talking easily with the waiters. Dick sat down. "Lucchese's coming over," Johnny said.

Dick was no shrinking flower. He knew how to handle himself

around important people. But Tommy "Three-Finger Brown" Lucchese was a different matter altogether. As the head of one of the original Five Families, he'd survived the Mafia wars and government efforts to put him away for life. There's no way to know for sure how much death and injury could be attributed to him, but he was known to be Lucky Luciano's favorite hit man. He'd played a pivotal role in the Castellammarese War, setting up the strutting Maranzano for assassination by a hit squad pretending to be IRS agents.

When Lucchese arrived, Dick was surprised to see a stooped, almost shy man who shambled over and stood behind a chair, eyeing the room. He locked eyes with Johnny, almost as if to ask if it was okay for him to sit down.

As he did, he gave Dick a nod and mumbled greeting, "Nice to meet you." Lucchese never shook hands because of the two fingers missing on his right hand that earned him his nickname.

He was dressed formally in a dark suit and kept his sunglasses on, even though the room was in shadow. His thinning hair was slicked back. He kept his right hand in his pocket.

Dick thought a more appropriate name for Three-Finger Brown would have been Three-Words Brown, for all the talking he did. Johnny carried the conversational load, talking about everything from sports to wiseguy politics while Lucchese nodded and smiled.

Johnny ignored the menu, ordering for the three of them. The first dish, *zuppa di pesce*, was a thick fish soup with mussels, shrimp, and white fish. This was followed by *saltimbocca alla Romana*, veal cutlets with ham, mozzarella, and sage. The name translates "jump into your mouth," and it truly fit that tender, delicious dish.

While Dick was enjoying the food, Lucchese was distracted. He stabbed at his meal almost randomly. The dessert was *zabaglione*, whipped egg yolks with sugar and Marsala wine. Lucchese passed on it, Johnny took a spoonful, and Dick finished everything.

The lunch lasted two hours. It was one of the most intimate glimpses Dick would ever get of the interior life of one of the founders of the Mafia. Johnny never explained the reason for the get-together, but it's likely he was trying to shore up support with one of the most powerful gang leaders of his era. Tommy had saved Johnny at least once already and Johnny would likely need him in the future. Johnny had been hoping, with Costello's retirement, that he could be transferred to Lucchese's family. But the Mafia, like the armed services, didn't operate democratically.

As Dick and Johnny grew closer, Johnny began opening up to his son-in-law about his frustrations with his Mafia brethren. He was openly dismissive of the younger generation, many of who had gotten in not by doing the work required of an aspiring soldier, but by paying off a boss. Anastasia and his underboss, Frank Scalice, who didn't know how to make a living other than with a gun, sold dozens of memberships.

Johnny referred to the new breed as the "ice cream mob."

"They couldn't rob a blanket off a horse," he said.

Johnny began talking about retiring, about getting into a legitimate business and finally leaving behind the bloody feuds and petty vengeance that characterized the Mafia in the wake of Frank Costello's retirement. But at the same time, he went right on operating the way he always had. He kept his hand in his Bronx and Manhattan gambling and union rackets. He shied the shylocks. He wouldn't walk away. That was the real trick about the Mob. It's not that you can't get out. It's that you won't. The Mob is one industry in which you can't be semiretired.

"There are no part-timers in this business," Scatsy said. "You're in or you're out. Johnny thinks he's going to be the first one."

The more time Dick spent with him, the more he found himself admiring his father-in-law. On one level, that surprised him, given that Dick was a straight shooter who had grown up in a household in which crime was an alien concept. For good or ill, he judged people by the way they conducted themselves in his presence. Nobody he'd ever met had done more for those around him than Johnny. Given that Johnny came from poverty, Dick admired his refusal to take the little that that life offered and be satisfied with that.

He'd been nothing. Now he had a lot, much more than his father could ever have had back in Italy or this country. To have was better.

But for the common people in America, those who followed the rules and worked diligently, life was hard. Unlike many mafiosi, whose greatest goal was to make money any way they could, exploiting the weak without a second thought, Johnny didn't think wage slaves were chumps to be shorn like sheep. He seemed sincerely regretful over the realization that there were, in his view, two ways to get ahead: cheat and steal or be born with a fat bank account. He was generous to anyone with a hard-luck story. He saw them as people who had tried to do it the right way, only to get chewed up in the machinery of commerce.

FBI agent Peter Clemente said that one time when he was tailing Johnny, he saw him outside a public phone booth on a street corner. The booth was occupied and Johnny paced with increasing agitation until he ran out of patience. Finally, he reached into the booth and dragged the caller out. As he did so, the guy dropped a brown paper bag and apparently the bottle inside broke when it hit the pavement. Johnny reached into his pocket and stuffed a wad of cash into his hand as compensation, patting him on the back as he took over the phone from the man. He was not a man to step on little people.

Dick once started complaining about all the law enforcement attention they were getting. Besides the locals, the FBI was hounding them and taking pictures everywhere they went. "I just wish they'd disappear," Dick said.

Johnny wasn't having it. "No cops? I wish that's all we had to worry about. What a fine world that would be," he said. "We'd be okay, but what about the teachers, garbage haulers, the average working guy and the two-dollar bettor? Who's going to protect them?"

The bond between Dick and Johnny went deeper than Dick's admiration for his father-in-law's common touch. Despite their differences in age and life experience, they had similar characteristics. Both had forceful personalities but preferred to remain in the background, out of the spotlight, whether it was in a meeting with made men or movie stars. Both were loyal and generous and knew the consequences of both.

Johnny's attitude toward Dick was always paternal, but it could range from appreciative respect at Dick's firm moral compass to amusement at his habit of self-examination. While Johnny was a humanitarian of Gandhi-esque proportions compared with most mafiosi, he didn't spend much time navel-gazing. He was amused by those who did.

"The worst beatings are the ones we give ourselves," he said. Coming from a guy who knew beatings, Dick took note.

One thing that's not generally understood is that belonging to the Mob didn't guarantee you a nice living. It offered protection from other crooks and a clan to belong to, but you had to make your own living, legal or illegal. As far as the bosses were concerned, it didn't matter. You had to give them a piece of everything.

Johnny was what they called a good earner. There was little doubt in Dick's mind that if he'd been legit people would have respected his name the way they do a well-known businessman in a small town. The kind who paid for concerts in the park and Christmas parades and, when he died, had a crowded funeral in a good church.

As Dick saw it, Johnny never gave himself enough credit for what he'd achieved. In Johnny's view, his willingness to cut corners made his achievements phony. That's why he was always dreaming of going straight, to see if he could make it the right way.

Dick respected that. He also respected the fact that Johnny was nobody's flunky. He was his own man. Of course, the hardest thing to justify was the violence. He'd killed, but Dick reasoned that they were only men in the life and this was the life they had chosen. He was certain that Johnny had never, even as a young man on the make, embraced the kind of mindless, animal behavior of people like Vito Genovese and Albert Anastasia, who killed straights and thugs alike without any feelings about them.

Johnny had developed a closely reasoned hierarchy about crime and the criminals who committed them. At the bottom of the pile, in his mind, were pimps and drug dealers, vermin that he would personally squash under his shoe, if he could. Next came wiseguys who bought their buttons, paying their way in to the Mob like coddled children buying into Ivy League schools, and who were almost as incompetent when it came to doing the work. Facing a man and taking him down, that took guts. That's why some of the people he admired most were burglars and people who had the balls to take their victims head-on, knowing at any second they could be unmasked and hurt, even killed. They took the greatest chances of all.

One of Johnny's favorites was Sammy the Hustler, about whom Scatsy said, "He earns an honest living cheating at cards." Sammy's technique, especially when he fleeced cruise-ship passengers, was to bring along a beautiful girl, who would stand at the table while Sammy played. At a signal from Sammy, the girl would let her dress strap slip, flashing a little skin, and distracting the other players while Sammy palmed a card.

One day in 1958, Johnny told Sammy the next time he went to Miami to stay at a hotel Johnny had recently bought into, the Bel Aire. It was a nice place, right on the beach.

"I usually stay at the Fontainebleau," Sammy said. The magnificent 920-room Fontainebleau was a showplace on a par with the finest hotels in New York. From the trio of Belgian chandeliers in the lobby, each with eighteen hundred pure crystal strands, to the marble-floored ballroom large enough for a royal wedding, the Fontainebleau was the place to be. It was always filled with the kind of high-rollers that Sammy trimmed like kids getting their first haircuts.

"I know you like the Fontainebleau," Johnny told Sammy.

So did Johnny. "But I own the Bel Aire now. Stay there," he said.

Sammy knew when it was time to fold a hand, so he agreed. He checked in at the Bel Aire, but left a few days later.

"Johnny, I want to know, who am I gonna rob down there? Big Nose Sam? Charlie the Blade? Joey Potatoes? I'm going to get killed there."

The clientele at the Bel Aire was like a lodge meeting of wiseguys. If Sammy tried to cheat them, he was going to end up floating face-down in Biscayne Bay.

A big smile crossed Johnny's face. "Okay," he said. "Go to the Fontainebleau."

A little later that year, Johnny went to Dick with a proposal to go to work at a carpet company Johnny had on the arm called Allen Carpet Shops. Despite its location in a nondescript warehouse in Queens, it was the largest retail chain of carpet stores in the metropolitan New York area. The company had just landed a contract to do the Copacabana, a nightclub Costello owned. Business was so good that they could use another salesman, Johnny said.

Selling rugs to apartment dwellers wasn't Dick's idea of a step up, career-wise. He still had dreams of making his mark in the entertainment business, even though Dick's efforts in the music business were struggling.

Johnny told Dick he was letting him in on the ground floor of something very big. He saw the carpet business as a potential escape from the Mob. His vision was to leave New York, with its clannishness and endless vendettas, and make a clean start with a legitimate business. Putting Dick there would also give him someone on the inside who could be his eyes and ears with Johnny's partner, Fat Jack Herman, whom Johnny did not trust.

Fat Jack was a compulsive liar. With most people, lying was a way of avoiding conflict or shifting responsibility. With Fat Jack, it was an addiction. He was so good, he could con you out of your socks while you were walking. Johnny thought the work could be good for Dick, giving him a steady paycheck at a time when Dick and Joanie were about to start a family. He promised that Dick could keep his hand in the music business in his spare time.

It was hard to say no to Johnny. After a couple of months learning to measure rooms and working in the warehouse, Dick went out on the sales floor. By far, he was the youngest salesman there. They had some very aggressive, very tough salespeople who immediately shortened his mouthful of a last name to "Cami." Dick learned not to judge a person by his looks or dress. Some of the least impressive people were the most successful. Big blowhards dressed to kill meant nothing. His very first day on the floor was proof. A guy dressed like a bum shuffled in. It was another salesman's turn but, looking at the guy, he passed the man off to Dick. "Take my turn, kid, you need the experience," he said.

He didn't intend to do Dick any favors. He didn't want to waste his time. It turned out the guy wanted to carpet a model home. Dick's first sale proved to be a monster. The other salesman tried to be gracious, but Dick could tell it was an effort. "You see what I do for you?" he growled.

Soon, Johnny and Fat Jack opened a new showroom at 515 Madison Avenue. It was called Leonard Carpets for Johnny's friend and frequent investor, Lee Ratner. The founder of the d-CON rat poison empire and a man with more good ideas in one day than most people have in their lifetimes, Ratner helped make Johnny rich. They'd done a hundred deals together. Johnny, in turn, protected Lee from shakedowns by other mobsters and helped solve problems that the cops wouldn't go near. The showroom symbolized the start of a big change.

"We're going legit," Fat Jack said. "Very few wiseguys will be coming around. We're going after Mr. and Mrs. America now."

To design the showroom, Johnny brought in James Mont, the famous interior decorator, whose style was variously described as violent, or even murderous, with bloodred hues and purplish touches. Mont was the unofficial designer to the Mob, having worked with both Luciano and Costello. For the right price, he would design furniture and rooms to conceal illegal activities, such as collapsible gaming tables and secret compartments. The new carpet showroom was every bit a Mont production, reeking with sex and danger. Customers sat at an open bar as their orders were processed.

As Dick settled into his new career, Joanie delivered her first baby. Named for Joanie's father, the baby gave Johnny a male child bound by blood. The naming was celebrated in a ceremony held at the Atlantic Beach house. Dick was understandably proud. Johnny tried not to show his delight, displaying his usual nonchalance as the guests gathered around the squirming baby. True to his nature, the child's grandfather bestowed a sardonic nickname on the child, affectionately calling him "Johnny the Louse." Later, whenever he inquired about Dick's family, he would ask, "how's the little louse doing?"

Dick invited his partner, Vinny Marchese, while a selection of Johnny's closest friends and allies rounded out the guest list: Eddie Falcone, Frank Salerno and his wife, Mary, Genovese *capo* John "Buster" Ardito, and a few of the other boys. The food, as usual, was plentiful and delicious. There was *bacala*, shrimp salad, stuffed peppers, baked mussels, stuffed squid, shellfish risotto, and fresh mozzarella and ripe red tomatoes with torn basil dressing. The hit of the affair was Mary Salerno's St. Joseph *zeppole*, deep-fried dough balls stuffed with a sweet vanilla custard and sprinkled with powdered sugar. One of the great Italian desserts, when it's made well, and Mary's were the best; few sweets could approach it for richness and delicacy.

Mary herself was a bit of an eccentric. She lived on the fifth floor of an old Manhattan walkup on Houston Street that had been condemned by the city, refusing to leave because her friends were nearby. Given no choice, her husband, Frank, accepted her decision and bought the apartment building for her.

As the party revved up, a gray-haired man with a ski-slope nose showed up. Scatsy saw him coming up the drive and tugged at Johnny, who met him at the door. It had been months since Frank Costello had been seen in public. He'd become a virtual recluse since the night he was gunned down by Gigante.

Dick had never met him; he'd only talked to him long enough to recognize the voice and hand the phone to Johnny when he called. Watching the two men together, Dick saw the mutual respect that had cemented their relationship for more than two decades.

If the FBI had planted a camera inside Johnny's house that night, they'd have seen nothing more than a friendly nod and a handshake exchanged between the two old friends. Costello also gave a nod to Dick and Joanie. He greeted Millicent with an affectionate smile.

Johnny and Costello retired to the den. After a few minutes, Johnny came out and motioned for Salerno and Ardito to join them.

Johnny never disclosed the purpose of the meeting, but the plot against Genovese was a likely subject. Within months, Genovese would be sent to prison. An hour later, Johnny was back at the party, sitting in the dining room, sharing espressos with friends. Nobody at the party saw Costello leave. He went out through the kitchen and garage.

Mandy's death aside, the future looked bright. Johnny had survived Vito's bloodletting. His second daughter was well and finally married to a man who was everything he wanted in a son, and they had given him a grandson to carry his name.

Business was good and Johnny decided it was now time to build a plant that would manufacture custom carpet. With Allen Carpets selling the new line of Leonard carpets, Johnny and Fat Jack anticipated plenty of business. Johnny's friend Ratner agreed to put up the money for the new plant. His one demand was that it be in Florida, where Ratner lived. As the construction work proceeded on the plant in Hialeah, part of greater Miami, Fat Jack traveled south frequently to supervise the work.

Fat Jack wasn't just a gifted salesman and con artist, he was also a pathological bully. The manager of the plant in Hialeah was Fat Shelly, who was, if anything, fatter than Fat Jack. When he drove, his car listed badly to the left and, when he leaned forward to change a station on the radio, the horn beeped.

The first time he met Fat Shelly, Dick was sitting in Fat Jack's Hialeah office, when Jack picked up a work order and started yelling. "Shelly, you fat fuck, come in here right away."

In a few seconds, in waddled Shelly. He could barely wedge his body through the doorway.

"Did you order the wool for the Harris job?" Jack said.

"I think so," Shelly said.

Fat Jack exploded. "Try looking at me when you're talking, you fat piece of shit," he said.

He rumbled out from behind his desk and started bombarding Shelly with overhand rights and lefts. It wasn't playacting, either. He put his weight behind each punch.

"You think so?" *Bam.* "You think so?" *Thwack.*

Red-faced, Shelly screamed, "No, no, Jack, please, not the face."

Dick leaped in to break it up. His history with Lou Albano gave him experience in this sort of mayhem.

"Wedging myself between those two cows weighing nine hundred pounds between them was no easy task," Dick said. "But I managed it."

Having restored the peace, Dick was again shocked, but less so, the next day, when it happened all over again. *Bim, bam, boom*—another beating in the office. He soon learned this was a daily routine. Dick stopped trying to intervene.

One day, Fat Jack became so enraged that he took a paper spindle from his desk and threw it at Shelly. It tumbled over and over through the air and stuck in Shelly's skull behind his left ear. Shelly calmly pulled it out.

"Give me back my spindle, you fat piece of shit," Jack said.

Shelly put it back on the desk like nothing had happened.

Scatsy once asked Shelly why he took it. "Why do you let that fat prick get away with that? If you ever gave him just one good shot, you'd put him on his ass," Scatsy said.

Shelly had no answer.

Chapter 9

Why Don't You Call It Peppermint Lounge?

Around this time, Johnny ended up with another New York club on a fluke. An old pal from Brooklyn, Sibbey Mamone, had to go on the lam and asked Johnny to take over his club, a few doors down West 45th from Johnny's other club, the Wagon Wheel.

The place, before Sibbey had it, had been a gay bar named Harry and Larry's. It was closed down after a scandal involving a U.S. senator's son. Sibbey reopened it under the name the Gangplank, hoping the nautical touch would help him shanghai the overflow of sailors spilling out of the Wagon Wheel.

Johnny gave Sibbey $30,000 for 90 percent of the club. The other 10 percent remained with Sibbey's wife, to give her an income while her husband hid out.

Dick and Joanie were newly married when Johnny called his crew together in the early spring of 1958 to make plans for the new club. Dick fought his way through mid-Manhattan traffic and the cold, windy night. At last, he turned into Kinney's garage, threw the keys to the attendant, waved at Emil the manager, and pulled the collar of his coat against his chin before facing the chill.

Al Prisco met him at the door of the Wagon Wheel. "I made a *fil-letto* sauce," he said. "You want a plate?" God forbid he should say no.

At the table, Johnny was seated with his usual cast of characters. Sam Kornweisser, known as Sam K., was the nuts and bolts expert behind all Johnny's businesses. Next to him was Fat Jack Herman. He'd been with Fat Tony Salerno, a boss in the Genovese Family, until the Mafia transferred him to Johnny.

Also at the table were Scatsy and Big Sal Triscaro, a bouncer from the old neighborhood in the Bronx who was like family. Big Sal, who Scatsy liked to say was "six feet fourteen inches" tall, settled a lot of Johnny's arguments with an overhand right. He never carried a gun and was smart enough not to become a made man.

The table was covered with platters of all the usual food. The meal was finished off with big baskets of Zito's bread. As they sipped Sambucas, Johnny got down to business.

First off, he said to Dick, "We're taking over a joint a few doors down the street. I'm letting you have a rooting interest." Rooting interest meant a small percentage.

Johnny wanted to know what kind of entertainment they should feature. To Dick, this was one of those rare moments when you feel you're in exactly the right place at the right time. He told Johnny exactly what he thought.

"Don't use the same tired old jazz bands you have here," Dick said. "Everybody in town has jazz. What you should put in there is rock-and-roll."

"That bullshit noise," said Scatsy. "You call that music?"

"You guys have no idea what's happening in the music business," Dick said, drawing on his hard-won education. "The kids love this music. There's no other rock-and-roll clubs in the city. We'll have the only one. Kids will come from miles around."

Sam K. looked interested. "Can you get these bands?" he asked.

"Absolutely," Dick said. Even better, they worked cheap.

Johnny hadn't said a word. He just nodded, and that was it. That decided, the whole crew ambled into the chilly New York night, heading toward Times Square. They stopped in front of the Knickerbocker. A small sign over the door at 128 West 45th Street read: GANGPLANK.

Dick peered inside. It looked small, cramped, only big enough for, maybe, a hundred (the exact number turned out to be 178). "What are we going to call the joint?" Sam said.

"How about the Ha-Ha Club?" said Al Prisco.

"How about Your Mother-in-Law's Balls Club," Scatsy said. He knew Al was breaking his balls about a gay club Scatsy had worked at in Florida.

"The Celebrity Club?" said Big Sal.

Fat Jack had been silent. He was busy struggling to open a pack of blue-and-white peppermints. He finally got the package open and popped one in his mouth.

"Why don't you call it the Peppermint Lounge?" he said.

As soon as Dick heard it, he knew that was it. Everybody waited to hear from Johnny.

"That sounds good to me," he said. "Peppermint Lounge it is."

The license was in the name of Ralph Saggese, a retired NYPD lieutenant who spent his entire career being friendly to the boys. Saggese had his name on the permit from when Sibbey owned it. He used to tell people he'd been working for UNICEF since leaving the force, but he actually had been working in the restaurant business as a maitre d' around town. Although Saggese was the owner of record who fronted for the club and was its spokesman, Sam K. ran the place.

To keep the doors open and the cops off their backs, they shelled out $900 a month in payoffs for each place. Those services covered basically nothing. It was a pure shakedown. Johnny never complained about the payoffs. He considered it part of the cost of doing business. Scatsy had a different attitude.

"I feel like I'm at the Academy Awards," he said. "Every month I'm passing out the envelopes."

When the Peppermint first opened, it didn't look like the bet on rock and roll would pay off. They booked the music, but the kids took their time discovering the club. Scatsy kept complaining. "I hate that noise," he said. "The other night a waitress dropped a tray of glasses and six couples got up to dance. Don't they know any wop songs?"

Dick didn't give the place much thought. At best, he figured it would be another bucket of blood. When he and Joanie went out on the town, it was the last place he'd ever think of going.

For Johnny, the club was a convenient place to do business. In the early afternoon or after midnight, people would come and go from the back room, soliciting Johnny's blessing, asking permission to put money out on the street, where to go to fence a piece of swag. There was also union business handled and the financing of bookmaking operations—tallying the bets or big layoffs had to be done on schedule.

If the law walked in on any of this, it would look like any other office with a desk and a couple of guys sitting around. Everything was done by word of mouth. There were never any records, receipts, papers, or files of any kind. Nobody dealt in cash. There were undisclosed locations where drops were made for that. Occasionally, when a large meeting was scheduled, a room would be made available at the adjacent Knickerbocker Hotel, where the lobby served as the back entrance to the club. Such meetings were always brief and secret. Everybody who attended the meeting came alone.

About six months after it opened, as Dick predicted, the kids began discovering the Peppermint. With the legal drinking age in New York at eighteen, the bridge and tunnel crowd poured in from New Jersey and Connecticut.

Dick never knew what his percentage of the New York Peppermint was. Johnny from time to time gave him envelopes stuffed with money. Sometimes there would be a few hundred in it, sometimes a few thousand.

This was Johnny's standard approach to business. His practice was to give out partnerships, sometimes one or two percentage points, sometimes more. It was cheaper than paying for a service, and better since the partnerships had value only as long as the place made money. He also sold points for cash, twenty to thirty thousand dollars at a clip, which he turned around and put out on the street in the form of loans. The money paid to investors was nothing compared to the interest Johnny earned loan-sharking.

It may have looked like a haphazard, not to say dangerous, way of running a business. But with Sam K. keeping track of everything, everybody always got paid.

Dick used the cash to make a down payment on a house in Massapequa, a hamlet on the south shore of Long Island that was almost as exclusive an address as Johnny's in wealthy, white, and well-bred Atlantic Beach. Massapequa was itself an enclave of the rich and famous where Mob boss Carlo Gambino would eventually settle. Joanie went shopping for furnishings appropriate to their new status. Only three days after Dick and Joan put the money down on their new house, Johnny announced that he wanted Dick and Scatsy to move to Miami. Nominally, Cami's task would be, once again, to keep an eye on Fat Jack. There was another, more personal reason. If Johnny was going to move his operation south, he wanted his son-in-law and brother with him.

With the carpet business doing well, Johnny Biello began to talk seriously of moving his entire operation to Miami and letting the younger members of his crew take over his rackets in the Bronx. He was fifty-two, young perhaps for retirement. But then, thirty years in the Mafia are hard, soul-scarring years. Johnny had survived imprisonment, Mob wars, the near assassination of his benefactor, and uncounted investigations by law enforcement. Who could blame him if he was tired?

Scatsy didn't want to hear about it. He was a New Yorker through and through, from his appetites to the cruelties he inflicted on the language. Outside of Miami, where he liked to spend the winter, anywhere beyond New York was foreign territory. "Fucking yokels" was his standard dismissal.

"The old man wants to move to Miami and get away from all the bullshit," Scatsy said. "I told him he's crazy. So the bookmaking operation got pinched. So what? I told him we should just open up again. We got the men to do the work."

"Johnny is the original change-your-life guy," Al Prisco said.

Dick could hardly complain about Johnny's request. Johnny was responsible for his success. Still, he figured his wife wouldn't like it, and he was correct. It made no sense to Joanie and she put up quite a fuss. Her father had met her every want, sent her to the best schools, given her addresses anybody would envy. But she wanted nothing more than to put a thousand miles between him and her. Her husband was supposed to be her escape. Instead, he'd cozied up to Johnny. She grew so angry that one Sunday she dragged Dick away from dinner before the *cannoli*, a serious breach of family protocol.

In the meantime, Johnny was having trouble with one of his Miami investments. He had a piece of a restaurant on the 79th Street Causeway in Miami called the Bonfire. Featuring a Wild West décor and displaying celebrity initials in the form of brands burned into its walls, the Bonfire was a fine restaurant with a good reputation. The owner was Radio Weiner. One problem with having lots of business partners was that Johnny didn't always choose them wisely. In this case, Weiner was being obstinate about paying Johnny his share. Scatsy suggested they burn the place down, bringing new meaning to the restaurant's name.

"You always want to be a fucking cowboy," Johnny said.

Johnny's idea was to get Weiner's attention without destroying the investment. The way to do it, he decided, was to throw a stink bomb into the restaurant. He'd had it done before with great success.

The mother of all stink bombs was called the Stink Bottle. Scatsy said it was invented by a pharmacist from the Bronx and consisted of more than twenty ingredients. It was so potent that a four-ounce bottle could chew into concrete and render a building the size of a warehouse uninhabitable. The odor was impossible to describe. You might call it a combination of sulfur, dead cat, and skunk spray, with a thick helping of sewage.

Johnny arranged for the delivery of the Stink Bottle. When it arrived, Scatsy held it up. "Look at this little fucking thing, will you," he said.

"I'd be careful how you handled that," Johnny said. "Not only is that the most powerful stink bomb in the world, but if you stick around after it's opened up you've got a good shot at getting sick."

Dick recommended that they put the Stink Bottle somewhere safe until it was time to use it. He knew a place in the carpet plant in Hialeah.

Not long afterward, a cold front from Canada pounded the Northeast, turning the cities into ice sculptures. People clogged the airports heading to Miami for the sun. It was January, the perfect time for the stink bomb. "I think it's time to turn on the radio," Johnny said.

In Florida, Scatsy took the wheel of the '57 Fairlane they'd bought from the late Little Augie. They headed to the carpet plant to retrieve the bottle and deliver it to Johnny, who had someone ready to throw it into the Bonfire.

A side door at the parking lot of the restaurant led to a long hallway that opened onto the main part of the dining room. The plan was to go in that way, smash the bottle inside, and be back in the car before the panic set in.

The carpet plant was in an industrial park on 32nd Street in Hialeah, surrounded by large warehouses. "Don't let that fat fuck Jack or that pig Shelly know what we're doing," Scatsy said as he parked the car.

Scatsy checked the rearview mirror a number of times before getting out. It was like he was on another caper from the old days. When they entered through the side door, Shelly looked up from his desk.

"Who's in the office?" Scatsy said, motioning him to keep quiet.

"Jack and Dorothy," Shelly said. Dorothy was Fat Jack's not-quite-so-fat wife.

Dick and Scatsy made their way to the back, where the carpet was stored. There were thousands of yards of carpet rolls stacked in huge piles that reached almost to the ceiling thirty feet above the floor. Scatsy went up on a ladder and pulled out a cardboard tube. Inside was the bottle, contained in its own box.

"Here it is," he said. He climbed down and, when he held it out, the bottom of the box gave way. The little bottle dropped to the concrete floor and shattered.

"Holy shit, Johnny's gonna kill me," Scatsy said.

"Let's get the fuck out of here," Dick said

As the dark chemicals started to foam, he grabbed Scatsy's arm and ran. The fumes were already spreading through the plant. Fat Jack ran in, demanding to know what the smell was. His fists were clenched, ready to exercise his anger on Shelly's face, so certain was he that his perennially incompetent employee must be to blame. "What's going on here?"

"Please, Jack," Shelly said. "It's their stink bomb."

Dick stepped between them, "Shelly had nothing to do with it, Jack."

Jack looked at Shelly. "You're so fucking lucky," he said.

After Dick and Scatsy helped evacuate the plant, they jumped back in the car and drove around the block, where they parked to watch the evacuation of the entire industrial park. The stench was so strong that when the police arrived, they thought it was a gas line break and called the fire department, which responded as if there were a five-alarm fire.

Crowds gathered in the street to watch the firefighters rushing here and there with their hoses. Scatsy and Dick sat in the car and watched quietly. There wasn't much to say. *Welcome to Miami*, Dick thought.

Sometimes Johnny's business decisions made Dick wonder. "We just bought a new joint," he said one day. It was a bar on Biscayne Boulevard and 123rd Street called the Old Mexico. "I put your name on as the owner."

Dick couldn't believe what he was hearing. Where, he wondered, was he going to find the time to look after the new business while he was holding down a full-time job at the carpet plant?

"We'll put Scatsy there and you'll only go by to see what's what," Johnny said.

What Johnny didn't know was that the seller, Bill Monte, had inflated the income figures. Johnny gave him thirty thousand for the bar, the land and everything. It wasn't a bad price. The place had to make only two thousand a week to cover the nut. Monte assured Johnny he was taking in much more than that with just a piano player for entertainment. Johnny knew Monte was a bullshitter, but he believed there was a legitimate business at the Old Mexico. The place had a nice atmosphere. There were miniature covered wagons on the back patio.

The first day under the new ownership, the bar took in about one hundred dollars. "Don't worry," Monte said. The second day take was a bit over two hundred. "This doesn't look so good," Cami told Monte, who stayed on during the transition.

Meanwhile, boosters and second-story men were going in and out, doing business with Monte in the back. Monte had every kind of scam going, including a length of string in the pay phone to get the dimes and quarters back. Even though there was a constant flow of thieves and burglars through the door, they didn't buy any drinks so the house made nothing.

On the third day, Bob Ball came in. He was an heir to a railroad fortune and lived off a trust fund, which mainly supported his drinking habit. Ball was Monte's patsy. He told Dick that what he should do was let Ball get bombed, then put him in a cabin in back when he passed out. While Ball slept, Monte said, Cami could take the man's credit card and "bang it out for around five hundred. Never make it an even figure. Sign his name to it."

Ball came in at least three times a week, Monte said. There was another guy he did the same routine with, busting him out for eight hundred a week.

"Between the two of them you can make over twenty-five hundred," Monte said.

Dick couldn't believe it. "Trust me these guys want it that way," Monte assured him.

"We don't do things that way," Cami said. "I'm not putting anyone to sleep."

When Ball came in, Cami and Scatsy let him drink but never stole from him or let him sleep it off in the cabin. The rule was he had to have a ride home or he couldn't drink himself into a stupor. The arrangement was working until one night when Johnny came in.

"Who's that guy over by the bar? He looks drunk," Johnny said.

"That's Bob Ball the railroad heir—he's a lush," Dick said.

"What's the matter with you? Why are you letting him get drunk. Doesn't he know liquor can kill you? Cut him off. No more drinks for him."

"Cut him off?" Dick said. "If we do that, there goes half the business."

"Who cares? No more booze for him and when he sobers up, tell him to come over to the Fontainebleau. We'll give him a steam bath and flush him out."

Only Johnny Futto would cut off the only steady-paying customer. When Dick told Ball that Johnny was cutting him off, Ball could only offer a blank, dumb look. He didn't know what to say. Ball was like a big basset hound, a harmless Harry type that wouldn't hurt a fly. He just wanted to get drunk and listen to what the guy on the next stool had to say. That was his whole life until he met a girl he fell in love with and married. Ball had no idea who Johnny was. He was simply amazed that someone wouldn't take his money.

Scatsy came up with a solution that worked for a while. They served him vodka in a Mountain Dew bottle so Johnny wouldn't suspect anything when he came in. Ball went for the idea. But after a little while, Dick went to Johnny and convinced him that Monte had sold him a pig in a poke. Johnny told him to get the money back from Monte.

When Dick went to Monte, he didn't like the idea. He kept saying, "Hey a deal's a deal."

Dick trumped that by reminding him who he was dealing with.

"You know who Johnny is, right?"

"I know who he is."

"Good, then you know how hard it is to see with a needle in your eye."

Monte sat up straight in his chair.

"My advice to you is to wake up," Cami said. "You're going to force Johnny to do something that he doesn't want to do. But for sure he'll do it. I'm advising you to reconsider and take the place back. Say yes. Don't be unreasonable. Remember, Johnny will respect you and the door will always be open to you."

Monte took back the bar, none too happily. A few years later, however, he sold the land for more than half a million. After that, every time Cami saw Monte, he got a big smile.

Bob Ball was also at the center of the trouble that Dick got into during his brief, unhappy experience with shylocking.

Johnny partnered Cami with Joe "Scootch" Indelicato, a Gambino man close to Meyer Lansky. Joe was a tough bastard with a gruff manner and a temper so volatile that Scatsy used to say, "If you think nobody cares if you're dead or alive, try missing a couple of payments to Joe Scootch."

When Dick met him the only thing Joe had going for him was a cigar store on Biscayne Boulevard and 79th Street in Miami. It provided him with a very modest income. Plus, the FBI was breathing down his neck. Johnny set him up in the shylock business to help him out. He thought putting Dick together with him would be a way for his son-in-law to earn a few extra bucks.

Joe Scootch went to Dick one day asking about Bob Ball.

After Cami told Scootch about Ball, Joe said the guy wanted to borrow $10,000. Was he good for it? He had plenty of money, Dick said, "But who knows? The guy is a bad drunk. Anything could happen with him."

All Scootch could see were dollar signs. He made the loan anyway. Everything went okay for a month or two.

Then Ball got arrested for shooting and killing the wife he had lost his heart to, along with the guy she was banging while Ball was out ruining his liver. Of course, Ball was bombed, so the first few shots were off the mark and only wounded the lover. Before he died, the guy got his gun from the nightstand and put a few bullets into Ball.

The next morning, Joe saw the story in *The Miami Herald*. All he could think of was his money. He called Dick and demanded that he meet him at his store. Right after that, Dick got a call from Johnny. "You read the papers this morning about Ball?"

"No, but Joe just called and he wants to meet me."

"You better go. Stupid head Bob Ball just killed somebody and he himself is in critical condition in the hospital."

Dick went to Joe's store. "We better go see what's what," said Scootch.

At North Miami General Hospital, Dick and Joe pretended to be relatives. When Dick saw Bob, he didn't know whether to laugh or what. It was like a movie where all you see is the guy's face because his whole body is covered in a plaster cast and one leg's held up by a pulley.

When he saw Dick, Ball tried to smile. In an instant, Joe Scootch dispensed with the niceties. "Listen you motherfucker, you got one day to come up with my money. Otherwise I'll bury you myself."

Jesus, Cami thought. *This guy's almost dead.* He took Joe by the arm. "Let me talk to him alone and see what I can do."

"The best thing you can do is pay back the money right away," Dick said after Joe left.

"Tomorrow. Come back tomorrow and I'll have it," Ball said through a mouthful of gauze. Dick warned he better not be telling a story, because Joe Scootch was not a man to play with.

The next day when Dick returned, there was a lawyer standing at the foot of Bob's bed. When Ball started to introduce them, Dick waved him off. "No introductions please. Just give me the package," he said.

The stranger handed over an envelope.

"Don't let me give this to Scootch unless all the money is in this envelope," Dick said.

"It's all there," the attorney said.

"I hope so Bob, for your sake." Dick nodded to Bob and left. He didn't stop to count the money until he got back to Scootch's cigar store. It was all there.

"It was one of the few times I ever saw Joe Scootch smile," Cami said.

With all his money, Ball went to the can on a second-degree murder conviction. His case wasn't helped by the fact that he'd gone back to his car to reload after running out of bullets.

That experience convinced Dick that the shylock business wasn't for him. It wasn't just the danger, or the pathetic look of fear on Ball's face. The whole thing was too nakedly predatory. With gamblers, at least you were giving them some entertainment. Even losers usually walked away with smiles on their faces. When Dick went to Johnny about it, he understood perfectly. That's why he'd gotten out of the business himself. By then, he only shied the shylocks.

One shylock Johnny shied was Julie Bender, a colorful character who came to Johnny for help buying a liquor store that he imagined would provide him with a reliable enough income that he could retire from his life of crime—that great criminal dream of settling down and making the mortgage without using the gun and knife. Johnny stood for him and Julie opened Sunshine Liquors.

Julie kept getting robbed. The store was in a bad neighborhood, adjacent to Liberty City, one of the toughest ghettos in America. Once a week, Dick would go to collect the money and Julie would crack him up with stories. But after he started getting robbed, he got angrier and angrier. He especially didn't like having a gun stuck in his face, which Dick thought was funny, considering his former line of work.

Johnny told Julie not to take it seriously. "Maybe they needed the money," he said.

"Maybe you should put a sign in the window: 'If you want to rob me, don't come in with a pistol. Call me and I'll meet you outside with the money or phone in the heist like a take-out order and I'll have the money ready for you in a bag when you come.'"

Johnny laughed but Julie was not amused. A little later, Julie was robbed again. This time, he lost it and followed the thieves outside and threw a couple of wild shots after them. One went through the window of a car waiting at the stoplight and struck the driver in the head. The man died instantly, with his wife and baby on the seat next to him.

Johnny was enraged. "He knows better," he said. "He was a thief once. He knows he's not supposed to do things like that." Johnny wasn't as upset about the accidental shooting of the bystander as he was about Julie's breaking the criminal code. Preventing a robbery was one thing, but shooting at a thief when you were one yourself was beyond the pale.

He ordered Julie to repay everything. Right away. That was the end of Julie's American dream. And Dick's career as a shylock.

While still holding down the job at Leonard Carpet, Dick next worked the phones for a few hours at night in a boiler-room operation, selling lots for Johnny's friend and investor, Lee Ratner.

After selling off his d-CON pesticide business, Ratner needed a good tax dodge. He bought 61,000 acres of grassland in eastern Florida and started his own cattle ranch. But Ratner quickly decided he didn't understand the business and broke up the ranch into quarter-acre and half-acre lots, creating one of the nation's first planned communities, Lehigh Acres.

Ratner's pitch was simple: ten dollars down and ten dollars a month. Who couldn't afford that? But that wasn't the real hook. Lee never sold price. He sold lifestyle.

And he lived the lifestyle he sold, making buyers feel they could be him. To reinforce the image, he always left a big tip, even for a cup of coffee. Lehigh Acres became a boomtown as New Yorkers flooded south for the winters.

On the night of the 1960 presidential election pitting Richard

Nixon against John F. Kennedy, Johnny and his son-in-law received an invitation to join a small, elite group gathered to watch the returns on television at Ratner's palatial home. At precisely eight o'clock, after waiting several minutes and checking his watch, Johnny pressed the buzzer outside the tall gates.

Lee Ratner flipped a switch and the gates swung open. Ratner's mansion was huge, with a marble fountain out front and a double-wide stairway leading to the main floor. A Venetian glass chandelier cast its light on an imported Carrara marble floor. In the evenings, a breeze came off the ocean through the open terrace doors. Below that was a seaplane ramp on Biscayne Bay, the only one of its kind in Miami Beach.

Ratner floated down the grand staircase to greet his guests. Also in attendance was a man Cami had never met before, Charlie "the Blade" Tourine, a formidable organized crime figure in his own right. Tourine was close to Meyer Lansky; he'd operated several casinos for Lansky in Cuba, including the famed Havana Casino de Capri. When Fidel Castro routed dictator Fulgencio Batista's troops and took over on New Year's Day 1959, Tourine is said to have escaped in a private plane with a half dozen suitcases stuffed with cash.

Ratner asked Dick if he would pick up someone at the airport who was going to watch the election returns with them. "He's an older guy. A little man. He'll be wearing a cardigan sweater, blue. His name is MacArthur," said Ratner.

John D. MacArthur to be precise, one of the country's richest men. He made his first fortune in the insurance industry. In 1954, he purchased 2,600 acres of land for $5.5 million in northern Palm Beach County that today includes Lake Park, North Palm Beach, Palm Beach Gardens, and Palm Beach Shores. For years, he conducted his business affairs at a table in the Colonnades Beach Hotel on Singer Island, where he lived in a penthouse apartment overlooking the Atlantic Ocean on one side and the Intercoastal Waterway on the other.

Dick knew none of that. Ratner hadn't told him anything about his rider. The guy was quiet and unprepossessing on the ride to Ratner's place. They arrived at nine o'clock, just as the returns were starting to come in. The network anchors boasted about a new RCA computer they were using, which they said would enable them to be first to predict the winner.

"I hope they're fucking right with that machine," Tourine said. "I've got seventy thousand dollars bet on this election."

"I hope they're right, too," MacArthur said. "My office in Chicago just leased three of those computers for that price."

Ratner nodded knowingly. "Don't worry. If they don't work, we'll send Johnny to get your money back." Johnny winked at his son-in-law.

The computer called the election for Kennedy and everyone in the room was happy. "I didn't want the prick to win," Tourine said. "But I knew he would."

The group celebrating Kennedy's election could not know that as soon as the new president took office he would turn his brother Bobby loose on the Mob that helped him win the election.

MacArthur left early. Dick expected any friend of Lee's would be staying at an expensive place on the beach, but his directions took them to a nondescript place called the Biscayne Terrace Hotel on Biscayne Boulevard. As MacArthur got out, Dick noticed a hole in the guy's sweater. *Poor guy*, he thought, wondering how someone so obviously running on bare tires could afford to lease three RCA computers.

It wasn't until the next day that Lee told Cami who MacArthur was. When Dick asked why the guy would stay at a place like the Biscayne, Ratner's brows arched.

"He owns it."

Chapter 10

The Twist

S yd Nathan couldn't tell a hit from Shinola, but he put out some of the greatest rhythm and blues recordings ever made. Nathan was a frustrated jazz drummer who ran a store selling radios and, when a jukebox operator repaid a fifty-dollar debt with a truckload of used records and they sold faster than the radios, Nathan decided to get into the music business. In the forties, he launched his own record label, King Records, following up with a growing list of associated labels that included Federal, DeLuxe, and Beltone. Nathan presided over his modest empire from an old icehouse on Brewster Avenue in Cincinnati.

Dick Kline, who had been working in the Miami warehouse at Decca Records, sweeping floors and packing shipping boxes full of Domenico Modugno's big hit, "Volare," went to see Nathan about a job during the mogul's annual visit to the luxurious Harbor Island Spa in Florida. When he arrived at his room, Kline found Nathan wearing a Harbor Island bathrobe, lying on his back on the bed with one leg in the air, his foot cradled by a man carving off calluses. The attendant was Marvin "Falsie" Novack, Nathan's childhood friend, who also happened to be the Miami branch manager of King Records. He would soon be Kline's boss.

Nathan, five-foot-five, two hundred and fifty pounds, had an unlit cigar jammed into his face. He squinted through Coke-bottle lenses at Kline.

"So you want to be in the record business? There's two things you need to know to make it in this business. First, everyone's a liar until they prove themselves true. The second thing is, fuck the artist. Take the song."

Publishing was where the money was. Publishers earned money not only every time the record was sold, but every time it was played on the radio. The money came in the mail. Publishers did not have to go city to city to pick it up. Some called it crooked, but it was the record company, after all, that took all the chances and gave the performers the opportunity to have their songs heard and to make a living on the road.

When Kline got the job, he serviced three hundred and fifty accounts across the state of Florida, earning a salary of seventy-five dollars a week, plus a five-dollar daily allowance for hotels, three dollars for meals, and gas money for the un-air-conditioned old Chevy that served as the company car. But he was in the record business.

Kline's territory covered some of the smallest, most remote R&B stations in the nation, dotted across the expanse of Florida. He represented the King line to rural, small town deejays who were glad to see anybody from the big city. Kline brought along sandwiches and a pint of whiskey to share with the lonely overnight jocks as he pitched his new releases.

One of the most popular King artists was Hank Ballard and his group, the Midnighters. Born John Henry Kendricks in Bessemer, Alabama, Ballard never really achieved the recognition or rewards due him as one of music's great originators. His greatest hits were called "smut" by *Variety* and *DownBeat* and were mostly banned from the airwaves. That didn't stop them from selling large numbers of records for Nathan's company.

Rhythm and blues talent scout Johnny Otis discovered the group that would become the Midnighters at an amateur contest in Detroit, when they were still called the Royals. Otis also wrote the Royals first record, "Every Beat of My Heart," released by Nathan's Federal Records in March 1952. A little more than a year later, after recording four more equally luckless singles on the label, lead vocalist Henry Booth stepped aside for a new member, seventeen year-old Hank Ballard.

The group knew Ballard from the neighborhood, dating to their gospel-singing days. Ballard was a shy, thoughtful man with a rough, almost harsh voice. His first record as the group's new lead vocalist, "Get It," made the top ten on the *Billboard* R&B charts in 1953.

In January 1954, the group went into the studio to record a new song Ballard wrote titled "Sock It to Me, Mary." Producer Ralph Bass complained the title was too strong. While Ballard was working on changing the song, the engineer's pregnant wife, Annie, walked in the room and, within minutes, Ballard had completed "Work with Me, Annie." Nathan changed the group's name—without mentioning it to them—to the Midnighters, to avoid confusion with the "5" Royales, a popular group on the Apollo label that Nathan was courting and would soon sign.

"Work with Me, Annie" brought the raunch out from between the lines ("give me my meat"), where it had been hidden by other rhythm and blues artists. Despite being virtually blacklisted off the radio, the record's success spawned a host of answer records exploring the further adventures of Annie. At one point in September 1954, all three of the Midnighters' records in the "Annie" trilogy—"Work with Me Annie," "Sexy Ways," and "Annie Had a Baby"—were in the *Billboard* R&B top ten at the same time. The "Annie" records on Federal were among the most crucial recordings to introduce white teenagers to the illicit pleasures of Negro rhythm and blues.

Rock and roll would grow different from Hank Ballard and the Midnighters, but never better. Within a year, the music world was turned on its head as rhythm and blues artists stormed the pop charts.

Fats Domino, Little Richard, even Big Joe Turner were selling records to a white audience that had never existed before, and in volumes never dreamed of by the performers. Numbers told the story about the difference between black and white radio. A hit on the *Billboard* R&B charts sold perhaps 7,500 records. A hit on the pop charts had a good chance to sell a million. While their peers went on to success, the Midnighters were left behind in the rush down trails the group helped blaze.

"The Twist," which Ballard first took into the studio in 1958, was supposed to be a rejuvenation for the Midnighters. Hank Ballard thought he finally had found the rock-and-roll hit that would break him on the pop charts. The song came to them by way of Brother Joseph Wallace of the gospel group the Sensational Nightingales. He brought the rudiments of the song to Ballard when they were sharing a hotel in Tampa, Florida, while on tour. Wallace was a fan of the Midnighters and knew his group couldn't use the gritty, secular tune. Ballard and his guitarist Calvin Green sat down and worked the number into "The Twist," borrowing liberally from the latest Midnighters record, "Is Your Love for Real?" (itself based on a Clovers record). Guitarist Green gave the tune a Jimmy Reed–shuffle feel.

Ballard, who believed his contract with King Records had expired, explored the possibility of releasing the song through Chicago's Vee-Jay Records, the home of popular black recording artists such as the El Dorados ("Crazy Little Mama") and the Spaniels ("Baby It's You"). Miami record man Henry Stone, who ran Tone Distributors, took Ballard into the North Miami Armory with some remote recording gear and cut a bluesy, driving version of "The Twist." Vee-Jay liked the idea of releasing the record until the company heard from Nathan, who claimed Ballard still owed him $300 and promised to sue anyone who signed him.

Ballard returned to Cincinnati to record the song with King's staff producer, Henry Glover. At the last moment in the studio, Ballard, sensitive perhaps to censorship issues, changed the lyrics from "You should see my baby do the Twist" to "You should see my little sis."

When the record came out, the sole songwriter credited was Hank Ballard. Syd Nathan had the publishing.

Nathan moved the group to the King label for the release and changed their name, once more, to Hank Ballard and the Midnighters. Although Ballard thought "The Twist" sounded like the hit, Nathan decided to promote the mundane ballad on the other side, "Teardrops on Your Letter." The A-side did well, going all the way to number four on the R&B charts.

The B-side made it as far as number six on the R&B charts, a strong showing that reflected sales and airplay in Baltimore, Pittsburgh, and Philadelphia. The dance that grew out of the song first surfaced in Baltimore on the popular afternoon TV dance party, *The Buddy Deane Show*. Rock-and-roll singer Freddy Cannon, from nearby Philadelphia, saw the black teens doing the dance when he performed his latest single, "Way Down Yonder in New Orleans," on the Deane show; he brought word of the phenomenon back to Philly. Interest in the dance was sustained enough that King decided to re-release "The Twist" in July 1960. It went back on the R&B charts a week before the version recorded in Philadelphia by a young man named Ernest Evans, going under the name Chubby Checker.

Evans was a light-skinned, oversized nineteen-year-old with a winning disposition who went to the same South Philly high school as teen idols Fabian and Frankie Avalon. He famously worked as a chicken plucker in a poultry market before his music career kicked into gear. Raised by churchgoing Baptists, he said his prayers every night and sang in a doo-wop group in high school, where he was known as Fat Ernie.

Checker ended up recording the song that became a sensation through a series of events that began with Dick Clark looking for someone to record a Christmas message for fans in 1958. Clark was riding high at the time. His Philadelphia-based teen dance show, *American Bandstand,* had gone national the year before. Clark went to a friend and associate, Bernie Lowe of Cameo Records, to find a performer who could mimic popular rock-and-roll singers.

Lowe recommended Evans. He sang "Jingle Bells" for Clark and his wife, Barbara. His Fats Domino impression was so good that Barbara Clark dubbed him Chubby Checker. Cameo had Chubby repeat the impressions on a novelty record called "The Class," which made a modest showing on the charts the next spring.

There is no overestimating the power the youthful, handsome Clark wielded over the musical tastes of the teenage nation in the early years of rock and roll. His show was watched by millions of kids who rushed home after school to tune in. If he plugged a record, it had a great chance of becoming a hit. And as he expanded his grip on musical tastes, he began to dabble in the business side of the industry. It was Lowe again who introduced him to the music publishing game, giving him a piece of the copyright to Cameo's first rock-and-roll hit, "Butterfly," by Philadelphia rocker Charlie Gracie. After that, the singer made twenty appearances on *Bandstand*. When he sued the label for royalties, he got a small settlement, but he never again appeared on *Bandstand*.

Clark's involvement with Ballard and "The Twist" began on June 22, 1960, when Hank appeared on *American Bandstand* to lip-synch and finger-snap his way through a song called "Finger Poppin' Time." On the strength of that appearance, the record soared into the top ten, which is where it was sitting when King reissued "The Twist."

All the record needed was a push by Dick Clark to give Ballard his long-awaited breakout hit. But Clark, who had ordered the cameras turned away when he first saw kids on his show doing the Twist, had his own ideas. The last thing he wanted was another dirty record from Hank Ballard. He called Bernie Lowe and suggested he find someone to cover the Hank Ballard dance song.

Lowe recorded the song with Chubby Checker, who, once again, put his skills as an impressionist to work on record, singing it almost exactly like Hank Ballard. Clark introduced Checker's version on his highly rated, prime-time Saturday evening TV show, *The Dick Clark Show*, on August 6, 1960. Chubby gave the nation its first Twist lesson on network TV. "Just pretend you are wiping your bottom with a towel and putting out a cigarette with both feet," he said. His record—a note-for-note copy of the Hank Ballard original—zoomed all the way to number one on the pop charts.

Ballard was floating in a motel swimming pool in Liberty City in downtown Miami when he heard the Chubby Checker recording on the radio. For the first few bars, he thought it was his record and that he had finally made his pop radio breakthrough.

Dance records came and went with some regularity at this time. In the months that Clark had been broadcasting *American Bandstand*, his dancers had spread the word on a lot of new crazes, each invariably illustrated by its own record. Clark was not above calling a friend who managed the vocal group the Diamonds, squeaky-clean squares from Canada, and suggesting that a record to go with the popular line dance the kids were doing on the show, the Stroll, could be an automatic hit. It was.

Chubby Checker's next number one hit, in fact, was another dance song, "Pony Time," released early in 1961. By that summer, he was already looking back on the Twist as history in "Let's Twist Again" (". . . like we did last summer"). The hit parade had moved along and the Twist was relegated to places where teenagers danced, like the Peppermint Lounge.

One September night in 1961, Lee Ratner took his paramour, Grace Palmer, along with him when he went to meet Johnny Futto at the Peppermint Lounge. While Lee and Johnny talked in the back office, Grace, dressed in a full-length mink Ratner had given her, witnessed the raucous scene in the club. The bridge and tunnel kids from Jersey, with their bouffant hairdos and rolled-up jeans, went at it on the dance floor, doing this unique dance she'd never seen before.

"I can't believe what I saw in there," Grace told Lee when he came out. "I wanted to stay and try out that dance myself."

That set Lee to thinking about what he saw and what his girlfriend said. He called Al Miniaci, who spoke to his friend Gene Pope, the owner of the *National Enquirer*. The paper's columnist, Alex Freeman, thought it would be better if the item appeared in a real society column and gave it to his girlfriend, a young journalist named Liz Smith, who worked as an assistant to Cholly Knickerbocker at the *Journal-American*.

Knickerbocker's real name was Igor Cassini, younger brother of Oleg Cassini, the designer who dressed Jackie Kennedy, giving her that smart look of studied glamour that women across the country were emulating. Never in his brother's shadow, Igor Cassini wrote a hugely influential column about café society, which he memorably dubbed the "jet set." Newspapers all over the country carried his column. The Hearst Corporation, which owned the rights, boasted that twenty million Americans read the Knickerbocker column every week.

The item—a small note to the effect that Prince Obolensky had been seen dancing the Twist at New York's "chic" Peppermint Lounge—appeared in the September 21, 1961 edition of his "Smart Set" column. "The Twist is the new teenage dance craze. But you don't have to be a teenager to do the Twist," he wrote.

It wasn't much. It wasn't even true. The Russian aristocrat had never been near the joint—that was a total fabrication. And calling the seedy little off Broadway nightclub on West 45th Street "chic" was hyperbole, even by gossip-column standards. But the small entry in the Knickerbocker column set off a chain reaction. Other columnists picked up the fiction. Eugenia Sheppard, fashion columnist for *The New York Herald Tribune*, mentioned the Peppermint Lounge and its specialty dance a couple of days later. Earl Blackwell of *Celebrity Register*, as well as Sheppard's great friend and next-door neighbor in the same building, started frequenting the place.

Actual socialites, curious to see what they were missing, came to the West 45th Street dive in their diamonds and pearls. Since the club was in the Theater District, Truman Capote, Marilyn Monroe, Judy Garland, Shelley Winters, and Tallulah Bankhead started dropping by. A writer asked screen goddess Monroe if she did the Twist.

"I do the Twister," she said. "I put something extra in it."

Johnny Biello and his family on the set of *The Dolly Sisters*; Betty Grable, Barbara, Johnny, Joan, June Haver, B. S. Pully, and Millicent Biello, 1945. *(Dick Cami)*

Johnny (left) and one of the guys called Mopy Dick, mid-1950's. *(Dick Cami)*

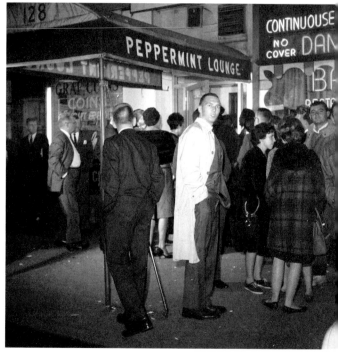

The crowd on West 45th Street outside the Peppermint Lounge, 1961. *(Corbis Images)*

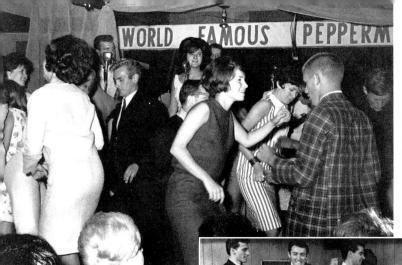

Twisting at the Peppermint Lounge. *(Corbis Images)*

Joey Dee and the Starliters on the band-stand. *(Dick Cami)*

The uncred-ited costar: the Peppermint Lounge — "Filmed Where It Happens Every Night." *(Dick Cami)*

Eighteen-year-old Veronica Bennett, Ronnie of the Ronettes, on the Peppermint Lounge dance floor, 1961. *(Dick Cami)*

The original Peppermint Twisters (Janet Huffsmith, second from right), 1962. *(Dick Cami)*

Janet Huffsmith, a rail dancer who helped invent go-go dancing. (Note fur stole on customer.) *(Dick Cami)*

Newspaper ad for the opening of the Peppermint Lounge in Miami Beach, 1961. *(Dick Cami)*

Peppermint Lounge van that Dick Cami used as a moving billboard on the Causeway in Miami Beach. *(Dick Cami)*

Keely Smith does the Twist at the Miami Peppermint with John J. Miller of the *National Enquirer*, 1962. *(Dick Cami)*

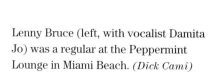

Lenny Bruce (left, with vocalist Damita Jo) was a regular at the Peppermint Lounge in Miami Beach. *(Dick Cami)*

Conway Twitty at the Peppermint Lounge, Miami Beach, 1963. *(Dick Cami)*

Dion at the Peppermint Lounge, Miami Beach, 1963. *(Dick Cami)*

Rail dancers at the Peppermint Lounge in Miami Beach. *(Dick Cami)*

Scatsy in his domain, the Peppermint Lounge kitchen, Miami Beach. *(Dick Cami)*

Sam and Dave, surrounded by white people, at the Peppermint Lounge, Miami Beach, 1963. *(Dick Cami)*

Alice In Wonderland billboard, announcing the 1963 season in Miami Beach. *(Dick Cami)*

The Angels, Miami Beach, 1963. *(Dick Cami)*

Louis Lomardi bids goodnight to John Lennon and his wife, Cynthia, 1964. (*Corbis Images*)

George Harrison, John and Cynthia Lennon ringside, and Paul McCartney and Ringo Starr at the next table. Peppermint Lounge, New York City, 1964. (*Getty Images*)

Ringo hits the dance floor with Peppermint Twister captain Marlene Klaire. (*Corbis Images*)

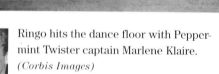

The Beatles with Hank Ballard and the Midnighters at Miami. (*Dick Cami*)

"Body of Slain John Biello Lies Sprawled on Car Seat," 1967. *(Miami Herald photo by Bob East)*

Chubby Checker, Thunder Valley Casino, January 2012. *(San Francisco Chronicle photo by Lance Iversen)*

Noël Coward and his artsy gay crowd came by to laugh. Tennessee Williams and his fellows dropped in for drinks. Café society, such as the Duke and Duchess of Bedford, and Bruno Paglia and his wife, film actress Merle Oberon, started showing up. Noted playboy Porfirio Rubirosa, one of the first of his crowd to discover the Peppermint, switched his allegiance from Le Club, the suddenly oh-so-stuffy East 55th Street club that had been the city's first European discotheque when it opened the year before. Elsa Maxwell, the dowager queen of New York society, made her way to the dance floor. "I hear people saying it's sexy, but of course it isn't," she reported. "It's too tiring to be sexy."

In the tinderbox of Manhattan society, the Twist was suddenly ablaze. By the middle of October, when Louie Lombardi summoned Johnny and Dick from Miami, crowds waiting for admission to the club jammed the sidewalk every night. Crosstown traffic clogged the street. It all happened with breathtaking speed. One week, the place was nothing but a sleazy hangout for teenagers and the motorcycle set; the next week, it was jammed with a whole new crowd.

"One week in October 1961, a few socialites, riding hard under the crop of a couple of New York columnists, discovered the Peppermint Lounge and by next week all of Jet Set New York was discovering the Twist," wrote Tom Wolfe in the *Herald Tribune.* "Greta Garbo, Elsa Maxwell, Countess Bernadotte, Noël Coward, Tennessee Williams, and the Duke of Bedford—everybody was there, and the hindmost were laying fives, tens, and twenty-dollar bills on cops, doormen, and a couple sets of maitre d's to get within sight of the bandstand and a dance floor the size of somebody's kitchen."

Outside on 45th Street, a candy-striped awning covered the entrance, while lines of people four deep stretched down the sidewalk to Broadway and around the corner. The doormen could be gruff and short, especially when some celebrity they didn't recognize tried to throw their weight around. Scatsy went nuts when he found out the Terrible Turk had turned away Ethel Merman—he was a fan—until Turk told Scatsy she told him to fuck himself. "Fuck her then," Scatsy said.

Maitre d' Joe Dana was a dark-skinned man with short jet-black hair and hawklike eyes who seemed taller than his five-foot-eight. He was making so much money in tips from swells looking for tables, he rented a room at the Knickerbocker so he had a place to empty his pockets. He told everybody he kept the room to sleep over instead of spending time driving home, but he would dash upstairs and dump the cash on his bed several times a night.

Inside the dingy, *L*-shaped room led to an elevated dance floor surrounded by mirrors. There were ostensibly two lines divided by a rope inside—one leading to the dance floor and the other to the exit—although that never worked in practice. Because the club levied no cover charge or admission fee, the only revenue came from the drinks, so the staff developed something of a sensitivity around keeping the aisles cleared to the bar, although the men who worked at the club were hardly sensitive people. The collection of mugs and thugs that staffed the club could have been rejects from a *Guys and Dolls* audition, large, ungainly men, many of them professional wrestlers.

Louie Lombardi was one of the other owners of record. He was in his mid-fifties, bald, and could fracture English with the best of them. He knew nothing about rock and roll. When someone said something to him about getting the Coasters, the rhythm and blues group famous for "Yakety Yak" and "Charlie Brown," Lombardi didn't know what they were talking about. "I ordered a new case last week," he said.

As you came in the door of the Peppermint, the long front part of the room was the bar, presided over by large, genial bartenders with a lingo all their own. "What's your pleasure?" they'd say. "What did you have for dinner? Where did you eat?"

Dana, from Bensonhurst, Vinny Marchese's tough neighborhood in Brooklyn, was as smooth and refined as the rest were ragged and unpolished. Like most of the crew at the Peppermint, he was no mobster, just a guy who caught on to Johnny's coattails somewhere along the line and, knowing a good thing, hung on.

The outside doorman was the Terrible Turk. Because there was no cover charge, even after the place got famous, it was first-come-first-in, at least in theory. The club did have a back entrance through the lobby of the Knickerbocker Hotel, guarded by two large doormen. VIPs were slipped through the crowd into reserved tables, where the club often stationed another beefy security guard to keep autograph seekers away from rock-and-roll celebrities such as Clay Cole, the twenty-two-year-old host of a popular Saturday rock-and-roll dance program on New York City television. Nobody asked the Duke of Bedford for his autograph.

The Turk and some of the other doormen earned extra cash by letting people in for the right price at the back door, in the Knickerbocker Hotel. The customer would walk up to Turk at the front door and reach out to shake his hand. As he did so, he sneaked a fifty-dollar bill into it. That was a lot of money, but just enough to get into the hottest club in the nation.

The Turk would take out a business card and write down a daily code on it, which the customer would hand to the bouncer at the rear door. It was a nice little scheme and Johnny never caught onto it. Dick once mentioned to Scatsy that he suspected the Terrible Turk and the others were taking bribes.

"Tell me about it," Scatsy said. "Hey Turk, Dick wants to give you a tax number."

"For what?" the Turk said.

"Because you cocksuckers are in business for yourselves out there on the door."

"I don't know what you're talking about," the Turk said.

Years later, Scatsy lit into the Turk one last time. "Stop bullshitting and tell me how much you were making out the back door."

"About two thousand a week," the Turk allowed.

Scatsy wasn't angry. He was impressed. "That's a lot a clams," he said.

So much money was gushing into the club that it was nearly impossible to keep track of it. Which constituted a temptation that Johnny's ragged crew of ex-wrestlers, con men, and thieves had trouble resisting. One night, Scatsy said he'd been watching the liquor closely and the costs came to nearly 44 percent of the take. Scatsy proposed that they bring in a character nicknamed Vinnie the Squint to watch the bartenders at work. Louie laughed.

"He's blind. What's he going to see?" said Louie, who thought Scatsy was just paranoid.

"It don't matter what he sees," Scatsy said. "It's what they think he's seeing."

The plan worked perfectly. For three days, Vinnie sat at the bar, drinking a little, staring vacantly in the direction of the cash register. When Scatsy looked again at the figures, the liquor costs had plummeted to 16 percent.

"Now you want to tell me they ain't stealing?" he said.

To Sam K. and Louie Lombardi, keeping the aisles clear became an obsession. They looked at it like it as taking money out of the register.

"What are you guys? A bunch of sissies?" Louie said to the bouncers. "If they don't keep out of them fucking aisles, grab 'em by the balls."

"What if they're broads and don't have balls," said the Turk, another ex-wrestler employed as a bouncer along with Alley Oop and Captain Lou Albano, Dick's old college pal.

Louie gave him the slow burn. "Then let Albano handle it, you dumb cluck. You only know what balls feel like anyway." Turning his back, Louie swiftly kicked his right foot backward toward the Terrible Turk like he was wiping something off his shoe and walked off muttering, "Faggot."

The place was so crowded that when a patron asked Joe Dana where the men's room was, he answered, "Go in your pocket—you'll never make it."

The waitresses were mostly young women, college students, aspiring hairdressers, and transplants from the Midwest who loved the music and sensed something important was going on in the dingy little club. One night, the service bartender got sick and Joe Dana asked his father to fill in. Dana's father was young-looking and did a great job. One of the waitresses took an interest.

"That new bartender is really cute," she said. How about fixing me up with him?"

"I'll have to ask my mother first," Dana said.

Janet Huffsmith was typical of the group, a young girl bored with small-town Pennsylvania life who wanted to experience the thrill of New York. Though underage, she was working at a club called the Champagne Colony when a friend told her the Peppermint was looking for waitresses. When she started there it was nothing but a sailor hangout.

One night, she recalled, the columnist Alex Freeman brought some society folks in. As she remembers it, he was fascinated watching her do the Twist. The next night, more society types came with him. Soon, the place was jammed with celebrities and chauffeur-driven limos were parked out front.

Janet's favorite was John Wayne, "the biggest sweetheart." He didn't do the Twist; that wasn't his style. But he wanted a souvenir. "He asked for my stockings," Huffsmith said. By this time, the dancers were in costume with sleeveless tops and fringed skirts, along with theatrical mesh stockings. Janet disappeared demurely backstage and removed her stockings, handing them to a grateful Wayne.

One Sunday, the *Today* show, hosted by Dave Garroway, was broadcast from the Peppermint Lounge. Frank McGee anchored an edition of his *Here and Now* from the club. Jack Paar ranted about the Peppermint Lounge for six full minutes coast-to-coast on his TV show. The management at the Peppermint held mixed feelings about all the publicity. They certainly didn't court the press. Bouncer Lou Albano was now Captain Lou Albano, who worked at the club between wrestling matches, watching for cops. One night, Albano tugged on his earlobe—the sign police were in the house—as a guy in a shiny suit wandered in, looking flustered. The guy said he represented a New York TV show.

"This place is a phenomenon. I had a devil of a time getting in," the man told Louie Lombardi. The visitor proposed doing a show from the club, "maybe late at night when things settle down some." Louie walked to Johnny's office, where he was relaxing with Dick and Sam Kornweisser. Sam was an unprepossessing, grandfatherly type, but very canny when it came to keeping tabs on the bottom line. "We don't have the room," Sam said when Louie outlined the proposal.

Dick couldn't believe it. "This could be great publicity," he said.

"Look out there," Sam said. "We don't need more publicity. We could use a little less if you ask me." Later on, Dick looked at the business card the visitor had left behind. It read Mike Wallace, the future *60 Minutes* correspondent. At the time he was hosting a TV show called *PM East*.

Anything could happen at the club. Intrigued by all the fuss, some of Johnny's mobster friends began stopping in to catch a glimpse of the freak show. A few even ventured out onto the dance floor. One of the most energetic wiseguy Twisters was Vincent Alo, known as Jimmy Blue Eyes. Unlike so many wiseguys Dick was meeting, who tended toward short and stumpy, Alo was tall and handsome. He didn't stand out as a thug, but he had the reputation, which he'd earned the hard way, working for Joe the Boss before joining up with Meyer Lansky. Alo went at it like he was kicking a man to death.

When he was done, he came off the floor dripping wet and asked Scatsy for a bar towel. "Whatta ya lookin' at kid?" he growled at Cami, who was studying him.

"Nothing," Dick said, looking away. "I was just admiring your dancing."

"I love to dance," he said. "Hey, Scatsy, gimme another fuckin' towel."

When Alo returned to his table, Dick said he couldn't help noticing Jimmy's eyes weren't blue. "Everybody thinks that," Scatsy said. "They were never blue. He got the name from all the beatings he took as a kid."

One night an interior designer with a shaved head was seen shaking his hips on the Peppermint's dance floor. The guy bore an uncanny resemblance to Nikita Khrushchev, the shiny-pated premier of the USSR who had scared Americans only the year before by pounding his shoe on a desk at the United Nations. Lee Ratner sent a photograph of the guy to all the newspapers with the caption, "Even Khrushchev does the Twist at the Peppermint Lounge."

Between all the waiting in line, tips for favors changing hands, the overcrowding, and all the bad tables or, worse, no tables, there was a lot of grumbling among Upper East Side types who made the trek across town. The scene had gotten so out of hand that Cholly Knickerbocker, the columnist who lit the fuse in the first place, felt compelled to defend his discovery in his column. "We can only say that among the people we have seen there are members of the first family, top business, society, theatrical names, and lots of respectable John and Jane Does from suburbia," he wrote.

"But the point is that we never said the P.L. was El Morocco or the Stork. Whatever 'charm' made it catch on must have been due to the very fact that it wasn't. What people wanted was something a little rugged and different—a place where social credentials didn't count.

"One also has to take into account the pressures of the owner of this West 45th Street nightspot. As a result of his big success, he is overcrowded, understaffed, can't equate supply with demand, and can't control all the abuses which undoubtedly exist. Also he is a constant state of surveillance by police and fire officials who want to enforce certain city laws.

"We never said the P.L. was perfect—nothing is. We found it amusing. But if you're looking for a nice, calm, civilized place where five dollars to the maitre d' will solve all your problems and no rock 'n' roll will shatter you, go East."

By the end of the year, the Twist had swept the nation and the rest of the world. Everywhere the Twist was danced—and where wasn't it?—the name of the Peppermint Lounge was known. It was the source of a phenomenon that had loosened the world's libido and gotten everybody shaking their asses. It wasn't much, but it was a start. Life seemed better. World peace was still an issue, but the Twist offered the bright promise of pleasure and frolic. Syndicated columnist Earl Wilson summed it up. "If it wasn't for the Twist," he wrote, "1961 would have been a sad year."

Chapter 11

The Twist Takes Over

The Peppermint Lounge had become the center of the rock-and-roll universe. Rhythm and blues singer Sam Cooke spent an evening in the club and, amazed at what he saw, bounded out of the club anxious to write a song about his experience. The result was a smash hit, "Twistin' the Night Away."

"Like, one night I went to the Peppermint Lounge, and wrote down what was going on around me," Cooke explained.

The Twist had conquered New York society. Next came Middle America. On the Sunday night television institution *The Ed Sullivan Show*, where America first had met Elvis Presley five years earlier, Chubby Checker made a critically timed appearance on October 22, singing a medley of his two Twist hits, again offering the entire nation a free Twist demonstration. His summer hit, "Let's Twist Again," sparked a nationwide revival of the dance among kids. Checker's 1960 hit, "The Twist," rose from the dead like Frankenstein's monster and headed for the village. Radio began playing it again like a new record and it started back up the charts, the first record ever to reach number one twice. The recording industry paid attention.

On the bandstand every night during the Twist era at the Peppermint Lounge, in the eye of the hurricane, was the house band, Joey Dee and the Starliters. An altar boy from Passaic, New Jersey, who went to the same high school as the girls who became the Shirelles, Joseph DiNicola started his band in 1957. The girls in the Shirelles introduced him to the chief of their record label, Florence Greenberg of Scepter Records, and made a couple of singles with the band.

Already a hot attraction on the northern New Jersey bar circuit, Joey Dee and the Starliters were finishing a two-month run at Oliveri's in Lodi, New Jersey, when booking agent Don Davis happened across the group and offered them a weekend at the Peppermint Lounge. The Starliters were initially booked to play for three nights, starting October 13, 1960, but they went over so well that they were hired the following Monday and became the house band, playing six nights a week for $600.

Peppermint Lounge regular Ahmet Ertegun was enamored of the band and wanted to sign the group to his label, Atlantic. That was never going to happen. As the Peppermint Lounge exploded and the spotlight fell on the house band, Morris Levy and his Roulette Records always had the inside track on signing the group. Levy was widely known as organized crime's front man in the record business. He knew Johnny Futto and had grown up with Vincent "the Chin" Gigante, fingered as the hitman who shot Frank Costello. As a teenager, Levy ran a photo concession in several Mob-controlled nightclubs. His underworld connections were part of the operation when he opened Birdland, the city's 52nd Street jazz headquarters, in 1947. It was Levy who commissioned pianist George Shearing to compose "Lullaby of Birdland" for one of his music publishing companies. The song went on to become a standard.

Like Syd Nathan, Levy was fond of copyrights. He once tried to copyright the term "rock-and-roll." Levy also acquired the publishing rights—and eventually added himself as co-writer—to the landmark Frankie Lymon and the Teenagers hit, "Why Do Fools Fall in Love?"

Despite all his past successes, Levy needed to sign Dee and

capitalize on the Peppermint Lounge phenomenon because Roulette was on the verge of bankruptcy. The challenge for Levy was to get some Starliters product out on the market before the Twist craze ran its course. That job fell to Levy's musical director, Henry Glover, a thirty-nine-year-old industry veteran who had left King Records the year before. He'd played trumpet for the Lucky Millinder and Tiny Bradshaw bands and brought both bands and their vocalists, Bull Moose Jackson and Wynonie Harris, with him when he started working for Syd Nathan in 1947.

It was Glover, not Nathan, who made all those great rhythm and blues records. He had also produced the original version of "The Twist" with Hank Ballard and written the A-side of the single "Teardrops on Your Letter."

Glover showed up at the Peppermint one afternoon and batted out a song at the piano backstage with Dee that they called the "Peppermint Twist." The song incorporated the signature "1 . . . 2 . . . 3 . . . kick . . . 1 . . . 2 . . . 3 . . . jump" part from one of the previous Starliters singles. In the studio, recorded at the soundstage where Dee and the Starliters were making the Peppermint Lounge movie, Starliters vocalist Dave Brigati didn't have the sound Glover wanted. Dee, who had never before sung on a record, took over the lead vocals.

"Peppermint Twist" hit the charts on November 26, 1961, one week after the Chubby Checker version of "The Twist" reentered the charts. "The Twist" reached number one again on January 13, 1962, where it stayed for two weeks. It would have been longer except it was pushed off the top spot by Joey Dee's record. "Peppermint Twist" spent three weeks at the top of the charts. The Twist phenomenon was officially crowned.

When Johnny asked Dick who he thought should record the Peppermint Lounge album, Dick recommended Chubby Checker, who had been hanging around the club, hoping to get the chance at making a record there. "If we go with him we'll have a million-seller for sure," Dick said.

Dee got the nod instead. "Doin' the Twist at the Peppermint

Lounge," was recorded on a single microphone and quickly released on a long-playing album to further capitalize on the hit single.

Free of their contract with the Peppermint at the height of the Twist boom, Dee and the Starliters spent a couple of weeks doing holiday shows for Murray the K at the Brooklyn Fox, then flew to California to play a private New Year's Eve party for the Hollywood elite at Romanoff's thrown by department store magnate Alfred Bloomingdale. Jimmy Stewart and George Burns and Gracie Allen were among the celebrants. The band stayed in Hollywood to play a six-week engagement for $23,000 at the Crescendo Club, a big step up from the $900 a week they'd been earning at the Peppermint, after getting a raise.

After thirteen months, Dee was out at the Peppermint. Danny Lamego, who was leading a rock-and-roll band that had been installed in the Wagon Wheel, took over the bandstand and changed his name to Danny Peppermint.

Ronnie Bennett was a seventeen-year-old high school senior that fall when she decided to make the trek to the Peppermint Lounge from her Washington Heights home with her sister Estelle and their cousin, Nedra Talley. The girls dreamed of a singing career. Ronnie and Estelle had been doing shows on Saturday nights at home for their family since Ronnie was eight years old. They'd recently taken the first step toward a professional singing career by recording a single for Colpix Records as Ronnie and the Relatives, called "What's So Sweet About Sweet Sixteen?"

As they got ready that night, Ronnie recalled, their mothers and aunts fussed over the girls, layering on makeup and mascara, stuffing their bras with Kleenex, trying to make them look old enough to get in the front door of the Peppermint. They wore matching yellow dresses, taffeta and ruffles down the front. They teased their hair as high as it would go, took the subway downtown, and joined the line outside the club.

Inside, club management was on the lookout for three girl dancers that agent Don Davis had promised to send over. Impatient, Louie Lombardi went outside and scanned the line. Seeing the three girls in their bright yellow matching dresses, he pulled them out of line. "What are you waiting in line for?" he said. "You're already late."

Ronnie didn't hesitate. She knew they'd been mistaken for someone else, but she wasn't going to miss her chance. It was something she'd been preparing for, in private, for years. The girls had taken singing lessons from, of all people, Dick Cami's father at his studio on 44th Street off Broadway. Ronnie recalled Richard Camillucci Senior's rigorous workouts, making them sing "When the Red, Red Robin Comes Bob, Bob, Bobbin' Along," over and over.

Lombardi brought the girls into the loud, crowded club and pushed their way through to the stage. "You're dancers," he said to the girls. "So dance."

They climbed onstage and started shaking it. Every eye in the place was on the three girls. Starliters vocalist David Brigati started singing Ray Charles's "What'd I Say." Ronnie moved next to him, shaking it like crazy. She knew the song well. They did it in their shows at sock hops and parties. Almost as a joke, Brigati offered Ronnie the microphone. That was no joke to her. She grabbed the mike and started belting. The place went nuts. Even the band was applauding when the song ended. They were sitting at a table during the break when the club manager walked over and offered them a job at $10 a night per girl.

The job called for the girls to sing a couple of songs, then spend the rest of the evening dancing on the rails that surrounded the Pep's dance floor. By this time, thanks to waitress Janet Huffsmith's inspired idea, rail dancing had become a part of the scene. Ronnie, her sister, and her cousin were now officially in show business, playing a signature role in the Peppermint Lounge cast.

Seeing all the attention the girl dancers were getting, Sam K., who Dick said had little understanding or appreciation for the niceties of show business, finally brought in a choreographer and put together the Peppermint Twisters, a team of four house dancers who worked as shills and freelance dancers. The fringe on their dresses was once measured at eighty miles per hour. Huffsmith had impressed Louie and Sam enough that they made her one of the official Twisters. The Peppermint Twisters began to land jobs outside the club, doing a Twist show at the fashionable Bourbon Ball at the Plaza Hotel, among other places. But waitresses still broke into dance on the job. At any hour, the whole staff was encouraged to pile onto the dance floor and shake it.

The Peppermint Lounge had been the town's only real rock-and-roll nightclub, but with its sudden ascendancy in the fertile world of New York nightlife, a dozen others sprang up practically overnight around Manhattan. Morris Levy's wiseguy hangout on upper Broadway, the Roundtable, converted to rock and roll. Alan Freed's East Side Twist opened on the site of the former Camelot Club, canceling a show in rehearsals to open as a dance club. The Polynesian restaurant the Lanai featured its own set of dancers, the Lanai Twisters, doing their own version of the Lanai Twist in the club's front window. Honeymoon Lane, one of Broadway's better known dime-a-dance establishments, hung a sign outside advertising Twist dancing every night. When Dixieland jazz guitarist Eddie Condon was told that his Greenwich Village nightclub now featured Twist dancing, he said, "It won't last longer than a sore throat."

Swinging socialites even made it uptown as far as Harlem's Smalls Paradise at East 135th Street and Seventh Avenue to Twist to the music of saxophonist King Curtis. "These white people come to ·Twist. This is the best Twist spot in town," said basketball star Wilt Chamberlain, who owned the club.

Opened by a former elevator boy named Edwin Smalls in 1925, the club sat at the center of historic Harlem, on the same block where Bessie Smith once sang, Father Divine preached, and Willie Mays played stickball. Smalls sold the club in 1955 (although he continued to operate a big liquor store on 154th Street), long before Chamberlain took over.

Chamberlain found himself hosting European royalty, United Nations diplomats, New York politicians, and other rich, powerful white people the blacks didn't recognize. "That Peppermint Lounge is so-o-o white," said actress Sally Kirkland, hopping out of a red sports car to make her way to the Smalls dance floor.

As soon as whites started turning up looking to do the Twist, Chamberlain hiked the prices. Admission to the downstairs club now cost $2.50 with a $2.50 drink minimum. Locals tended to drink in the upstairs bar or mill around on the sidewalk in front of the club. Around eleven o'clock every Tuesday, long lines of limousines waited outside the club after depositing their charges for the weekly Twist contest, featuring a dance troupe, Mama Lou Parks and the Parkettes, who had been around the scene since the Lindy Hop.

As the Twist returned to its black roots, Mama Parks and the Parkettes challenged the Peppermint Twisters to a dance contest. Shaking it for clueless celebrities was one thing. But the cute, young white girls who comprised the Peppermint Twisters knew they were no match for the Parkettes. When the Harlem troupe came downtown for the competition, the Peppermint Twisters were a no-show at their own club.

The club sometimes hired other dancers. Two of the most popular danced as a team using only their first names, Barbara and Stevie. They'd started out as customers dancing at Trudy Heller's, a hipster dive in Greenwich Village. The two young, good-looking kids were not boyfriend and girlfriend; in fact, Stevie was gay. But they were so good that Trudy hired them as a dance team. They started getting calls to dance at the Peppermint and began landing jobs dancing at society parties. Barbara's father was the maitre d' at the Copacabana and one of the few who knew what kind of people were actually behind the Peppermint. He took a dim view of his daughter working there until he found out she was pulling down two grand a week between the club and the parties.

This was no longer just another teenage dance craze. When New York society adopted the Twist, it gave the go-ahead to the rest of the grown-ups. The Twist made rock and roll safe for adults. When Norman Mailer hit the Peppermint Lounge dance floor with Lady Jeanne Campbell (granddaughter of Lord Beaverbrook), columnists everywhere took note. That literary lions and British aristocracy were shamelessly embracing this vulgar, low-brow music made it seem all the more sordidly wonderful.

Even Hank Ballard found himself the beneficiary of a new status as he played his first society event ever for hotel tycoon Carling Dinkler at his sumptuous home in Atlanta. Kay Gable, Clark Gable's widow, was the guest of honor. Soon Ballard was playing a debutante party at New York's St. Regis Hotel opposite white-glove society bandleader Lester Lanin. The Dinklers also arranged for Ballard and his band to play the opening of the exclusive Surf Club in Miami. Mrs. Dinkler was a big fan of the Twist. "It's so 'un-stuffed up,'" she said, "and most of us are so 'stuffed up' from the frustrations of life. The Twist 'unstuffs' us."

After Kennedy sister Jean Smith made a visit to the Peppermint Lounge, the Twist wriggled all the way into the White House that November. Jackie Kennedy danced the Twist at a party for her sister, Princess Lee Radziwill, in the Blue Room of the White House. A roomful of more than eighty guests—fashion designers, politicians, journalists, and diplomats—did the Twist until the wee hours to the strains of the Marine Corps Band and the Lanin dance band. This shocking behavior was controversial enough, press secretary Pierre Salinger felt it necessary to deny. "I was there until three A.M.," he said, "and nobody did the Twist."

After New York society and political Washington fell under the spell, the phenomenon touched down on the West Coast, where gossip queen Hedda Hopper gave her readers in the *Los Angeles Times* a list of the best Twisters in town, as ranked by socialite Wanda Henderson. Her credentials were considered unassailable because she "took her basic training in the Peppermint Lounge and believed enough in her vibrations to insure the dance's acceptance in the inner circles of Hollywood and L.A."

Henderson's honor roll of the best Twisters swiveling in "the poshy salons of Beverly and Bel Air" included Denise Minnelli, the Italian wife of the celebrated director Vincente Minnelli, who shimmied in slow, luxuriant motion. Princess Soraya, the former wife of the Shah of Iran, took a "sophisticated approach" to the music. She didn't ignore the men, praising the inimitable style of actors Cliff Robertson and David Janssen, the frozen-faced, soon-to-be-star of *The Fugitive* television series. But Fran Stark, wife of the film producer Ray Stark and daughter of the actress and comedienne Fanny Brice, won the award for best shaker outside the San Andreas with her patented "turbo jet action."

Hollywood could hardly wait to cash in on the Twist. According to the story he liked to tell, talent agent Harry Romm had read an article in the morning paper about the Twist, so when he spotted a long shot named Let's Twist later that afternoon at the track, Romm was inclined to make the wager. When the long shot came in, he took his wife that night to the scene of the crime. They fought through the crowds of teenagers and socialites, but when Romm actually got inside the club and heard Joey Dee and the Starliters rock the place, he was gone. On the spot, he decided he wanted to make a movie.

Romm was an old-time show-business hand who had been around forever. He handled the Three Stooges for decades and, after their reemergence as after-school television fare in the late fifties, he produced two feature films by the senior citizen Stooges, *Have Rocket— Will Travel* in 1959, and *Stop! Look! And Laugh!* in 1960. He also produced a couple of equally low-rent Louis Prima–Keely Smith vehicles, *Senior Prom* (1958) and *Hey Boy! Hey Girl!* (1959).

At the Peppermint, Romm braced bandleader Dee on his break and told him he wanted to sign him to make a movie. Dee summoned his agent and within an hour, a deal was struck. Romm, who knew to move quickly, contacted the screenwriter of *Senior Prom*, Hal Hackady, who delivered a full treatment with the robust storyline that Romm demanded the next Monday. By noon, the story outline was on its way to six major film companies. Within two hours, four companies said they wanted to make the movie. Romm made a deal with Paramount Pictures.

As Joey Dee's brother, he cast Teddy Randazzo, a singer who had played musical parts in Alan Freed's rock-and-roll movies and the big Hollywood studio production *The Girl Can't Help It*. Jo Ann Campbell, a cute and perky twenty-three-year-old who had a couple of singles out and had been on *American Bandstand*, was picked for the ingénue role. Campbell practiced her Twist moves on the floor of the Peppermint Lounge to prepare for the part. Former Italian leading man Dino Diluca canceled a planned trip to Italy after reading the part of Papa, proprietor of the run-down delicatessen that turns into—what else?—the Peppermint Lounge. Greg Garrison, a TV director from *The Milton Berle Show* and *Playhouse 90*, was assigned to the picture.

Romm knew he had to beat the other studios to the market. Columbia Pictures had signed Chubby Checker for a movie. With the film already scheduled to open over Christmas, *Hey, Let's Twist!* was shot in three weeks, mostly at Pathe Studios on East 106th Street. On Tuesday, December 5, 1961, a scant three weeks before the opening, Paramount took over the entire Peppermint Lounge to throw a party and, simultaneously, film the final scene. Bulging by even Peppermint Lounge standards, the club was lit for the film crews and packed twice as full as usual. But they got the film in the can and the movie opened on New Year's Day. With a few exterior shots thrown in and the footage from the party in the final scene, the movie was advertised "Filmed where it happens every night!" The Peppermint Lounge was an uncredited co-star.

Dick hated the movie, feeling it poorly served the club and the music. But *Hey, Let's Twist!* was a big success. Only Ronnie Bennett, her sister, and her cousin didn't like it. The girls were thrilled when Joey Dee and David Brigati suggested they play their girlfriends in the movie, but hurt and depressed when the casting director told the multiracial girls they were too dark to play white and too light to play black. They would go to the studio, hang around and watch the filming, and they were part of the crowd scene in the Peppermint Lounge, dancing in the corner of the screen, but they couldn't hide their disappointment. They went to see the movie and watched from the balcony. "We were probably the only girls in New York who cried all the way through *Hey, Let's Twist!*" said Ronnie.

Romm only barely beat the competition. Producer Sam Katzman, a Hollywood low-budget specialist, opened his Twist movie, *Twist Around the Clock*, three weeks later, paired on a double bill with *The Three Stooges Meet Hercules*. Katzman brought Chubby Checker, Dion, and Clay Cole, the handsome, young, popular New York disc jockey, out to Hollywood in November to film, after catching Cole's Saturday night rock-and-roll show on New York TV in his hotel room while he was in town casting his movie. The movie, shot in seven days for $250,000, was lifted straight from Katzman's 1956 potboiler with Bill Haley and His Comets, *Rock Around the Clock*. When *Twist Around the Clock* pulled in more than $6 million at the box office, he rushed ahead with *Don't Knock the Twist*, a carbon copy of his Bill Haley follow-up, *Don't Knock the Rock*, which hit theaters by April.

Cole meanwhile went on to put together an act, Clay Cole's Twist-a-Rama, a variety-style revue that debuted hopefully at the Camelot Club on the East Side. The short-lived enterprise had a couple of good runs there and a big weekend at Skinny D'Amato's 500 Club in Atlantic City before crashing to a sudden end on a gig at Harmon Air Force Base in Newfoundland, when members of the troupe were arrested for carrying marijuana into Canada.

Romm and Katzman weren't alone in the Twist movie land rush, although they were the class of the field. Louis Prima, divorced from Keely Smith, paired with buxom British blond *Playboy* model June Wilkinson for *Twist All Night*. Not only was it the worst of the Twist movies, it hit the theaters months too late and was stillborn at the box office.

Chubby Checker, of course, was the star and chief booster of the Twist. Joey Dee used to invite Chubby to the bandstand whenever he showed up at the Peppermint. He made scientific note of the difference in their dance styles from studying his television appearances. "He grinds his feet into the floor," said Dee. "I execute more of a shift of weight from one foot to the other—a little more footwork rather than a pure swiveling of the feet alone. Chubby Checker throws his hands very hard from side to side. I prefer a smoother movement executed from side to side and occasionally backward and forward . . . His technique is not incorrect. That's just his way of doing it."

Checker was jointly managed by songwriter Kal Mann of Philadelphia's Cameo Records and Henry Colt, the ambitious businessman who discovered young Ernest Evans singing while he worked at Colt's Philadelphia poultry shop. Colt took out a $6,000 full-page advertisement in *The New York Times* in late November 1961, just as the snowball was starting to roll, looking to put his chicken-plucker to work as a pitchman. "MANUFACTURERS ATTENTION: A new nationwide name to presell your product . . . The Twist with Chubby Checker (king of the Twist) who created the greatest nationwide dance in years! LICENSES AVAILABLE . . . BIG NAMES MEAN BIG BUSINESS."

Checker, not yet twenty-one, chafed under the strict control of his manager. He still lived at home with his dockhand father, Raymond, and seamstress mother, Eartie, and two younger brothers, Tracy and Spencer. He made do on $150 a week spending money, although by the time "The Twist" hit the top of the charts a second time, he was pulling down $2,500 a night for performances and suing his manager. Under the stress of success and constant performing, the two-hundred-plus-pounder lost almost thirty pounds.

Henry J. Saperstein of Television Personalities Inc. in Los Angeles, took charge of marketing Chubby Checker merchandise. Saperstein, who represented famous names such as Wyatt Earp, Lassie, Debbie Reynolds, and the Three Stooges, thought Checker could be another Elvis Presley, whom he also represented to the tune of $45 million in merchandise sales (including a half million tubes of Elvis Presley lipstick). Manufacturers of scarves, hats, and jewelry lined up to license Chubby Checker's name.

Melville Shoe Corporation not only produced Thom McAn black and red "His Twisters" tennis shoes at $8.99 (and "Her Twisters" at half that), but Chubby demonstrated how effective the shoes could be in a television commercial. There was a Twist necktie, a Twist hat, and a Twist Kit, complete with foldout map featuring footprint guides to doing the Twist. Ten one-minute Twist instructional films were produced and edited into a commercial for Duncan Hines Fudge Mix. Saperstein offered only twenty licenses. "We don't take in much more money on fifty products than we do on twenty," he said. "And there's just so much space available at a counter for Chubby Checker merchandise."

Chubby Checker wasn't alone in the market. There were Joey Dee board games and Peppermint Twist dolls. Somebody made Joey Dee socks with spiral stripes. A hat manufacturer offered a fetching peppermint-striped Joey Dee sailor cap and, as a publicity stunt, decided to give away 1,012 of the hats to the first 1,012 people to show up one December night at the Peppermint Lounge. The mob outside the club was like New Year's Eve. Extra police had to be summoned.

One dressmaker came to Dick with a proposal to license skintight Peppermint Twist dresses with fringes that shimmered like tinsel on a Christmas tree as the girl danced. Another guy wanted to manufacture split-proof Twist pants. A baker came to them with a Peppermint Lounge roll. Another visionary wanted the go-ahead to manufacture a Twisting dildo. The thing had a battery inside that made it do the Twist, like the dancing mushrooms in *Fantasia*. The inventor was lucky he made his pitch to Dick; Johnny would have given him a beating. Like all good Mafia men of his generation, Johnny hated everything that had to do with the sex trade. It offended his belief in the sanctity of womanhood and the man's role as protector and law-giver.

It was a licensing free-for-all because Johnny never registered the Peppermint name as a trademark. Johnny wasn't the type to go around enforcing trademarks. He was just happy the NYPD hadn't shut him down for undisclosed ownership.

Peppermint Lounges soon sprang up in every corner of the globe, from Toledo, Ohio, to Sydney, Australia, as well as all over Los Angeles. There was a Peppermint Lounge on the Pike in Long Beach, an amusement park on a pier. There was the Peppermint Stick in the San Fernando Valley, and there was Peppermint West on Cahuenga in Hollywood, which was the hot place to go dancing for a while. Blond bombshell Mamie Van Doren and her baseball player boyfriend Bo Belinsky danced frequently at the club. Princess Marusia Toumanoff, the Polish designer who worked in the movies, opened the Peppermint West, and even brought out dancers like Stevie and Barbara from New York.

Marusia was a big fan of the Peppermint in New York. She asked to host a birthday party for Hedda Hopper at the 45th Street club. Because the celebrity-studded guest list of two hundred was too large for the cramped confines of the Peppermint, the party was moved to the larger Wagon Wheel.

As with the Peppermint, the Wagon Wheel's bouncers were ex-wrestlers who always wore suits and ties. The maitre d' and floor-seating captains wore tuxedos. The bouncers implemented a policy of control that Dick referred to as "firm but fair," meaning anyone who got out of line faced the likelihood of an emergency-room visit. Admittedly, it might not have always appeared fair to guests who were out of order, but it was invariably firm.

Where the Peppermint started life as a place hoping to catch the overflow from the Wagon Wheel on the corner, the situation was reversed. The Wagon Wheel had its own Twist band and team of four Twist dancers. It wasn't any classier than the Peppermint. As Dick recalled, there was no décor. The walls were painted black. Mismatched tables and chairs crowded the cheap tile floor. The walls were lined by vinyl booths of an indeterminate color. Seventy-six-year-old Hedda Hopper arrived in a wheelchair, her head drooping onto her chest, wearing a big hat with daisies shooting off in every direction.

The most beautiful actresses filed past. Dick stood watching the panorama, trying to decide who was more beautiful, Arlene Dahl or Rhonda Fleming. In no time, the place was jammed. Noticing a commotion at the front door, Dick raced over to find that one of the bouncers, known as Johnny Superman because he bore a slight resemblance to the TV actor George Reeves, was blocking the entrance of Loretta Young.

"What's the problem here?" Dick asked, smiling at Miss Young, one of his favorite actresses.

"The problem is we ain't got room," Johnny S. said. "Prisco told me not to let anyone in." The guy had no idea he was preventing the entrance of an Academy Award–winning actor who was one of the most popular performers of her era. Dick told her he would find a table, which proved harder than he expected, requiring him to commandeer a spot already being occupied. When he got back to the door Loretta Young balked at usurping someone else's table. Instead, she handed him a note and asked him to deliver it to Hedda Hopper.

"Are you sure?" Dick said as she turned to walk toward Sixth Avenue. She gave him a smile and walked on. Giving the note to Hopper was a challenge. The famed columnist didn't raise her lolling head when Dick spoke to her, so he slipped the note into her pocketbook. She remained in that position the whole night. Dick wondered if she even knew she was there.

Almost as soon as the Twist became established, variations appeared. The Bowler's Twist used a pendulum arm swing. The Oliver Twist employed a side-to-side arm motion. The Pulley involved imagining using a weight-lifting machine. In the Peppermint Twist, the body moves to the left, while the hands move to the right. The Fight features shadow boxing. In the Back Scratcher, the dancer pretends to scratch his back against an invisible pillar. The Organ Grinder's Twist combines the Pulley with the Peppermint Twist, with a circular flourish by the hands. On the Jockey's Twist, the dancer pretends he has a whip in his hand. The Lasso . . . the Seventh Inning Stretch . . . the Oversway . . . the Fly (the latter variation actually was the subject of a Chubby Checker single the month before his version of "The Twist" came back).

The record industry applied the same copycat philosophy. With Chubby Checker's "The Twist" and Joey Dee and the Starliters' "Peppermint Twist" holding down the number one slot on the charts consecutively through the first month of 1962, a flood of Twist records followed—"Dear Lady Twist" by Gary U.S. Bonds, "Soul Twist" by King Curtis, "Twistin' the Night Away" by Sam Cooke, "Twistin' Matilda" by Jimmy Soul, "Twistin' Postman" by the Marvelettes, "Twist and Shout" by the Isley Brothers. Even Chubby Checker's next record was "Slow Twistin'," which featured an uncredited female vocalist named Dee Dee Sharp. Chubby Checker had six albums on the charts and three in the Top Ten, alongside other Twist albums by artists as far afield as Louis Prima and the Ventures. Atlantic's Ahmet Ertegun packaged up old tracks by two Atlantic stars recently signed to other labels: *Do the Twist with Ray Charles* and *Twist with Bobby Darin*.

Saxophonist King Curtis was a one-man Twist army. Not only did he lead the house band at Harlem's Twist headquarters, Smalls Paradise, and have a hit instrumental called "Soul Twist" (the first chart record to use the word "soul" in the title), but he was all over other people's Twist records. The Arthur Murray Twist album for RCA Victor was performed by the King Curtis Combo. Curtis laid down the requisite raspy solos on society bandleader Lester Lanin's Twist album on Columbia and cut more Twist albums of his own such as *Doing the Dixie Twist* or *The Shirelles & King Curtis Give a Twist Party*, for different labels around town.

The entire record business turned its attention to the Twist. Even Frank Sinatra joined the fray with a record he always wished he could forget, "Everybody's Twistin'." If you were in the record business in the beginning of 1962 and not making a Twist record, you weren't paying attention. Suddenly, everybody was doing the Twist. Rob and Laura Petrie on TV's *The Dick Van Dyke Show* did the Twist. So did Fred Flintstone. Mercury astronauts were seen in a grainy black-and-white transmission from their spacecraft doing the Twist in weightless outer space. Even Bob Hope got into the act. "If they turned off the music," he cracked, "they'd be arrested."

Word of the new craze beamed around the earth from 45th Street as the Twist went global. In France, the cast of the Broadway musical *West Side Story* arrived at the chichi Parisian nightclub Chez Régine straight off the plane and carrying a bunch of Twist records, thus igniting the craze in the French capital. Johnny Hallyday, the French Elvis, recorded a Twist album. There was a hit French cover version of Joey Dee's "Hey, Let's Twist!" and former British child star, Petula Clark, living in France, combined the Twist with the popular French ya-ya music in "Ya Ya Twist." German record companies pumped out homegrown Twist records, including the popular "Liebestraum von Liszt Twist," which put a rock-and-roll beat to old Franz Liszt. *Life* magazine showed performers in Rome on the set of Elizabeth Taylor's extravaganza *Cleopatra* doing the Twist on the set. Jackie Kennedy even taught the dance to a group of polo players on a tour of India.

The threat to the accepted order was met with predictable resistance. The Twist was denounced by religious figures as evidence of moral decay. The Soviet Union banned the dance as Western decadence. Even former president Dwight D. Eisenhower addressed the issue in a speech he delivered at the opening of his presidential library in Abilene, Kansas, in May 1962, in which he invoked the pioneers who first settled the land. "I wonder if some of those people could come back and see us today doing the Twist instead of the minuet," said Ike, "whether they would be particularly struck by the beauty of that dance? Now I have no objection to the Twist, as such, but it does represent some kind of change in our standards."

Around the world, in the republic of Vietnam, a small country few

Americans had even heard of, president Ngo Dinh Diem not only out-lawed the Twist, but also the singing of Twist songs. He asked the U.S., French, and British embassies to refrain from playing Twist records at embassy functions, lest the infection escape the diplo-matic compounds.

The Twist apparently unwittingly tapped into some vital global need for self-expression in an anxious world beset by nuclear brink-manship. More than mere dance step, the Twist had somehow stepped on an intersection of lines in time and history. Caught in an incipient rising tide of sweeping social and moral change, the Twist brought to the foreground simmering conflicts that would break more fully into the open before long. Somehow this goofy dance managed to articulate a growing divide in the world—energizing people who embraced the future and threatening those who would safeguard the past. Having a teenage dance adopted by high society and, subse-quently, middle America, was only a taste of things ahead. A new world was coming and the Twist was a first, tentative line drawn in the sand.

Johnny Biello hadn't planned any of this. When he opened the Peppermint he just wanted cheap entertainment and to be left alone to run his rackets in the back room. He wasn't particularly happy about all the attention. But he had rarely let an opportunity to make money slip by. He and Dick Cami quickly finalized plans to open a second Peppermint Lounge in Miami Beach.

The Original World Famous
New York Peppermint Lounge
in Miami Beach

If New York was the center of influence as America entered the sixties, Miami Beach was the preferred playground. Not only did it attract the young and affluent in America, but it was also a watering and frolicking spot for the international playboy crowd.

Action went all night. You could hop from one club to the next until seven in the morning, catch Billy Daniels or Frank Sinatra at the Fontainebleau, Harry Belafonte at the Cafe Pompeii in the Eden Roc Hotel, finish off with Lenny Bruce's hip, outré comedy at the late show at the Le B. Big names worked the big rooms at the Deauville and the Carillon. When Elvis came out of the army, Sinatra broadcast his final Timex TV special—featuring Sammy Davis Jr., Joey Bishop, and Peter Lawford, along with Elvis—from the Fontainebleau in March 1960.

For those with more exotic tastes, Collins Avenue featured the latest in strip shows. San San was a twenty-two-year-old girl from Moultrie, Georgia, who gave up finishing school to find fame as the interpreter of "the Vampire Dance." It began with her stalking across the stage to creepy music and ended with her shedding bat wings. For wildlife exhibitions, there was the Gaiety Club, where Zorita performed her snake dance with a real python. Not to be outdone, a girl named Siska stripped with a macaw for a partner.

There was the Penthouse, a popular bay-front restaurant; the Top Draw, where mobsters mixed with the locals; and the Bonfire, Radio Weiner's joint. Dino's was a fancy restaurant and lounge on 79th in North Bay Village owned by Dean Martin, a regular in South Florida. The Place for Steak was popular with Mafia beefeaters. Most infamous of all was the Dream Bar, owned by one of the top mobsters in the south, Pasquale "Patsy" Erra, where you could get your head busted for taking the wrong table.

Florida had a reputation for crime and graft that compared favorably to any place in America. Florida's governor, Fuller Warren, was elected with a treasury bulked up with money from the racetrack industry, despite a state measure outlawing that very practice. Dade County Sheriff Jimmy Sullivan, an ex-prizefighter, told a congressional committee investigating organized crime in Florida that his failure to report $50,000 in earnings from various "little deals" was just an oversight. He denied a charge by his own deputies that they were dispatched to deliver $36,000 in payoffs to the sheriff's wife. Sheriff Walter Clark of neighboring Broward County admitted that fully a third of his income came from a firm that operated a numbers racket. Johnny Futto felt right at home. It was a perfect place for a new Peppermint Lounge.

Dick and Johnny returned from their trip to New York and immediately went hunting for a location. They found a building they liked, formerly Colonel Jim's Restaurant in the heart of Restaurant Row along the 79th Street Causeway on Biscayne Bay, just down the highway from the Fontainebleau. Jerry Brooks, who owned the Famous Door on 52nd Street in New York, had just signed a lease on the building but was only too happy to give it up to Johnny Futto.

Johnny made Dick the owner of record and, as a sign of his growing respect for his son-in-law's business acumen, designated him manager. It was to be Dick's big chance at running a club that was going to be 100 percent legit. As he did in New York City, Dick was going to be bringing rock and roll to a nightlife scene in Miami that was ready to rock.

Because Dick had no experience in running a nightclub, Johnny brought in Morris Levy as a partner, giving him 30 percent of the club. In exchange, Morris would teach Dick the ropes, drawing on his fifteen years of experience operating Birdland, New York's top jazz spot. Morris wasn't the only wiseguy with his beak in the trough. He was attached to a lot of mobsters all the way up to Carlo Gambino, head of his own Mafia family, reputed to be a $500 million illegal enterprise.

Dick was thrilled about working with Levy, into whose club he sneaked as a boy to see the procession of jazz greats Levy paraded through the tiny basement off Broadway, from Coltrane to Monk, Mingus to Miles.

Sam K. and Louie Lombardi transported some of the original Peppermint crew to the South. The Turk came down to work as a floor captain and bouncer. Anthony "Okey" Salvato, a former bookmaker for Johnny, who had just retired from his jewelry business in Manhattan, came down to Miami and, virtually straight off the plane, started working as the steward for the new Peppermint Lounge. Johnny was determined to make this a legitimate, first-class operation all the way, promising to stay away from the club to avoid, as he put it, "stinking up the place."

Among the lessons Levy imparted was a stern warning against messing with the booze. That ran counter to long-established practices Scatsy oversaw at Johnny's other nightclubs, but Morris insisted. It might be okay to screw with the booze in a dive bar, but if you wanted to attract the class tourist clientele, you had to play it straight, he said.

"If some businessman orders Cutty Sark, he's going to know it as soon as it hits his throat," Levy said. "Then he's going to think, 'This guy's a bullshitter.' You've lost him forever."

To Cami, this advice made sense and he never touched the liquor.

They did, however, take advantage of every opportunity to buy booze cheap that was smuggled in, or sometimes stolen, from the Caribbean. A load of stolen precut one-pound prime sirloin steaks was another delicacy they got at a bargain. Okey, known around the club as a serious penny-pincher, handled the negotiations with the thieves.

"To tell you the truth, we don't even need the stuff," he said. "If Johnny knew I was thinking of buying any more he'd go crazy."

When he'd negotiated the price down far below wholesale, Okey would add, "That's prime, right?"

After giving the place a final once-over, Levy declared the bar unsuitable. He said he knew where they could get a better one. He'd once owned the Five O'Clock Club, a hangout in the late fifties for Sophie Tucker and actress Martha Raye. It was one of Miami's first strip clubs; for a three-dollar minimum, from 10 P.M. until five in the morning, patrons were titillated by the likes of Cookie Cooper, who began her act clothed in a full wedding gown. Levy recalled they had a round bar there that would be perfect for the Peppermint. "I can get it for a song," he said. That meant some poor sucker was going to give it to Levy for nothing.

The Miami Peppermint was three times the size of the New York club, accommodating nearly five hundred people altogether. A red-and-white striped awning greeted patrons at the front door. As you entered, you were confronted by a full-sized stand-up picture of the guy who looked like Khrushchev doing the Twist. There were two doors on either side of the stand-up. The left led to the bar, the right to the main room, which seated three hundred and fifty. To the right of that was the kitchen and service bar where Scatsy ruled with a wooden spoon in his white apron, a gnome with a troll's tongue.

The walls were painted black and from the ceiling hung dozens of Styrofoam candy canes. At the back wall was the dance floor, two feet above the main floor. Above that was the stage, framed by two massive Altec speakers, powered by the biggest McIntosh amp available. Morris Levy insisted on good sound.

Behind the stage was a sliding glass door that led out to the patio and the dock. Just outside the back door, Dick kept a twenty-four-foot boat tied up so they could go fishing whenever the mood arose. Dick would use that boat to take bands out fishing right after the club closed at daybreak, the perfect time to fish. They could go straight from the bandstand to the Gulfstream.

The doors to the Original World Famous New York Peppermint Lounge in Miami Beach opened on December 1, 1961. They were packed to the air vents on opening night. There wasn't a seat available anywhere and the crowd waiting outside stretched as long as the mobs in New York, maybe longer. Wildman Louisiana rockabilly king Dale Hawkins ("Suzie Q.") was the featured attraction. The club flew down the Ronettes—as they were then known, having changed their name from Ronnie and the Relatives after they went to work at the Peppermint—and their parents to stay for the entire run of the first season (the club closed after Memorial Day).

The music was blasting and customers were throwing back drinks when a dozen state beverage agents and Metro detectives descended on the place like a swat team. Right at the front entrance, between the maitre d' stand and the bar, a skinny, bug-eyed agent boomed, "Stop serving liquor . . . this establishment is being closed down."

Dick was standing nearby. "For what?" he said.

"Failure to obtain a restaurant license."

Dick caught a glimpse of Morris Levy, slinking out of sight. Liquor laws in Miami were very restrictive. No reason for him to surface or let anyone get the wrong idea, which would be totally correct, that he had a piece of the club. Dick told the agent they'd applied for all the proper licenses. He had a lawyer do it and had been assured that everything was in order. How much does a restaurant license cost anyway? Dick asked.

"Twenty-eight dollars," the agent said.

"Are you fucking kidding me?" Dick said. "You bring an army in here to close us down for a lousy twenty-eight bucks?"

As soon as the words were out of his mouth, Dick regretted them. He was getting his first taste of how they did things down South. He was lucky Johnny was there. He alerted Benny Cohen, a noted Mob attorney who happened to be sitting next to the stage, and put him together with the head agent in the office. Cohen called a friendly judge, who granted an injunction over the phone so they could stay open.

"That just cost us five thousand dollars," Johnny said. "The judge will probably get a case of whiskey out of it, but you know what? Any time you can give a case of whiskey to a judge, that's a good day."

Dick found out later that he'd been right. You couldn't get a liquor license without a restaurant license. The raid was a pure shakedown. Dick wanted to go to court over it, but Johnny told him to forget it.

"You think they give a shit for you or what the law is," he said. "They can do whatever they want to do. Remember you don't own a liquor license—you're only renting it."

Murray the K, the top New York rock-and-roll disc jockey from WINS, was backstage on opening night, where he introduced himself to the Ronettes. He told the girls he loved their show. "Too bad you girls are from Florida," he told them. "I could use you on my shows in New York."

"We live at 149th and St. Nicholas," Ronnie said. "We listen to you every night."

He hired them on the spot for his Easter 1962 shows at the Brooklyn Fox, which is where Phil Spector—the famed record producer and Ronnie's future husband—first saw the girls. (When the Ronettes eventually auditioned for Spector, who would make the girls stars, the only song they could think to sing was "When the Red, Red Robin," straight from Mr. Camillucci's lessons. They never knew that their voice coach was Dick Cami's father and Dick never knew the girls studied with his dad until he read Ronnie's autobiography, *Be My Baby*, many years later. The Peppermint Lounge was where it all started for them.)

One night, the great blues singer Dinah Washington approached Ronnie in the Miami club's ladies room. The backstage dressing room was so small, it didn't have a toilet. Washington told Ronnie that she wanted to take her away for a solo career, but the teenage girl couldn't even think of performing without her family around her. Two years later, when the Ronettes first heard a deejay play "Be My Baby," the brilliant Phil Spector record that would change their lives and rock and roll, they were playing Wildwood, New Jersey, still working as part of the Joey Dee and the Starliters revue.

There was a long tradition of enjoying black music in the South. It was completely socially acceptable for an all-white fraternity to hire a black band for the house party. Young Southerners didn't mind the Negroes singing and dancing and providing entertainment, as long as they didn't have to eat next to them at a lunch counter. The South always kept its dirty little secrets and it was difficult for someone like Dick Cami, raised in the melting pot of New York City, even after his experience at the University of South Carolina, to navigate the tricky waters of race relations in the Jim Crow world. This was the unrepentant South. There were no freedom riders in Florida, no sit-ins. The club was an instant success on the Miami scene, but there was always tension between New Yorker Cami and the segregationists. The club hired the best rock-and-roll bands and that always included a lot of black musicians and entertainers. But they were not allowed to be served as customers. The Florida state beverage commission was vigilant about that rule.

Which was why Cami was surprised a few months after the Miami club opened to get a call from Levy in New York, informing him that a special guest was coming down, a VIP with a distinction. "He's a colored guy," said Levy.

"You're kidding, right?" Dick said.

"I know what you're going through down there, but you've got to do this," Levy said.

Now Dick was as much intrigued as shocked. "You know we might take a pinch for this, don't you?"

"I know," Levy said. "Just put him at a table in the balcony and spend some time with him to make him feel welcome. Who's headlining now?"

It was the Coasters. One of the most popular groups that played the Peppermint, the Coasters were a novelty group best known for comic R&B songs. They went over well with white audiences in the South. "If anyone asks, tell them he's the Coasters' manager and tell their singer, Speedo, so he'll know what to say," Levy said.

Cami decided to talk it over with Johnny. Knowing his father-in-law's attitude about telephones—"The biggest stool pigeons in the world"—Dick drove over to Johnny's house on Biscayne Bay. Johnny had already talked to Levy, so he knew what was up.

"Who is this guy?" Dick asked.

"He's Bumpy Johnson, the boss of Harlem," Johnny said. "Take care of Mr. Johnson. Anything he wants."

This didn't mean much to Dick, but Bumpy Johnson was a legend in Harlem. Not only was he a staunch ally of the Genovese family, he fought Dutch Schultz to a standstill when the Dutchman tried to move in on the Harlem numbers rackets when Bumpy was little more than a kid. This was at a time when blacks were routinely intimidated and exploited by the Jewish and Italian mobs. By the early sixties, Bumpy was aristocracy in Harlem society, friends with Lena Horne, Bill "Bojangles" Robinson, and Sugar Ray Robinson. "It's good you should know him," Johnny said. "There's a lot he can do for you with acts."

The following Friday night, the Terrible Turk came hurrying into Dick's office. "That colored guy here?" the Turk said. "That's Bumpy Johnson. He's a bad cat. I know a guy who was in the can with him."

"Go tell him if he gives us any trouble, you'll throw his ass out on the street," said Dick. The Terrible Turk went away laughing, only to be replaced by Scatsy.

"Are you out of your fucking mind with that colored guy out there?" he said. "The fucking beverage agents will be all over us."

"The old man sent him in," Dick said. "He's a big shot from Harlem, Bumpy Johnson."

"Holy shit, that's Bumpy Johnson?" Scatsy said. "He's the guy who straightened out Vincent Coll, when we was kids."

Scatsy proceeded to tell a stunned Dick Cami the story of his friendship with Mad Dog Coll and how they used to go shooting in Harlem.

"I only drove the car," Scatsy said. "You know Coll was a nut. Why do you think they called him Mad Dog? When Bumpy heard that Coll was shooting people in Harlem with an air gun, he sent word that if he shoots any more, he's going to hunt his ass down and kill him and his entire family. I never saw Coll afraid of any man, or ten. But we never went shooting in Harlem after that."

"Why don't you come over to the table and let me introduce you as the guy who was driving the car when Coll went to Harlem," Dick said. "I'm sure he'd love to meet you."

Scatsy threw his hand down. "Why don't you go where you got to go?" He turned and walked away.

With all this in mind and a smile on his face, Cami made his way over to the table where Johnson was sitting. He was dressed in a custom-made suit, a diamond stickpin in his tie. His girl was a Lena Horne look-alike in a hundred-dollar dress and an ermine fur stole. "You Futto's son-in-law?" Johnson said.

"I'm Dick Cami," he said. "I want to welcome you to the Peppermint Lounge. It's important to Johnny that we make you happy. Otherwise, he told me he's going to give me a beating."

Bumpy roared with laughter. He and Dick hit it off. As Johnny expected, Bumpy did help with black performers. The club became known as the one place down South where African Americans could play and feel welcome. Of course, as a result, the state beverage agents regarded Dick as a "nigger lover."

One night a young, African-American saxophone player went to Dick and asked if his family could come and see him perform with his band. He was a good kid, well mannered. Cami said sure. He sat the kid's parents and sister in the balcony with Joanie, who was in that night.

Sure enough, a state beverage agent came in. "Any niggers in here tonight?" he asked.

"No," Cami said. The beverage agent nodded and went around to inspect the bar. He came back around and gave the room a last once-over, then stopped in his tracks. "I thought you said there were none here tonight," he said, pointing upstairs.

"They're not customers," Dick said. "They're a band member's family. They're my guests."

"I don't care," he said. "Get them the hell out of here."

Without thinking about the consequences, Dick refused. "I'm not throwing them out. They're in the middle of watching their son play."

"You better think twice, boy," the agent said. "If you don't get those niggers out of here, I'm sure as hell going to violate you."

After the set was over, Dick went to the kid and laid it out for him. "You see that ugly bastard over there," he said. "He's from the beverage department. He saw your family and he's threatening to violate us unless they leave. I'm sorry. I don't know what to say. I'll leave it up to you."

"No, I understand," the kid said, so quietly Dick could barely hear him.

"You understand? I wish you'd explain it to me, then," Dick said.

The sax player talked to his family. One of the family members got up and went to the waitress. She glanced at Dick, who shook his head. The man handed her some money, and from her reaction, Dick was sure it was a good tip. As they left, the family gave him looks that made Cami feel sick. It was one of the worst things he'd had to do in his life. Dick never forgot the look on the faces of the family as they filed past him on the way out.

Dick wanted to plant the Peppermint Lounge flag on the Miami Beach nightlife scene. He knew the club represented a new sound and a new world, and he wanted to be accepted by the local show business community. When Cleveland mobster Morris Kleinman called Johnny and asked if he could send over one of the Peppermint groups for his annual charity fund-raiser, Dick was glad for the chance to inject a little rock and roll into a program featuring the biggest names in entertainment.

Every year, Kleinman, a longtime partner with another Cleveland mobster, Moe Dalitz, in the Desert Inn in Vegas, threw a big event at the Fontainebleau in Miami to raise money for research into Parkinson's disease, with which his wife was afflicted. Just as Johnny did for his mentally retarded daughter Connie, Kleinman turned his personal tragedy into a national cause. The fund-raiser was a major stop on the charity circuit. Every entertainer who could clutch a microphone would be there, from Sinatra to Tony Bennett, Nat King Cole, Don Rickles, and on and on. Bob Hope was master of ceremonies. Hope and Kleinman grew up together in Cleveland and remained best friends, despite Morris's reputation.

With the Peppermint Lounge fresh on the scene, Cami sent his house band, the 7 Blends, and the Ronettes, no longer timid little girls but increasingly polished entertainers in slinky, cheongsam dresses who could rock any house. Cami saw Hope backstage, smiling and shaking hands, and made his pitch. "Why don't you let my group open the show. They'll wake up the crowd, I'll tell you that."

His real purpose was to get them out of there early and back to the club. "Morris told me you'd be coming over," Hope said. "I think that's a good idea. Let's open with a bang."

The 7 Blends came out and slammed into "Shout," the Isley Brothers' rave-up. Right in the middle, the Ronettes rocketed onto the stage like they'd bounced off a trampoline. Ronnie grabbed the mike and ripped into their signature version of "What'd I Say?"

"How about those girls? Aren't they something?" Hope said. "The last time I saw anything shake like that was when Bing tried to get into one of Dorothy Lamour's dresses. And what a band. No wonder the Twist is so popular."

Race remained an issue. Cami had to pick his way carefully through the minefield of race relations. One of Dick's best friends in Florida was a flamboyant nightclub owner named Johnny Lomelo.

Known as Big John by the amused local press, Lomelo was the color-ful, scandal-tainted mayor of Sunrise, Florida. With seven marriages behind him and almost as many indictments ahead, Lomelo was once asked who he'd like to play him in a movie about his life. "I'm conceited enough and egotistical enough to portray myself," he said.

Lomelo's club, the King of Hearts, was on NW Seventh Avenue in the Liberty City ghetto. Cami met him when he came into the Pep-permint one afternoon with two black guys in dark suits and skinny ties, looking a lot like salesmen in a men's clothing store. They called themselves Sam and Dave.

Samuel Moore and David Prater, both small-town Georgia boys, worked independently on the gospel circuit in the fifties before meet-ing at the King of Hearts. Both were struggling when they teamed up one night on the Jackie Wilson hit "Doggin' Around." It was a revela-tion. Their voices, Moore's tenor and Prater's rich baritone, blended beautifully. Sam & Dave was born.

Lomelo brought the pair to Cami because he thought they de-served a bigger stage and hoped the Peppermint would give it to them. Dick had Dale Hawkins call them up to the stage to do a num-ber. When they went into their act, he was impressed by their energy and their call-and-response vocals. But from their looks he doubted they would go over with the Peppermint crowd. He was wrong, wildly wrong. Sam & Dave didn't just get the crowd out of their seats, they got them onstage, something Dick had never seen before. The sight of flagrant race-mixing terrified Dick and the rest of the crew at the Peppermint.

"I'd have booked them in a second," Dick said. "But I was already having enough trouble with the beverage agents. Imagine what would have happened if they'd seen a stage full of white girls dancing with Sam & Dave."

Another time, the great Clyde McPhatter, founder of the Drifters, was onstage when a fair-skinned brunette yelled, "I love you Clyde. I really love you."

McPhatter knew where he was, even if the girl didn't. He put his hand over the mike and leaned close to her. "Thank you, darling, but you know this is the South, don't you?"

The cops were frequently around the Peppermint. But Johnny had ways of keeping them off their backs, even if Dick Cami tended to ignore some strongly held local customs. Patti LaBelle & the Bluebelles pulled up to the club in a van the day before they were set to open. The four black girls from Philadelphia, all teenagers, had a big hit with "I Sold My Heart to the Junkman."

Their manager and founder was Bernard Montague, an older man who sold his printing business to run R&B shows. He handpicked the group's members and handled them with special care. When he asked Dick if he could park their van in the lot, Cami didn't understand what he was getting at. When it became clear that the manager planned to stay in the van with the girls overnight, Cami was surprised, but he understood.

At that time, black performers had only two choices of places to stay. One was the only hotel in Miami Beach that allowed blacks, the Blackstone, or Liberty City. They weren't even allowed on Miami Beach after sundown. Segregation was strictly enforced.

Dick agreed to the request. He directed Montague to the back of the parking lot facing the bay, where there was plenty of room. He gave the manager a key to the back door of the club, so they could use the restroom after everything was closed.

Dick Cami didn't much care what the police thought about the arrangement. If the Bluebelles wanted to camp out in his parking lot, that was fine by him. Scatsy had a different idea.

"What's with these people, are they gypsies?" Scatsy said. "Ain't we got enough shit to worry about without getting heat for putting up these people in the parking lot?"

"Shut the fuck up," Cami said. "They're there and they're going to stay there. I'm not going back on my word with them." Scatsy walked away.

It was the first time Scatsy and Dick had words. Scatsy went to

Johnny the next day, but Johnny told Dick not to worry about it. "We're sitting pretty good with the police," he said. "I don't think they'll be bothering you."

One good thing about Florida cops—they stayed bought—although some were more trouble than others. It wasn't long before the beverage agent Dick had so many problems with returned.

"You guys got a full house tonight," he said. "A lot of the other places are empty."

The agent wondered why the Peppermint was jumping and the other clubs on the Causeway were struggling. Cami told him it was probably the entertainment.

"You mean that nigger music," the beverage man said.

Just then, the Ronettes finished their last number and ran off the stage, going by Dick and the agent as they headed into the kitchen, which connected to the dressing rooms.

"Those nigger girls are cute," he said. The Ronettes were actually a mixed-race group, partly black, partly white, partly Native American. Ronnie once said that when she was growing up she was confused over whether she was black or white.

"How about fixing me up with one of them?" the agent asked.

Dick couldn't believe the son of a bitch had the balls to ask a question like that. He knew he had him. He wasn't a cop or anything. He was a beverage agent who was no longer "just doing his job." He had crossed way over the line.

Dick invited him back to his office. He let him go in first, positioning himself behind him, back to the door. When the agent turned around, Dick hit him with a forearm shiver. He'd thrown a lot of them in his football-playing days, but this was the best one he'd ever landed. The guy sank to the floor like the bag of shit he was. Dick called Scatsy to take the guy out into the alley. The beverage agent still in a fog, Dick shook him by the shoulder and told him that if he ever showed his face in the place again, he'd get worse than a broken jaw. If he thought he was joking, he was welcome to come back and find out.

Dick didn't put the guy down because of the Ronettes alone. He hadn't been able to put out of his mind the memory of having to put the black sax player's family out of the club. Scatsy and the Turk helped the agent into his car. They never saw him again. The next agent was a decent guy, but just as inflexible about the race rules. That didn't change until the new civil rights law was passed in July 1964. Running a rock-and-roll nightclub in the South was posing challenges Dick hadn't imagined. This was just the first season.

Miami Beach,
the Second Season

When he opened the second season in Miami Beach on Labor Day 1962, Dick Cami sensed the Twist was losing steam. Sam K. thought it was going to last forever. In his view, the dance had tapped into something so deep and rich in the culture that it would not give out in his lifetime. He wasn't alone. As keen an observer of the scene as Atlantic's Ahmet Ertegun seemed to agree. He told *Billboard* in February 1962 that he was introducing an entire label devoted to the Twist, called Twistime Records.

"The Twist is going to be with us for a long time," Ertegun said, "certainly for another year at least."

They were both wrong. Soon enough, the Twist was buried beneath the cultural rubble of the Mashed Potato, the Monkey, Frug, Watusi, and dozens of other dances. Three months after Ertegun's forecast in May 1962, *Billboard* headlined a story: "Has the Twist Had It? Trade Sees Fad Fading Fast."

The Twist was over as suddenly as it emerged. The title of the new Joey Dee and the Starliters movie, which during production had "Twist" in the title, hit the theaters with a new, Twist-less title, *Two*

Tickets to Paris. Twistime Records, announced confidently by Erte-gun in February, halted releases and folded in May. In November, in the wake of the startling public reception to Brazilian music from guitarist Charlie Byrd and composer João Gilberto, *Billboard* won-dered, "Is Bossa Nova the New Twist?"

One of the last people to realize the fad was on its way out was the president of the United States. For Jack Kennedy's forty-sixth birth-day in May 1963, Jackie arranged a party aboard the presidential yacht *Sequoia.* Unaware that the Twist was out of fashion, the presi-dent continued ordering more Chubby Checker tunes whenever the band played anything else. Jackie, who knew better, cringed at her husband's side.

New York Herald Tribune columnist Tom Wolfe revisited the Peppermint Lounge two years after the Twist hit high tide. "The Jet Set has moved on from the Peppermint Lounge, but the Jersey teen-age cycle is continuing," he wrote.

Inside the Younger Brothers and the Epics are on the bandstand . . .
A few leggy kids, in red satin shorts, and waitresses are standing around the sides miming the Monkey with their hips, shuffling to themselves. While out in the center nine girls from Jersey, all with exploding hair and Dick Tracy eyes, have a table and watch the danc-ing with that same old dead-serious look. Nobody is doing the Twist. Everybody is doing something like the Monkey, in which you make some motions with your arms like you're climbing the bars of your cage, or the T-Bird, in which there is some complicated business with the hands about opening the front door, going inside and mixing a cocktail. Every now and then, Larry Cope, who is one of the Younger Brothers, will introduce a pure Twist number, but he has to use a historical preface, sort of like they do at Roseland or some place when they say, "Well, now we're going to have a good old-fashioned waltz." Out in the club the Epics, with four electric instruments go-ing, are playing "Doing the Dog," and Misty is doing the Dog, and

Janet is doing the Mashed Potatoes, and Geri Miller is doing the Monkey . . .

Even if the swells no longer gathered there and the Twist was only one of the dances on the menu, business was still good at New York City's most famous rock-and-roll dance club, as well as at its Miami Beach branch. Dick understood something that Sam didn't. Rock and roll was the thing, not the Twist.

Beginning with the 1962–63 season, Dick hired Broadway choreographer Wakefield Poole to create a forty-five-minute stage show called *Crazy Crazes*, which told the story of the history of American popular dancing, starting with the Black Bottom and moving up to the Twist and all the other modern dances. The show did big business, which caused Dick to recommend that Sam adapt it for New York. But Sam insisted on "driving the Twist into the ground," Cami said.

It was only after business started slacking off in New York that Sam finally agreed to scrap the Twist and bring in the *Crazy Crazes* show. It did good business for a while.

Unlike the New York place, the World Famous Peppermint Lounge in Miami Beach was never based on the Twist. From the day the club opened, the Miami branch was a different animal—a legit, class nightclub that featured the best live rock-and-roll performers on the scene, from Chuck Berry to Jerry Lee Lewis. It was the greatest rock-and-roll club in the country—there was nothing else like it.

Morris Levy slapped out live albums during the first season by both Dale Hawkins and his Escapades and the 7 Blends, plastering "Recorded Live at the Miami Beach Peppermint Lounge" on the cover. Not that either sold much. But in one quick season, the Peppermint in Miami had not only found a place on the rock-and-roll road map, but also was a glittering star of the Miami nightlife scene, the only club where white people could go to hear this music.

The Peppermint also soon developed a reputation for not only great rock-and-roll music, but for their quarrelsome, authentic New

York staff. Snooky came down from Brooklyn with maitre d' Freddie Pace, and they put him to work in the kitchen under Scatsy. John "Snooky" Palumbo, a man with a perpetual smile, could handle without complaint Scatsy's continual tirades and stream of abuse. He, in fact, became something of a straight man to the crabby chef and surprised everybody in the place one night when the lady eating dinner with Burl Ives keeled over choking by performing mouth-to-mouth resuscitation on the old dame (turned out he used to work as an orderly in a Brooklyn hospital). He did all kinds of chores, including driving home a shit-faced Gary Merrill to his wife, Bette Davis, one Christmas Eve.

Davis was so grateful, she invited Snooky and his family over for a drink on Christmas day. "What a classy lady" he said when he came into the club that afternoon.

All Scatsy wanted to know was where was the bread that Charlie Zito had flown down from New York for Johnny's traditional Christmas dinner. Snooky had forgotten it. He dashed out as Scatsy got on the phone with Johnny. "Jerkoff's on his way," he said.

Okey, the retired jeweler who bore enough resemblance to Johnny that they sometimes tricked the FBI agents who tailed Johnny by dressing him up like the old man, turned out to be the perfect crusty foil for Scatsy. In his role as steward of the club, Okey kept a careful eye on rising expenses. He was particularly vigilant of the cost of bar napkins. "When are they going to stop raising the prices?" he asked Scatsy.

"They're only three cents each, for Christ's sake," Scatsy said with a snort. "How many napkins can we use?"

"You'd be surprised," said Okey, who knew exactly how many napkins they used.

Not long after this conversation, Jerry Lee Lewis was headlining. The afternoon of the show he was rehearsing his band. Anyone who ever saw a Jerry Lee show knew how hard he worked, hair flying, feet dancing, fists pumping. His rehearsals were just as energetic.

When the rehearsal ended he came down from the stage and

grabbed a bar napkin to wipe the sweat from his forehead. Okey watched him wiping with one napkin, then another, a muffled fury building inside him. Finally, he could take it no longer.

"You know those napkins cost three cents each?" said Okey.

"No, I didn't, horse," said Lewis, reaching again for the stack of napkins.

Every day running the Peppermint was an adventure. One afternoon, maitre d' Freddie Pace came into Cami's office and announced that Nat King Cole was out front. Cole was one of Cami's favorite performers, a man with the smoothest and most soulful voice ever. Dick, who was just a kid to most of the staff, thought Freddie was playing another joke on him. Freddie insisted, "I'm telling you he's here."

When Dick went out he couldn't believe his eyes. "Nat, what a pleasure, you wanted to see me?"

Nat extended his hand, "I need a favor from you. I was wondering if I could sit in with one of your bands."

The raucous music featured in the club couldn't have been more different from Nat's rich baritone and supple jazz-flavored pop music. "You want to play here?" said Dick. "With one of our bands? What for?" Dick couldn't understand what was happening.

Cole explained that he wanted to get the feeling of rock and roll and the only way he could do that was to play with a band.

Dick asked if he was going to sing. "No. I'm under contract at the Deauville." The Deauville was one of Miami's grande-dame hotels, a beachfront hangout and playground for the Rat Pack and the international dilettante crowd.

Dick agreed and walked over to the bandstand, where a musician named Jimmy was playing the Hammond B3 organ.

"Get off," he said. "I'm replacing you tonight with another piano player."

When the musician saw it was Nat King Cole, he almost fainted. Nat sat down at the B3 and quickly found a groove. The rest of the band members were beside themselves and trying not to show it. Cole came back all week.

Another night while Cole was onstage, Sam Cooke and Jackie Wilson stopped in. While they were talking, Cami watched Cooke scan the room and do a classic double take. "Am I seeing Nat up there?" he said.

"The piano player got sick and I asked Nat to fill in."

Everyone broke up.

Johnny's connections sometimes helped straighten out problems that a newcomer like Dick couldn't solve on his own. The first time Dick booked the Coasters, who became one of the club's signature groups, lead vocalist Earl "Speedo" Carroll said they wouldn't perform unless they were paid in advance. The group had just finished a date in Pittsburgh before heading south and the owner of the club had stiffed them. Speedo was angry and determined not to be taken advantage of again. Dick was sympathetic, but he wasn't going to agree to Carroll's demand. No nightclub would survive very long if it paid its performers up front. However, he agreed to look into the problem.

"What you going to do, get my money for me?" Speedo said sarcastically. "That motherfucker wouldn't pay his own mother."

"It won't be his mother who will be asking," Dick said. Two days later Speedo got his money in a cashier's check. He could hardly believe it.

The Peppermint Lounge quickly became a favorite stop for nighthawks. When the shows in the big rooms—Sinatra, Martin, and the rest—ended at two in the morning, it was a tradition to head over to the Causeway to continue the party at the Peppermint until seven.

One morning, Dick ushered out a voluptuous blonde in a low-cut dress as a school bus loaded with children drove by. One of the little kids stuck his head out the window and shouted, "Hey, Mom—it's me." The city council got wind of the incident and later moved up the closing hour.

"If her big bazooms weren't falling out and hitting the pavement, nobody would have noticed," Scatsy said.

The performers during the second season, as the club hit its stride, were a varied group. The Chiffons, who hit the top of the charts twice in 1963, with "He's So Fine" and "One Fine Day," sang well and did their jobs with no fussing. The Angels, on the other hand, white girls with teased blond hair who did "My Boyfriend's Back," a number one record, were nice enough kids who couldn't sing. They also didn't know what to do onstage. Conway Twitty was so stricken with stage fright, Dick had to talk him into stepping out in front of his band. Jerry Lee Lewis, who broke four or five piano strings a night, worried backstage privately to Dick that his career was over.

"I keep tryin' but I'm beginning to think it will never happen for me again," he said. Not long afterward, Lewis went country and his career took off once more.

In the South, there was a rhythm and blues underground beyond the radio. When Cami booked Doug Clark and the Hot Nuts at a venue he leased with Steve Palmer near the Fort Lauderdale Airport that they called the Place North, all he knew about the bad boys of Southern frat rock was that they were popular with college kids. Formed in Chapel Hill, North Carolina, in 1955, they had started out doing standard rhythm and blues. Under the influence of the boozy party circuit, they embraced outright, flagrant raunch decades before rappers. Palmer knew, but Cami was astonished when they walked out onstage wearing nothing but jock straps.

As outrageous as Clark and the Hot Nuts were, they were tame compared to a group out of the wilds of the North Carolina mountain country called Thirteen Screaming Niggers. By the time Cami located them, after wandering down nameless North Carolina back roads for hours, he realized a more appropriate name would have been thirty or forty screaming maniacs. That's how many players they had, all related in some way that Dick had trouble understanding. It didn't really matter because there was no set lineup. Whenever they got a job, you could never tell who was going to show up. What's more, it didn't even matter, because they were always great. Like Doug Clark and his Hot Nuts, they made a living playing college dances around the South without making a name on the radio. Cami considered representing them with his partner Vinny, but realized it would have been impossible to put together a traveling band.

Cami was seeing so many groups that it was hard to predict who was going to make it. Major talents found ways of slipping through his fingers. One day Dick joined a young singer name Len Barry for hot dogs at the Fun Fair, a famous beach hangout where you could dine on pizza burgers and fries. Barry was a member of the Dovells, who were riding the crest of popularity with a dance record called "Bristol Stomp." Barry said he would be leaving the group after their Peppermint engagement. Cami urged him to reconsider.

"You guys had a hit record. You rang the bell. You know how rare that is?" Dick couldn't talk sense into him. A few months later, Cami was driving home and listening to local deejay Rick Shaw gush about a new record he expected to go right to the top. It was "1-2-3" by Len Barry.

Dick slapped the steering wheel. The son of a bitch had done it.

In 1962, a young guitar player from southern Indiana arrived at the club to back up Troy Seals, part of a musical family that included Jim Seals of Seals and Crofts and Dan Seals of England Dan & John Ford Coley, both groups that would have hit records later in life. The guitar player could play anything from gut-bucket blues to Hank Williams country. The band came for two weeks and stayed for the season. That guitarist's name was Lonnie Mack, a nice kid who spent his childhood on a small subsistence farm in Indiana that didn't even have electricity.

He described his childhood as being "beyond poverty." There was no money, but there was a primitive, battery-powered radio, which pulled in the *Grand Ole Opry* from Nashville. After the rest of the family was in bed, Lonnie would reach out for different kinds of music: gospel, and the black R&B sounds of the city, which inspired him to teach himself to play guitar on a battered acoustic he got in trade for his bicycle.

When Mack walked into the Peppermint carrying his Gibson Flying V guitar, he was just twenty-one. Dick mistook him for Seals at first glance. "No sir," he said. "I'm Lonnie Mack, the gi-tar player."

Mack had a powerful, gospel-style voice, which he let loose on occasion, to sometimes surprising effect. Seals's band was backing Steve Alaimo, a Miami-based blue-eyed soul singer best known for the 1963 hit "Every Day I Have to Cry." In the middle of a song, Alaimo stopped the show.

"What the hell is that?" he said, turning to look at Mack, who stepped back from the mike.

Near the end of the engagement, Mack played a record for Cami that he'd made a few months earlier at a session with the Charmaines, a girl group out of Cincinnati. The song was a somewhat reimagined version of the Chuck Berry standard "Memphis." Cami asked why he wasn't singing on it.

"I felt it as an instrumental," Mack said.

He'd worked up the song onstage one night when the scheduled vocalist failed to show. After it went over with the crowd, Mack began working it into the shows. The song as performed by Mack had seven distinct sections built around an unusually fast, twelve-bar blues solo.

Mack asked Dick if he knew of a label that might distribute the record. Dick wasn't sure there was much of a market for instrumentals in 1963. A few months later, "Memphis" was all over the radio, a top five hit, biggest instrumental of the year. The song was hugely influential on other musicians.

As difficult as it was to tell which musicians were going to make it, sometimes it was even harder to tell which ones weren't.

In September 1963, Cami found himself without a headline act after a last-minute call from Jay Black of Jay and the Americans, who had the hit "Come a Little Bit Closer." The popular band was scheduled to open the third season, but Jay asked Dick if he would let them out of their contract because he'd been invited on Murray the K's big Labor Day weekend show. New York deejay Murray Kaufman was at his peak of influence. All the kids in New York went to his sold-out shows at the Brooklyn Fox. Any performer would do a lot, or give up a lot, to play his shows, which also meant airplay on his top-rated nightly radio program. Dick agreed and Jay promised to make it up to him later. Dick started calling around for a replacement. A record producer named Bob Ury had a surprising hit on his hands called "He's Mine (I Love Him, I Love Him, I Love Him)." The record was number eight on the Miami charts.

Cami had heard the song and liked it. He called Ury, who was understandably thrilled at his success. The way the record business worked then, according to Dick's partner, Vinny Marchese, was this: "One hit could be a fluke; a second hit and people go 'Hmm, we might have something here'; a third hit and your career was made. You'd have decades of work in good rooms. No more scuffling and begging for coffee money."

It was possible Ury had nothing but a fluke on his hands. Still, the song was a regional hit and, in a pinch, that was good enough. The artist was a newcomer named Alice Wonder Land. Ury was happy to talk up the record, but started backpedaling when Cami inquired about live performances. "She isn't really a live performer," Ury said.

Cami was glad to hear that. It meant she was free of obligations. "I'd like her to come over and do a couple of shows for us this weekend," Dick said. "Friday and Saturday only." Ury couldn't really say no, but he kept reaching for excuses.

"Listen, Bob," Dick said, "when you needed help I was there. Now I need help and I expect you to be there for me. I don't want to hear any bullshit about her not being a performer. I expect Alice to be here Friday at two in the afternoon for rehearsal. I hope we understand each other."

That did it. Whatever Ury's reservations were, he set them aside. Alice showed up promptly at two on Friday for rehearsal. When Scatsy saw her, his rolled his eyes. Alice was a tiny black girl who couldn't have weighed more than a hundred pounds. She did a quick run-through with the house band, which didn't go so well. No matter.

By this time, the Peppermint had seen enough rock-and-roll bands to know rehearsals didn't necessarily matter, or to know whether a singer with a hit record could sing or not. That night the club was jammed when it came time for her to perform.

Alice was wearing a cheap, plain white dress that couldn't have cost ten dollars. Standing backstage waiting to go on, she was shaking so badly that Dick walked over and asked if she was all right. She didn't say a word, merely nodded her head. When she strode onstage the crowd greeted her with enthusiastic applause. The music started, but Alice didn't. She stood at the microphone, frozen with fear. She couldn't open her mouth. If it hadn't been for Ruby, the band's singer, grabbing the microphone and escorting her offstage, she might have stood there all night.

The band played on and Ruby finished the show. It was one of those nights when a nightclub owner wants to kill himself. Cami lifted the minimum so the crowd was free to pay for only what they drank. He felt no anger toward poor, pathetic Alice, collapsed in a chair in his office after the show. Dick paid her and told her gently that they wouldn't be needing her anymore. She showed nothing but relief.

Dick Kline, a local record promotion man who had befriended Cami, walked in that night and headed for the bar, where comedian Lenny Bruce stood, dressed in a trench coat. Kline asked him who the girl singer was. "I'm Alice," Lenny said. He opened his coat and pointed at his crotch. "And here's my Wonder Land."

Dick Cami tracked down Ury the next day, "Where were you last night?" he demanded.

"I tried to tell you she couldn't perform," Ury said, defensive.

"How the hell did you get her to sing on the record?"

Ury broke down and gave out with the story. "I had a record date over at Criteria but the singer I had ran off with the drummer from another band. I had to come up with someone quick," Ury said. The girl's name was Alice Faye Henderson and she worked as a maid for a neighbor of songwriter Stephen Schlaks. Dick couldn't believe it. "You're telling me I booked a fucking maid?"

"We doubled and tripled her and gave her voice plenty of echo," Ury said, "and it came out better than I expected. I gave her the name Alice Wonder Land. Who knew the record would take off? Then when you called I didn't know what to say."

Scatsy never let Cami forget the incident. "That Alice Wonder Land looked great up there, and what a way she almost had with a lyric not singing a song," Scatsy said. "Beautiful."

Chapter 14

Say Hello to the Milkman

It was dawn when Dick pulled into the driveway. By this time, he and Joanie owned a big house in Skylake, an upscale neck of North Miami Beach with gardeners, Jaguars, and swimming pools. It wasn't Miami Shores, where Johnny and Millicent lived. But there wasn't much to complain about, either.

Cami slipped the key into the front door and stepped into the house. *Boom.* Joanie brought a broom down on his head. "You son of a bitch," she yelled. "You come home at this hour?"

The broom came down again, but this time he got his hands up. He wrestled the broom from her and saw her tearstained face.

"Don't tell me you were out with my father this time," she said. "Mother told me you weren't with him."

"Joanie, please, you're waking up the neighborhood."

Dick explained that he'd gone to the Sir John to catch an act he was interested in. The Sir John Hotel put a microphone on the diving board over the outside pool so people could swim while being serenaded. After leaving the Sir John, Dick said, he caught Lenny Bruce's show at the Le B.

"Lenny Bruce?" Joanie said. "You went to see that degenerate without me?"

"You hate the guy," Dick said. "You told me the man's a pig."

Joanie had never wanted to come to Miami in the first place. Now that they were here, she took every opportunity to show her displeasure. Her once cheerful personality had congealed into disappointment and anger. She didn't want her husband spending so much time with her father. But when she and Dick weren't together she was equally upset, convinced he was cheating on her.

Dick was no choirboy. But he had learned a valuable lesson early: To be respected, a nightclub owner should never mess with the help or any of the women who came in. Johnny put him wise to this. You never know who was with whom or what consequences it might lead to . . . so to avoid making enemies Dick made an art form of dodging advances that came his way.

One time a stunning brunette came into the Peppermint with her boyfriend. Dick had seen her before but didn't know her name, and he had never spoken to her. He noticed when the boyfriend passed him that he got the dirtiest look. *What was that about*? he wondered. Later in the evening, as the woman passed Dick on her way to the restroom, she turned and grabbed his arm, whispering, "I told him we went out."

"What? I don't even know you . . . what did you do that for?"

"I wanted to make him jealous."

This, thought Dick, *is how innocent people got killed.*

Of course, Dick had to admit he could see Joanie's point. You didn't have to be crazy to be suspicious about a man who came home after the newspaper. Dick's excuse was a good one. The Peppermint shows ran all night long. All the clubs stayed open until seven in the morning on the 79th Street Causeway. Dick didn't usually close the place, but there were times when he needed to be there until the sun came up. He reminded Joanie he'd warned her he'd be late.

"Late, not eight in the morning," she said.

"What's the big deal?" he said. "I've come home a lot at this time. We're open till seven. You know that."

"I called the Peppermint and they said you weren't there. All Scatsy kept saying was, 'I don't know nothing.' Like he was on the stand. I had to remind him I was his niece."

"What did he say then?"

"Same thing. 'I don't know nothing.'"

Dick explained that he'd ended the night with his friend Victor at the Place for Steak. "That's it," he said.

"With those tramps at the Place for Steak, you mean," she said. Joanie jerked back the broom.

"So what's with the broom?" Dick said. "You going for a ride?"

"Don't push it," she said, and headed for the bedroom. As she passed the boys' room, they came spilling out like puppies.

"Say hello to the milkman," Joanie said.

Hearing about Dick's domestic problems, Johnny had trouble grasping the situation. The complaints of a modern woman, even his daughter, were beyond his understanding. His own wife never questioned anything. He urged Dick to consider divorce. That would happen, but not yet.

One thing Johnny was firm about, with his old-world attitudes, was keeping pimps and hookers out of the club. He'd seen what had happened to Charley Lucky. He didn't want to give cops even the appearance of impropriety. As a result, Dick kept an eye out for any single girls who looked like they were setting lures.

One night, the bartender, Johnny Defino, called his attention to an attractive blonde at the bar. Dick wasn't sure. She wasn't batting her eyes at the men hoisting drinks around her. But Defino had an instinct for these things, so Dick went over.

"Pardon me, miss, you're in the wrong place, aren't you?"

She did too good a job of acting shocked. Dick knew Defino was right.

"Listen, it makes no difference to me what you do for a living," he said. "But in here it does. You can finish your drink, but then you'll have to leave. There's no check for you."

"Okay, I'm a hooker," she admitted. Betty, that was her name, said she wasn't a bad girl. She was just turning tricks until she could afford to buy a charter boat. Her ambition was to be a fishing boat captain. Dick tried to picture her in rubber boots and flannel and discovered his mind couldn't safely expand that far.

She wasn't working in the Peppermint, she said. "The people performing here are my idols. I just want to hear the music. Please."

Dick ended up feeling sorry for her and decided to let her stay, but not at the bar. They put her at a little table off to the side, where they could keep an eye on her. She became a regular and everybody knew about her but Johnny.

One day some time later, she came running in with big news. "I got my captain's papers," she said. She'd bought her boat. "I'm calling it the *Betty B*."

Naturally, Dick was happy for her. He was just about to revise his opinion of human nature when a story in the local paper caught his eye. A charter boat named the *Betty B* had met with a serious accident in the gulfstream. "Charter boat collides with freighter," the headline read.

Captain Betty, who like her passengers had survived the accident unscathed, said she put the boat on autopilot because the fishing was poor. She was belowdecks with her all-male party when the accident happened. They must have been down there a while because she didn't see any boats on the horizon when she went down.

Dick felt a smile crossing his face. *Can't blame this one on the Bermuda Triangle*, he thought.

Over the years, Cami had kept up his partnership with Vinny Marchese, who by this time had shortened his name to Vinny Marc. Their record company, Cambria, had evolved into a promotional and management company. The first tour Cami organized in the South featured Betty Everett, riding high with "The Shoop Shoop Song (It's in

His Kiss)," and Garnet Mimms and the Enchanters, whose big hit was "Cry Baby."

One time, Garnell "Buz" Cooper and the Kinfolks found them-selves stranded in Miami by Etta James, whom they had been backing. As a favor to their manager, Hosea Wilson, Dick hired the band for a two-week stint at the Miami Beach Peppermint. The Kinfolks were big and boisterous and knew how to rock. They were an instant club favorite.

Learning that Dick managed groups on the side, Wilson ap-proached him to promote road shows in the black townships around South Florida. Since the Peppermint didn't do as much business dur-ing the off-season, Dick had free time to wander through the black villages, scattered throughout rural Florida, where gators prowled and people still ate possum. There were a lot of those clubs then. Dick could put on a show in a different club every night and not re-peat for a year. That was the chitlin' circuit.

Being the only white person in a black club could get sticky, so Hosea let it be known that the big white dude was a cop.

One tour was especially memorable. The show was in Belle Glades, a small sugarcane town west of Palm Beach in the Everglades. Fred-die Scott, a former songwriter who had recently struck gold as a vo-calist with the soulful "Hey Girl," was headlining. The Kinfolks were the band.

At the last minute, a bookmaker friend of Cami's named Bobby joined the caravan. "Bobby was a tough guy," Dick said. "He could hold his own in most situations where blood could be spilled. But like so many wiseguys, when you take them out of their element, they ain't so tough. That's what happened that day."

Bobby started out cocky, patting his jacket as he climbed in. "I got Old Betsy here in case we need her," he said.

Dick never heard anyone call his gun Old Betsy outside of a Davy Crockett western. He nodded, smiling to himself. As they drove, they reminisced, telling stories, reliving who failed and who succeeded, who got rich and who got nailed. After two hours of rumbling along pitted roads, through thick swampland forests, they reached the auditorium, a broken-down building with shattered windows. There were no fans, the floor was dirty, and the stage had no curtains. To Hosea, it didn't make any difference where they performed, what theater they played in, or what time the acts went onstage. Any time, night or day, open lots, stage or no stage, lights or no lights—all he was interested in was finding a place to set up a table and collect the money.

"This is the nastiest room I've ever seen," Dick said.

"Tell me about it," Hosea replied. "We're gonna make a nice score here and please don't stay by the table when we be taking in the money."

"Why not?"

"Because it don't look good for no ofay to be where we be taking in the money. And furthermore, this motherfucker you brought keeps hassling the sisters."

Bobby had been getting out of hand with the shabbily dressed girls waiting in line, looking them up and down and making comments.

"When one of the brothers breaks his leg, I hope he don't come running to me to save his ass," Hosea continued.

It began raining heavily, but that didn't keep the crowd away. There must have been two thousand people jammed into a hall meant for half that.

When the crowd heard the first drumbeat and saw the Kinfolks run onstage, the room exploded into a swarm of dancers moving in unison, on the beat. Dick had never seen anything like it.

When he saw Bobby again, he'd obviously gotten the message. He was shaken, white as a bleached sheet, and getting paler by the second. He said he thought he might sit out the show backstage, with Dick.

"Take Betsy with you and wait in the dressing room," Dick said.

On the way home Bobby was quiet. Then he started up and when he did he didn't shut up. "I ain't a good Jew you know. I steal. I don't go to temple."

He paused. "You know, tonight I was somewhere I'd never been before. I should have known better. I been around dangerous men all my life. But tonight I felt alone like I never did before. Those broads and everything. I'm lucky I'm alive."

"What the hell, we all learn," Dick said. He decided never again to take any of his buddies on the road with him.

Dick's partner, Vinny, ran into a different kind of trouble with one of his acts, a singer they handled named Barbara Chandler, who recorded "It Hurts to Be Sixteen" for Kapp in 1963. She was a real sweetheart, very talented. She tried everything to break through, even holding her nose as she sang on a record called "Fool's Errand," to get the proper nasal sound kids seemed to prefer. It went to number one in England, but flopped in America.

Vinny did everything he could for her, including walking her down the aisle. Barbara and Vinny were sitting in the audience watching Jack E. Leonard perform at a club called the Americana in Cleveland, when Vinny went to the men's room. When he returned, two mopes who looked a lot like wiseguys were sitting with his wife.

"Say hello to Carlo and Louie," Barbara said.

Carlo and Louie invited them to dinner with the underboss of the Cleveland Mob, Frank Brancato. At dinner, Brancato, who controlled loan-sharking and gambling in the Cleveland area, went to bat for his boys. He said they really liked Barbara.

"We're going to take her over and you'll get five percent," Brancato said. "For your trouble."

Vinny stalled him until he could get Dick on the phone. Their partnership worked well because whenever Vinny got in trouble, he knew Dick would be there to back him up. Of course, Dick's muscle was his father-in-law, who apparently outranked even bosses in Cleveland.

"I stepped on a land mine," Vinny told Dick.

Cami had one question. "Are they connected?"

Vinny was pretty sure they were. They threw their weight around like they were. After getting their names, Dick called Johnny. The next night, Carlo and Louie came over to Vinny's table again. This time they acted like old friends.

"What's the matter with you?" Carlo said. "Don't you know we were kidding about Barbara? Let us buy you a drink."

They were so eager to make up for their bad manners that they taxied Barbara to work, telling her that anything she needed, just give a call.

Something very similar happened in New York, with a singer Dick and Vinny managed named Tony Roma. He had a great voice, but Roma could never break through. Two wiseguys from Brooklyn named Joe Box and Buster thought they could handle him better than Vinny. Instead of bothering with the time-wasting formalities of actual negotiation, they told Vinny he was out and they were in. "I'm a little confused," Vinny said. "Tony never told me anything about this."

"Tony's got no say in this," Joe Box said. "We're hoping you don't give us no trouble. We're going to get him plenty of work. He's going to be a happy man, believe me."

That night, Cami got another call from his partner. "Why do these things keep happening to me?" Vinny said.

Once again, Dick called Johnny. Once again, Vinny got an apology.

"Yesterday they want to give me a beating and today they're giving me kisses," Marchese said. "These guys are real *cafones*."

He wasn't the only one who thought so. A month later, Buster was found in the trunk of his car, his life drained out of a dozen bullet holes. His balls were sewn to his lower lip, the classic sign of a stool pigeon.

Against Dick's advice, Vinny developed an unlikely friendship with John "Sonny" Franzese, the underboss of the Colombo crime family. Sonny knew Vinny from when he was a kid in Bensonhurst. Franzese was thrown out of the army during World War II because he had homicidal tendencies. But he liked the music business. He was a familiar presence around many label offices and occasionally handled groups like the Angels. In effect, he was the show business don. But that didn't soften him. He was once caught on an FBI tape giving lessons in murder to an informant.

"I killed a lot of guys," he said. "You're not talking about four, five, six, or ten."

He advised that with modern forensics it was foolish to leave bodies lying around. "Today you can't have a body no more. It's better to take that half an hour to get rid of the body" rather than leave it in the street.

His technique was to dismember the body, dry the parts in a microwave and then run them through an industrial-grade garbage disposal. When he did a hit, he said, he put nail polish on his fingertips to avoid leaving prints. He also suggested wearing a hairnet to keep from leaving stray hairs around.

Sonny Franzese was a bad man. He could also be charming and was invariably nice to Vinny, who returned the friendship. When the FBI showed up at his door, Vinny refused to help them nail him. "He's a friend of mine," Vinny said. "I've known him since I'm a kid from the neighborhood."

One night, Sonny invited Vinny to dinner at the Copacabana nightclub in New York. Vinny took Barbara Chandler with him but Sonny kept them waiting for more than an hour. By the time he arrived, Barbara was starving. She had met Sonny before but didn't know who he was. In a moment of aggravation she said, "Sonny, I'm so hungry I could kill."

"Take it easy, honey," the Mafia don said. "That's my job."

Chapter 15

Front-Page Rat

Picking up a rumor that Johnny Futto might be in trouble with the bosses again, the FBI made a run at him in 1962 in hopes he might become an informant. According to FBI records, two agents approached him outside his house in Miami Shores.

Johnny was surly at first. But after being told one of the agents had traveled all the way from New York and was entitled to common courtesy, Johnny's attitude changed. It was the perfect approach to a man like Johnny, to whom good manners were almost as important as not cooking with tomato paste.

He invited the agents in and offered drinks, which the agents politely declined. Biello described himself humbly as "a small man and a gambler." He admitted receiving income from the Peppermint, which he listed for tax purposes as coming from other sources. He freely told them what he thought of Sinatra—a degenerate—and admitted his health was a worry. He had a growth on his intestine that he feared was cancer.

As for once again being a target for assassination, Johnny told the

FBI men that he was a fatalist. Nothing he or anyone else could do would prevent his death if it was his time, he said.

As for becoming an informant, he repeated what he always said when the subject of his mortality was broached: "I was born a man and I'll die a man."

Johnny might have been a fatalist, but that didn't mean he abandoned himself to his fate. FBI files show that Johnny was on the Mafia's version of death row throughout the time the New York Peppermint Lounge opened and became the hottest nightclub in the world. It wasn't the logic of his arguments that repeatedly saved him, or his many years of service and loyalty to the organization; it was the men in high places he'd grown up with and whose friendships he'd cultivated over the decades. Lucchese had saved him at least once. Then there were times that he was saved by pure luck and the Mafia's relaxed work ethic.

In October 1962, the FBI in New York recorded a conversation between two hit men talking about how each had been given the job respectively to hit Johnny that summer. Although it wasn't stated, it was clear the FBI had wired the room where the hit men were staying. The incident was likely the genesis of the FBI visit to Johnny's house.

It was clear from the record of the conversation that Johnny escaped death that summer mainly because the killer assigned to the job was worried his wife would get mad if he wasn't home at the proper hour.

According to the records, the hit was ordered by Rosario "Saro" Mogavero, a longshoreman union executive who was close to Vito Genovese.

It's uncertain whether the hit was sanctioned by Genovese. As the top man in the Bronx, Johnny ran a lot of rackets in the rail yards. As a union parasite, Mogavero could well have wanted to expand his empire to include the rail yards. In other words, it was purely business, as conducted by the Mafia.

The Mogavero contract, which the hit men called a "trick," was given to Michelino Clemente and Charles "Bananas" Coppolino, both Genovese killers. Clemente got it first.

"Saro says to me. He says, 'tonight. We meet, you know, to get [Johnny's] movements.'" Clemente said. "I says, 'Saro, I got company over the house. Is this an emergency?' He says, 'No.' If it ain't an emergency then I don't want to meet now because my wife is gonna start an argument, 'Where are you going? It's Saturday night,' and all that stuff."

Any workingman could sympathize with Clemente. Getting in dutch with the wife was to be avoided if at all possible, even when your job involved assassination. There was an old Mafia saying: Friends help you move, but real friends help you move bodies. Clemente's scheduling conflict caused the trick to be put off for a while.

Dick didn't know about any of this. Johnny kept his anxieties to himself, at least until the day Georgie (Smurra) Blair, a hit man in Jimmy Blue Eyes's Harlem crew, came fast-walking into the Peppermint in Miami Beach with his hands held high, a gesture of peace.

"Johnny, they're going to kill you," Georgie said.

Dick kept a gun behind the service bar. Without thinking, he went for it, an extremely foolish move. If he weren't a friend of Johnny's, Georgie would have killed Dick without thinking. As it was, he only shot him a chilling sideways look.

"I know, Georgie," Johnny said. Dick was both relieved that Georgie was no threat, as well as deeply troubled to discover his father-in-law was in trouble again. They'd moved down to Miami not just to expand the carpet business and open a second Peppermint Lounge, but to get away from the New York Mob life. Johnny was supposed to be retired.

After Georgie left, Johnny turned on Dick. "This is my beef, not yours," he said. "Keep out of it."

This time, his father-in-law didn't whistle through his front teeth to signal his irritation, a common habit. Instead, he shifted gears and lightened the mood with a funny story about Georgie.

During World War II, Georgie Blair had to go on the lam for a murder rap. The FBI had put out an all-points bulletin on him. There were pictures in the post offices, and cops everywhere were on the lookout for him. The bosses set him up with a friendly family in San Francisco who had a secret apartment in their attic. The only time Georgie came out was to eat with the family. Hailing from the Sicilian village of Sciacca, the family were fishermen. "Fish was all they ate, morning, noon, and night," Johnny said.

Georgie was going crazy after a few weeks for some meat, any meat, Johnny continued. Perhaps sensing his mood, the couple told him they were going to have a special Sunday dinner in his honor. He thought of lamb. He imagined a big steak. Even chicken would have hit the spot. But when the Sunday came, they brought him his present wrapped in newspaper—a different type of fish.

"School was out," Johnny said. "Georgie couldn't take it anymore. He ran out of the house. The husband yells after him, 'George, where you going? It's too dangerous for you out there.' Georgie yells back, 'I don't care if I get the chair. I've got to get a piece a meat.'"

With the Peppermints reaching their peak of fame, Johnny was approached by the bosses to take over a Las Vegas hotel called the Last Frontier. Just because one boss wanted to whack him didn't mean they wouldn't do business with him.

A wealthy Texan named R. E. Griffith, and his nephew William Moore had built the hotel in 1942, making it the very first hotel on what would become the world-famous Strip. To make it a tourist attraction that would appeal to car-weary Californians, Griffith and Moore bought high-quality furnishings, authentic pioneer saddles, and antique guns for the lobby. They brought in stonemasons from the Ute Indian tribe to build fireplaces and patios of sandstone. They also purchased, at heavy expense, the nineteenth-century forty-foot long solid mahogany bar that for decades had been the centerpiece of the old Arizona Club in downtown Las Vegas.

Moore also built a facsimile Western pioneer town called the Last Frontier Village, which became a destination for families braving the desert heat in summer. Just as significant for the future of Las Vegas, the hotel opened the town's first wedding chapel, the Little Church of the West.

By the sixties, the place had fallen on hard times. Johnny was approached for a couple of reasons. The bosses knew he'd been in Las Vegas in the early days when he scouted the area for Costello. He was there when the Last Frontier opened. The other reason was that he was now seen as the genius behind the Twist craze. The offer came with a requirement that he open a Peppermint Lounge in the hotel.

Dick was excited by the prospect, but he was worried about Joanie's reaction. He knew she'd hit the roof again. In fact, she'd probably go right through the roof and into space, swinging her broom all the way.

Johnny was delighted at the Las Vegas prospect, as well. It would be like going back home for him. He still thought of the Southwest nostalgically, as a place where you could operate out in the open. FBI records show he made several trips out there, often driving a car and selling it once he arrived to avoid being tailed. Whether he was concerned about the authorities or his enemies was never made clear.

Johnny's partner in the venture would have been, as usual, Lee Ratner. In an FBI interview on August 20, 1962, Ratner denied knowing Johnny was a mafioso. He told the agents he considered Johnny to be retired.

"Retired from what?" the FBI wanted to know.

Ratner couldn't say.

He admitted to the FBI that he was interested in buying the Last Frontier. He offered $900,000 for the building and demanded a ninety-nine-year lease on the property. When the owner balked and asked for more money, Ratner withdrew. The hotel was later purchased by the eccentric billionaire Howard Hughes. Given what the Strip eventually became, the missed opportunity was costly. If they had gone forward on the deal Johnny and Lee would have made millions.

The real reason for Johnny's interest was not money. He never seemed to lack for that. He saw it as a way to get out of harm's way.

The conversation taped by the FBI made it clear, however, that those who wanted Johnny dead were fully aware of his plans.

Clemente and Coppolino weren't worried that he would escape his fate by fleeing west.

"We can get him better over there than here," Coppolino said on the tape.

"Easy," Clemente replied. "Because over there he wouldn't expect anything."

By January 1963, an informant told the FBI that Johnny was no longer worried about assassination. He'd once again managed to make the threat go away, or at least recede. It's likely any deal he made would have required him to finally give up any of his remaining rackets in New York.

One afternoon in the summer of 1963, Dick went to the club to make some phone calls and take care of paperwork. The Peppermint was like a tomb during the day, deliberately kept dark to keep the summer heat at bay.

At a table way in back near the empty bandstand, two dim figures huddled. Strangers meeting in the daytime was weird enough. Doing it in the dark was on the knife-edge of bizarre. Scatsy was coming up the aisle from them. Dick asked who they were.

"Santo," Scatsy said, referring to South Florida mob kingpin Santo Trafficante. "The old man called and told me to put them in back, real private. They wanted to talk, but didn't want to be bothered. That's Johnny Roselli, from the coast."

The way Scatsy talked, he seemed to think Cami should know the guy. "They were together in Cuba," Scatsy said.

Dick went into his office. Neither of the men looked his way.

Years later, a chill twisted its way down his spine when he read up on the Kennedy assassination and the role the Mob might have played in it. There were a lot of signs that the Warren Commission either missed, or chose not to see, that pointed at Santo and Roselli, along with a third man, Carlos Marcello out of New Orleans.

It's known that Roselli was the CIA's link to the Mafia back in 1960, when the agency decided to kill Fidel Castro. Charlie Tourine, Lee Ratner's guest the night of the 1960 elections, had offered $1 million to a career criminal named Frank Fiorini to kill Castro in 1959. Sandi Lansky, Meyer's daughter, confirmed that her father was also searching for someone to kill Castro. The Mafia ached to be back in Cuba, running their rackets, but they knew that would never happen while Castro remained in power. Roselli was involved because he, like Santo and Tourine, had been deeply involved in gambling in Cuba.

Supposedly, the planning advanced far enough that Roselli was given a handful of poison pills to be sneaked into Castro's food. After this and other plots, including the Bay of Pigs invasion, went awry, the Mob realized it was impossible to get to Castro. By 1962, they were stringing the CIA along.

Meanwhile, President Kennedy's brother, Bobby, as attorney general, was on a crusade against the Mob. Everybody from Chicago to Buffalo was getting indicted. Carlos Marcello was bundled off to Guatemala under Bobby's orders, returning to the States angrily vowing revenge.

Bobby's campaign was galling to the Mob, who felt they had put his brother in the White House. Dick wasn't on the inside enough to know all the ins and outs, but he was close enough to hear all the boys raging about the Kennedys. Not since Dutch Schultz wanted to hit Dewey had such dark threats been muttered. Mobsters especially hated someone who was one of them but now pretended to be above them. Old man Joe Kennedy was nothing but a bootlegger, after all. Beyond that, they were angry that Kennedy didn't follow through and get rid of Castro and restore their kingdom in Havana.

Kennedy's killer, Lee Harvey Oswald, was shot and killed by a local nightclub owner named Jack Ruby as he was brought out of jail in Dallas How Ruby managed to get so close to Oswald remains an enduring mystery. But one thing known is that Ruby considered Carlos Marcello a friend. On the day before President Kennedy was killed, November 22, 1963, Ruby was in contact with both Marcello and Santo Trafficante, supposedly over a problem he was having with the American Guild of Variety Artists.

Then there's the secret FBI wiretap of Trafficante, which was subpoenaed by the House Select Committee on Assassinations. He's overheard saying, "Now only two people know who killed Kennedy, and they aren't talking."

Finally, there's the remark that Trafficante's longtime lawyer, Frank Ragano, said he heard Santo make during an automobile ride on March 13, 1987, almost twenty-five years after the assassination. According to the account by the respected *New York Times* crime reporter Selwyn Raab, Trafficante, who was dying, blurted out, "Goddamn Bobby . . . We shouldn't have killed Giovanni. We should have killed Bobby."

But even if Marcello, Trafficante, or some combination of them and others were involved in the assassination, what would compel Trafficante to leave his favorite haunts for a meeting at a kids' night-club? The advantages of the Peppermint Lounge were actually mani-fold. Assuming that Trafficante knew he was being watched, he would want to meet Roselli somewhere outside his home but in a place that must be private. The Peppermint was a better choice than a restau-rant because the only windows faced the bay, not the street, where prying eyes might be watching. Trafficante knew he could trust Johnny Futto to keep his mouth shut. Not even Cami was supposed to be there. He had dropped in unexpectedly to take care of some busi-ness. Johnny had trusted the arrangements solely to Scatsy. And why were the two men sitting in the dark?

Clearly, whatever they were discussing was important, something they didn't want nosed around. Dick eventually got to know Santo pretty well. He is skeptical of Ragano's account. Santo never told Cami anything remotely like what he supposedly said to the attorney. Dick was only sure of this: Santo hated the Kennedys with a passion that strayed into obsession.

Johnny's respite didn't last. That October 1963, Cami walked in the office to find Okey sitting with Scatsy, who slammed his fist on the desk in the office and shouted, "Motherfucker." Dick hadn't seen the day's papers, but Scatsy filled him in.

"Valachi just ratted out the old man," Scatsy said.

A little-known thug named Joe Valachi, who was serving out a life sentence for murder, went to the feds after learning that his cellmate, Vito Genovese, was about have him killed, supposedly for being a rat. To save his skin, Valachi became one.

Before a Senate committee and in full view of a bank of TV cameras broadcasting his testimony nationwide to a rapt, astonished audience, Valachi revealed everything he knew about the Five Families, their businesses, and their blood feuds.

He revealed for the first time how deeply the Mob had dug its claws into American life. He described businesses and unions rotted through by the Mafia. He named names, among them three high-ranking mob chiefs in Miami: Tony "Goebels" Ricci, "Trigger Mike" Coppola, and Johnny "Futto" Biello. The next day, *The Miami Herald* front-paged the news that crime lords were living in their fair city.

Johnny walked into the office while Scatsy was still worked up. "A lot of people know about me," Johnny said, unconcerned. "What's the big difference?"

Scatsy wasn't mollified. "They put a rat like this on the front page," he said.

"If Genovese did the right thing this never would have happened," Johnny said. "If we're lucky, in a couple of days they'll be wrapping fish with those papers."

Instead, they found themselves under twenty-four-hour surveillance. Cami had trouble spotting the tails, but Johnny saw the agents a mile away. Don't look at the car, he counseled. FBI agents often used older cars.

"When in doubt, look at the tires. If you see a broken-down car with new tires, you can bet it's the feds."

Johnny was now somewhat semiofficially retired from the Mob, so he wasn't that worried about the FBI. Just be polite, he told his crew. Avoid confrontations and never, ever threaten them. Their ability to make things uncomfortable might not equal what the Mob could do— hence the ancient Sicilian maxim that "between the law and the Mafia, the law is not the most to be feared"—but they could still make your life miserable.

Chapter 16

The Beatles Come
to the Peppermint

The Beatles came to New York City in February 1964 to begin their first American tour. Despite the success of "I Want to Hold Your Hand," which sold 2.6 million records in two weeks, the band had been nervous about the tour. No British rock-and-roll musicians had ever succeeded in America. In advance of the first of three appearances on *The Ed Sullivan Show*, scheduled for Sunday, February 9, Sullivan was a little anxious himself. Although he was by then America's premier impresario, he wasn't sure the British rock-and-roll phenomenon would translate to an American audience. The first show, during which they performed five quite well-received selections, was viewed by seventy-four million people, 40 percent of the U.S. population, along with a continually keening studio audience. Beatlemania, American-style, was officially inaugurated.

The group had arrived in New York two days earlier to find their hotel, the Plaza, swarmed by hundreds of teenagers blocking the street. Barricaded in ten rooms lined up in an interconnected suite, the bewildered Beatles listened to stations blasting their records on transistor radios while they watched television coverage of their arrival at the recently renamed Kennedy Airport. The Ronettes, who knew the Beatles from London, came to visit, trailing disc jockey Murray "the K" Kaufman, who ingratiated himself as quickly as he could, taking charge of the Beatles' schedule for the evening, which is how the boys ended up later that night at the Peppermint Lounge.

The Twist might have been long gone, but the world-famous Peppermint Lounge was still the foremost setting to hear real American rock and roll. The Saturday evening, February 8, 1964, began with a whirlwind tour of New York's nightlife hosted by the self-promoting, often obnoxious Murray the K, who took everybody to dinner at '21,' followed by drinks at the Playboy Club, and then to West 45th Street, where Louie Lombardi greeted them at the door.

The group declined to participate in the club's Twist Revue, but Ringo climbed on the dance floor with Peppermint Twister team captain Marlene Klaire. While the house band, Seven Fabulous Epics, stomped their way through "Money," the sax player honking his guts out, Ringo and Klaire, a stack of brunette hair piled high on her head, did the Twist.

Documentary footage taken that night by Canadian filmmakers David and Albert Maysles showed the three other Beatles drinking cocktails, smoking cigarettes, and behaving like mature adult entertainers, somewhat shocking behavior for teen idols expected to behave as perpetual adolescents. Film director Richard Lester drew on the footage for a near-identical scene later that year when he made the Beatles' first motion picture, *A Hard Day's Night.*

A couple of days later, Dick Cami in Miami got a call from Sam K. in New York.

"The Beatles were just here," he said. "I told them Hank Ballard was playing down there. They really want to meet the guy, so they're going to see him when they get there."

The Beatles' second appearance on *Ed Sullivan* was scheduled for February 16 at the Deauville Hotel in Miami. The Beatles might have been excited to meet Hank Ballard, but Hank didn't feel the same way.

Ballard could be shy, sometimes a little bitter about his failure to break out on white radio, despite the fact that, as the writer of "The Twist," he made more money off the record than Chubby Checker did. He moved in different circles from the Beatles. The Peppermint was the only white club Ballard played. His audience was almost exclusively African-American and, in the segregated South, he was mostly confined to gritty black clubs.

When Cami proposed the meeting with the Beatles, his reply was succinct: "Fuck them."

Even less impressed were a couple of mobsters from Boston, Romeo "Scarface" Martin and Ronald "the Pig" Cassesso. As tough as they come, both were hit men and intimates of Johnny's good friend Boston Mob chief Raymond Patriarca. Cassesso and Martin, when they were in town escaping the Boston winter, liked to hang around the Miami Beach club, checking out the music and eating Scatsy's cooking.

On the day of the big visit, Scatsy fed the Boston hoods his special *penne filetto di pomodoro.* "You got more macaronis, they're great," Martin said.

"Take all you want, for crying out loud," Scatsy said. "And remember to be here tonight if you want to see the Beatles."

Romeo was suddenly, surprisingly upset. "It's my girl, Darlene," he said. "All she keeps talking about is that Ringo. Ringo this, Ringo that. I'm gonna clip that motherfucker Ringo's hair off. Enough already. I'm gonna bring her a souvenir."

Millions of red-blooded American men were jealous of the way their girlfriends swooned over the Beatles. But when these guys talked about doing violence to someone, it was usually no idle threat. Both had killed. A year later, Romeo Martin would himself be killed, leaving his golf clubs in Fat Vinny Teresa's car. Vinny used them until the day he went into witness protection and wrote a book about his career.

Mulling Martin's remark, Scatsy wondered. Nah, they would never. But still. "Do what you got to do with them, but do it after they leave," Scatsy said. "Let us get a little play out of them being here."

When the Beatles arrived in Miami, the local papers took note of every detail of the event. Thousands of kids rioted at the airport. The *Miami News* called the welcome smashing: "smashed doors, smashed windows, smashed furniture, and one badly cut teenager . . . The Beatles, who introduced a weird kind of hip-slinging, face-contorting rock and roll to Britain" planned to take a boat trip (where McCartney fobbed the captain's hat) and relax before Sunday's show.

At an airport press conference, they displayed the cheeky demeanor that even the dismissive American press couldn't fail to find amusing.

Reporter: "What do you boys plan to do after this?" By which the writer meant, what are your plans when you grow up? That was a still common question in the days when playing rock and roll was considered a lark and not a serious career.

Ringo: "What else is there to do?"

Reporter: "How much schooling did you have?"

Ringo: "Enough."

Reporter: "Where did you get your hairstyle?"

Paul: "From Napoleon and Caesar."

And so on. The paper called the event Twist-sational.

The Miami Herald took a more jaundiced view after its reporters followed the group around town. "The Beatles whisked through Miami Beach's swinging nightspots early Friday and created all the excitement of four flies at a picnic,"

At the Peppermint, the writer said, "The house band played merrily, ignoring their more famous guests. Twisters gyrated wildly on the dance floor" while John Lennon's wife, Cynthia, and the boys sipped Cokes and ate barbecue.

Dick was there that night. He could attest that they created more excitement than four fruit flies. That night, a car pulled up in front of the club. The driver was a Miami detective well known to Dick, Buddy Dresner. Dick started to wave hello when he saw the others in the car.

"All I see is a lot of hair and big noses," Cami said. "Holy shit, it's the Beatles."

Dick spent some time with them and came away with the feeling that they were good kids caught in the midst of a hurricane and doing their best to keep their balance. John said they were about to start filming *A Hard Day's Night.* This was a subject Dick knew something about. *Hey, Let's Twist!,* about two brothers who try to save their father's failing Italian restaurant by turning it into the Peppermint Lounge, had been a disaster in Dick's mind. "It was a stinker, let me tell you," Dick said.

Dick told John to make sure they got a good script. John said he thought they had one. He was right. *A Hard Day's Night,* written by Alun Owen, became a classic of the genre. Lennon also asked Dick if he would introduce them to Ballard. Dick went to fetch Hank who, at that moment, was finishing his set and was on his way to the men's room in the front of the club. When Dick said the Beatles wanted to meet him, Ballard's reply was again curt and pointed.

Dick rebuked Ballard. "That's not right." he said. "These are nice kids. They're looking to say hello to you like you're some kind of a hero. If you don't come over and say hello to them, I've got some news for you—that's just wrong."

Ballard agreed to think it over. When Dick told Scatsy what happened, he reacted with his standard term of derision, "Ooh, Fah." Like who gives a fuck?

Scatsy's opinion of the group was typically jaundiced. "That Ringo guy there. You turn him upside down and he looks like a toilet plunger."

Dick's next problem was finding a place to seat his famous guests where they wouldn't be bothered during the show. It was obvious that word had gotten out. The club was packed to the gills, far more crowded than it would have been for a normal Ballard show. To put John, Paul, George, and Ringo down front by the stage would have been crazy. Nobody would have paid attention to Ballard.

Cami decided to put them in the balcony overlooking the stage.

Even with the bouncers and the Miami cop watching over them, fans kept climbing the stairs and asking for autographs. Cami realized he needed more muscle. "Then I remembered Ronnie and Romeo," he said.

Finding them in the bar near the front door, he asked if they wouldn't mind lending a hand with the Beatles.

Romeo Martin loved the assignment. He became the Beatles' steadfast guardian. For the rest of the night, whenever Dick glanced into the balcony, Romeo grinned back. Standing behind Ringo, he waved and made hand motions over Ringo's head—*clip, clip, clip*—like he was giving him a haircut.

The Beatles had a great time, loved Ballard, and had their pictures taken with him. Hank managed to look pleased and happy. And nobody got clipped.

At the time, the club had a tradition of painting the names of celebrities on the backs of their chairs, allowing customers to feel their butts were special for sharing the same seat as a famous singer. When the Beatles left, Dick called the sign painter and ordered their names to be painted on the seats.

"Hell, I didn't know if we had the right chairs," he said. "To me it didn't matter."

One day not long afterward, Georgie Blair, the Genovese hit man, was in the place. He saw Ringo's name on a chair and showed surprising interest. "What does that mean?" Georgie said. "He sat in that chair?"

"It's a gimmick we do," Dick said.

"Give me the chair," Georgie said. "My kid loves that guy. How much you want for it?"

The chairs weren't cheap. They were wrought iron, with red cushions and backs. But there was no way Dick could charge Georgie. He was one of Johnny's friends and, even if he weren't, it wouldn't be smart to try to make a buck off him.

"Nothing, what are you kidding? Take it," Dick said.

Blair was thrilled. That wasn't the end of it. There must have been ten wiseguys that wanted Ringo's chair for their kids. Dick could never figure out why, but it was always Ringo. Cami never charged any of them. "I'd just tell Okey, 'Call the sign painter. Tell him we need another Ringo chair.'"

Change Is Gonna Come

The week after the Beatles came to the Peppermint Lounge, Dee Dee Sharp arrived to replace Ballard as the headliner. She was a feisty eighteen-year-old who was already an R&B veteran with four consecutive top ten hits starting in 1962 with "Mashed Potato Time," one of the myriad dances that came along to replace the Twist. It was recorded while she was still a student at Overbrook High School in Philadelphia.

A young prizefighter named Cassius Clay was spending a lot of time around the club. Clay loved R&B singers and was a huge fan of the music. He had been seeing Sharp, on and off, for several months while he was in town training for his shot at the heavyweight title against Sonny Liston on February 25, 1964. And no wonder—Dee Dee was cute and smart and had a mind of her own.

Because he was friendly with trainer Angelo Dundee, Dick had followed Clay's career since he'd won the Olympic gold medal in 1960. He told the staff to give the young fighter the run of the place. Freddy Fasula, one of the bartenders and a former fighter himself, complained about the way Clay swaggered around.

"Who the hell is this guy?" Freddy said. "I'd like to pop him one."

"Forget it. He's going to be the next heavyweight champ," said Dick. "This is the guy that's fighting Liston."

Like almost everyone else in the country, despite what he told his bartender, Dick didn't believe Clay had a chance. He was tall and rangy, while Liston was a prison-honed bull of a man who appeared to enjoy hurting his opponents.

"We don't even want to meet Liston walking down the same street," said Jim Wicks, the manager of Henry Cooper, a respected heavyweight who had nearly beaten Clay early in his career.

Fight experts had begun mentioning Liston in the same company with the greatest heavyweights in history. *Los Angeles Times* sports columnist Jim Murray reflected popular opinion when he said the only thing in which Clay could surpass Liston was reading the dictionary.

The buildup to the fight was enormous. Clay taunted Liston in poetry, predicting in the midst of the "space race" that he would make Liston the first human satellite. His standard term of derision was calling him "that big, ugly bear."

In the weeks before the fight, Clay parked his bus in front of the club. One night, he approached Cami. "I made a record I want you to hear," Clay said.

"You sing?" Dick said. People came up all the time and asked Dick to listen to their records, now that he was the Peppermint Lounge guy. Still he was surprised by Clay's request.

Clay invited him out to his brand-new Corvette. Cassius took out a new device called a compact cassette and slid it into a player on the dashboard. The music started and a raw, untrained but listenable voice started singing. Cami was doubly surprised. "That you?" he said.

Clay nodded. He sat back in his seat, his eyes half-closed, listening, head bobbing slowly with the beat. After his initial shock, Dick found much lacking in the production, music business professional that he was. "I don't think the record will get much play the way it is," Dick said. "But it's a funny business. You become the champ and anything could happen. If you want I can put you with a record company. Let me know."

Dick thought, *I hope he can fight better than he sings.*

Cami continually urged Dee Dee Sharp to get Clay up onstage, but he always resisted. Cami realized that Cassius was basically a shy kid. He was also very polite. When Dick shook his hand the first time, he offered only his fingertips. Among Italians, social conventions are very important, so Dick was dumbfounded, and a little miffed.

Clay noticed. "Nobody can squeeze my hand this way," he said.

It was hard to believe the often withdrawn kid was the same guy who appeared on television boasting how he was going to beat Liston ("You can't hit something you can't see").

One night, Dee Dee finally grabbed Clay and literally dragged him onstage. The crowd cheered and, like a switch had been flipped, the shy kid transformed into the bombastic character he portrayed in public.

"I'm too valuable to be here," he said. "People should be paying five hundred dollars to sit next to me."

Seeing Dick at the back of the room, he pointed. "And you. You owe me ten thousand dollars just for coming in here and making this place look good. I want a check right now."

Not feeling well one night, Dee Dee asked Cami if he would mind if Chuck Jackson filled in for her. The handsome, talented vocalist had managed to keep a string of chart records going since "I Don't Want to Cry" in 1961. A couple nights later, Cami found himself standing on one side of his desk with Sam Cooke on the other. Jackson was sitting in Cami's chair behind the desk and Dee Dee was sitting opposite. She was fired up. Being in the South, the seat of so much recent racial unrest and home to the kind of flagrant segregation that Sharp never experienced growing up in Philadelphia, she was exercised by the unfairness of it all. Famous as he was, Cooke himself had "problems" with his reservations at the ritzy Fontainebleau Hotel when he tried to check in only a few days earlier, until his white manager stepped in and berated the desk clerk.

Dee Dee Sharp ranted, but Cooke urged patience. "You're working in a whites-only club in the South," he said. "That's progress."

"Bullshit," she said.

Cooke was clearly uncomfortable. He was in a difficult spot. He'd won the approval of white audiences when most black entertainers still struggled. It was a double bind to be famous and rich while most of your people remained barred from the tent.

"I understand your frustration," Sam said. In fact, only a few months earlier, Cooke had written his most affecting song about the ongoing civil rights struggle, "A Change Is Gonna Come." Widely interpreted as being influenced by Martin Luther King's "I Have a Dream" speech, the deceptively simple yet profoundly moving song may also have roots in the drowning death of Cooke's young son in the swimming pool at the family home in Los Angeles only weeks before the historic speech in August, 1963. To Sharp, Cooke counseled patience.

"I'm a little older and I see changes, good changes," he said. "Keep the faith, sister. Good things are coming."

"I'm sure they're coming," she said. "But this is the only life I have."

Sharp was excited about Cassius Clay and not just as a prospective boyfriend. She said she thought Clay would do more for the brothers and sisters than all the Martin Luther Kings. Clay had been meeting secretly with Malcolm X, the Black Muslim leader who was terrifying mainstream America with his militant language. Even liberals who marched with Martin Luther King had a hard time with Malcolm.

The Black Muslim leader was in Miami as Clay's guest to attend the fight. Cooke seemed surprised to learn that Malcolm X knew the young fighter, who Cooke knew well, though he withheld his opinion about Clay's value as a civil rights champion. The two men met when Clay was just a goofy kid, fresh off his Olympics win in Rome. At a concert in Clay's hometown, Louisville, Kentucky, Cooke watched from the wings as Clay jumped onstage to sing "Hully Gully" with the rhythm and blues group the Olympics. Cooke and Clay spent a weekend partying together in July 1963 in Las Vegas, where they watched

Liston pummel former heavyweight champion Floyd Patterson, knocking him out in the first round.

Cami knew about Clay and the Muslims. One afternoon, he found Clay's corner man, Bundini Brown, standing outside the club, looking disconsolate. Brown was an underappreciated asset in Clay's career. It was he who authored the famous line, "Float like a butterfly, sting like a bee."

"Where's Cassius?" Dick asked.

"He's with Malcolm X," Brown said. "That's his man now. They got him and they got him good."

Brown also told Cami that when Cassius won the title, Elijah Muhammad, leader of the Black Muslims, intended to replace Angelo Dundee as trainer. Dick and Dundee had become close friends. Years later, Dundee told him that the Muslims did indeed try to replace him at a secret meeting with Elijah Muhammad. As discussions grew tense, the fighter put his hand on Dundee's shoulder and said, "Can you do what he do?" That was the end of the talk of replacing Dundee.

Clay's conversion had already been swirling in fight circles in the days leading up to the big fight. When the manager Bill Faversham got word that Clay flew to New York to address a rally with Malcolm X, he threatened to cancel the fight unless Clay put off announcing his conversion to the Nation of Islam until after the bout. Clay agreed. Only days after Dick last saw him at the club, Cassius went out and proved the experts wrong. Clay was declared the winner by technical knockout when Liston refused to answer the bell in the seventh round.

In the exultant moments of triumph, as the crowd mobbed Clay, he shouted out to Sam Cooke to come into the ring. "Let Sam in," said Clay. "This is the world's greatest rock-and-roll singer."

Ignoring the lavish victory party planned for him at the Fontaine-bleau, Clay, soon to change his name to Muhammad Ali, chose instead to go back to the Hampton House in the black section of town with Malcolm X, football star Jim Brown, and Sam Cooke.

A few months later, Cooke was dead, shot by the manager of a Los

Angeles motel in a struggle, the circumstances of which are still debated. Cooke's recording of "A Change Is Gonna Come" came out a
few weeks later.

> *I go to the movie and I go downtown*
> *Someone keeps telling me don't hang around*
> *It's been a long, long time coming*
> *But I know a change is gonna come . . .*

Dick could never hear "A Change Is Gonna Come" without thinking
of the young, impatient Dee Dee Sharp and Sam Cooke, only a few
years older, yet her tribal elder, telling her that change was coming.

Chapter 18

Star of India

It was the end of the 1964 season. Johnny and Dick were sitting outside the Peppermint, staring at the shimmering bay. All should have been well. The Beatles had come and gone, leaving an afterglow that had yet to fade. Above them, clouds bumped together and, when they did, dumped a few handfuls of rain. It didn't last long, so they stayed put, not saying much. Dick could tell there was something on Johnny's mind, so he waited.

"Maybe it's time for you to get into another business," Johnny said finally. "One where you won't be harassed by the feds. You know Matty wants to buy the joints."

Matty was Matty "the Horse" Ianniello. Dick knew him well. Matty loved the nightclub business and had a lot of clubs and dining houses on the arm, including a famous restaurant in Little Italy called Umberto's Clam House, which was popular with the Genovese family. Johnny said Matty knew people who wanted the Wagon Wheel and the New York Peppermint, along with the Miami Beach club. The Wagon Wheel in New York had become a moneymaker, so Johnny offered it to Dick first, if he wanted to go back.

This caught Dick by surprise. "Not without you," he said. He could tell Johnny was pleased. He didn't know the real reason that Johnny wanted out was that he was once again in the crosshairs. From Dick's perspective, the club was still doing well. The third season at the Miami Peppermint had been good, though the music was changing and the club was no longer a phenomenon. In search of another dance craze to rival the Twist, Dick had reached into the Caribbean and brought back Jamaican ska.

He sent drummer Freddie Scott, who played with Miami rock and roller Steve Alaimo, to Jamaica to audition dancers for an exotic revue. When Cami followed Scott down, he was met at the airport by bandleader Byron Lee, who was popular with tourists at Kingston hotels. Lee introduced Cami to Edward Seaga, a Harvard-educated music producer who was serving as minister of social welfare and economic development for the Jamaican government. Five years earlier, Seaga produced the first record by Byron Lee and his Dragonaires, "Dumplin's," and it was Seaga who had suggested the mainstream bandleader investigate the ska sound of the West Kingston ghetto.

Coincidentally, Seaga represented that same neighborhood in the Jamaican parliament, so it was natural for him to become a booster of the new homegrown musical style. Seaga now encouraged Dick to bring Jamaican ska to the Peppermint.

Ska was taking on the contours of a prospective new dance craze. Atlantic's Ahmet Ertegun came to Kingston (and brought his ace engineer, Tom Dowd) and recorded with Lee's band and other Jamaican vocalists for an album called *Jamaica Ska*.

In England, Jamaican singer Millie Small cut the worldwide smash, "My Boy Lollipop." Despite the arrangement by Jamaican guitarist Ernest Ranglin, the song was not much of a ska record. Still, it looked like this new musical style had all the makings of a craze. Byron Lee and the Dragonaires appeared in August 1964 at the World's Fair in New York City, along with the Blues Busters, Millie Small, Jimmy Cliff, and Prince Buster. Carol Crawford, Jamaica's 1963 Miss World, supplied the dance instructions.

Cami brought up a Jamaican drummer to teach Jamaican ska to the Peppermint house band, along with three breathtakingly gorgeous Jamaican dancers and the Blues Busters. They presented the "Jamaican Ska Revue" at the Peppermint, the first ska nightclub show in the country. After hearing the ska at the Peppermint, Alaimo, Miami's biggest rock-and-roll star, adopted the sound for his next album, *Starring Steve Alaimo*, featuring, "Everybody Likes to Do the Ska." The stars seemed to be aligning, but the ska turned out to be no Twist. The season ended with a whimper, not a bang.

The negotiations with Matty to take over the clubs were straightforward. Matty had two guys from New York put a chunk down on the Miami Beach Peppermint and agreed to pay the rest over five years. Dick didn't like the guys. They were fast-talkers who always paid late. Eventually the late payments and bullshit delays put them months in arrears. Dick let that slide, but the last straw came when he went to the club specifically to warn them a hurricane was coming. He urged them to take the precaution of bringing in the chairs and tables from the outside patio.

They didn't bother and the chairs became missiles that broke the sliding glass doors to the patio, letting several feet of water into the club. That was all Dick could take. The Peppermint was his baby. After he explained the situation, Matty told him to take the place back. He took it on only as a favor, he said. While Dick and Scatsy were up to their knees in the flooded club bailing water, a stranger walked in and asked about buying the place. Dick dismissed him, saying, "Unless you got a lot of money and a gimmick I'd stay away from the Causeway. It's a tough place to get a foothold."

Dick Murray wasn't worried a bit. "We've got both," he said. Realizing Murray was serious, Dick laid out terms for a deal and ten minutes later they were shaking on it. The new owners were Murray and Walt Daisy, a couple of businessmen out of Calumet City near Chicago.

The gimmick was Wayne Cochran and the C.C. Riders, a white soul group from Georgia. Cochran, who dressed flamboyantly and had a

white pompadour that made him look like a member of eighteenth-
century French royalty, was best known as the writer of the teen
death song "Last Kiss." Murray and Daisy overhauled the Peppermint
with a folksier décor and renamed it the Barn. They did a good business with Cochran for many years.

When he owned the New York club, one of Johnny's great worries
about all the attention the Peppermint received was that the authorities would discover the "undisclosed owners," which they finally did
in mid-1965. Even though the State Liquor Authority discovered that
an "undisclosed person" had a piece of the club, they didn't name Mafia chieftain Johnny Futto. It was Sam Kornweisser that they claimed
was siphoning off the profits. The list of charges included a failure to
keep proper books and concealing an owner's arrest record.

"The Peppermint Lounge, which became internationally known
as the original citadel of the twist, was dark and deserted last night,"
The New York Times said on December, 28, 1965, reporting on the
club losing its liquor license.

"The hectic popularity of the night spot has subsided considerably
since its early peak," the *Times* noted drily.

It wasn't just the music that was changing. Rock-and-roll nightclubs
were different. The Peppermint, where it all started, was old news.
There were new, trendy East Side clubs like Arthur, opened with
money from her divorce settlement by Mrs. Richard Burton, after her
husband left her for Liz Taylor.

Sybil Burton, whose photograph at the club's opening dancing
with Rudolf Nureyev was splashed in newspapers around the world,
shocked everybody a few months later by marrying Jordan Chris-
topher, the twenty-five-year-old leader of the house band, the Wild
Ones.

Ondine was another East Side hot spot that featured live rock-and-
roll bands. There was L'Interdit in the Gotham Hotel and Trudy Heller's Trik downtown. They were larger, fancier, and more hospitable

than the dingy dive on 45th Street and they even got a fancy new name, *discotheques*. It was the basic Peppermint Lounge blueprint with a continental accent and a stiff cover charge. All featured something that had come to be called Go-Go dancers, which was nothing more than an elaboration on the Peppermint Lounge rail dancers.

Go-Go dancing came to America from France, where it fled after the Twist went to Paris and settled in Regine Zylberberg's fashionable club, Chez Regine.

Zylberberg had begun her illustrious career as the queen of Parisian nightlife working as the women's room attendant in the Whiskey Au Go Go, an American-style nightclub opened in 1947, featuring whiskey in a wine-dominated culture. Go-Go may have been a shorthanded version of the French term *la gogue*, meaning "joy, happiness" or it may have been appropriated from a phrase the French hepcats picked up from American soldiers, "Go, man, go."

Regine's, which the by-now society matron Zylberberg opened in 1960, featured park-style benches and mirrored walls, with a disc jockey playing the latest sounds. When the Twist took over the club's playlist, Chez Regine suddenly was full every night with Rothschilds, Kennedys, and Rockefellers. Zylberberg stationed dancers in booths beside the stage, a practice soon picked up by her former boss at the Whiskey Au Go Go, where it was spotted by a shady character with Mob connections of his own, Elmer Valentine. Valentine had come to Paris in 1963 with a vaguely formed plan to open a club there and dive into the colorful life of an expat. In the end, the life was less colorful than he imagined and he returned to Los Angeles. But his trip had not been wasted. He was now determined to open a discotheque modeled on the Parisian clubs.

Valentine had made $55,000 when he sold his share of a club in Hollywood called PJ's that was very popular with the teens. He put $20,000 of it into refurbishing a place at the corner of Sunset and Clark called the Party that was stinking up the neighborhood. He renamed it the Whisky a Go Go and, unlike the European versions that featured disc jockeys playing records, went hunting for a live attraction that would help the club take off. He found Johnny Rivers, a twenty-one-year-old guitar whiz from Louisiana who was booked three nights a week into Gazzarri's, an Italian eatery on La Cienega.

Rivers agreed to become the Whisky's marquee act, playing three sets a night with a drummer and bassist. "Johnny was like the Pied Piper," Valentine said years later. "People were waiting in line to go in and dance."

Between sets, the audience would dance to records played by a deejay. But, in a combination of genius and pragmatism, Valentine decided the disc jockey would be a girl, attractive, of course. The Whisky was a small club. Dancers gyrated so close to the performers that they could literally reach out and strum their guitars for them. So to save space, Valentine decided the girl spinning the records would be suspended above the audience in a cage. It was a stroke of pure inspiration. Valentine couldn't help it if the sight of a beautiful woman twirling records above their heads touched something deep and sensual in patrons.

Valentine held a contest to find the right girl. But on opening night, January 15, 1964, the contest winner called in tears to say her mother wouldn't let her take the job. Thrown into the breach was Valentine's cigarette girl, Patty Brockhurst.

"She had on a slit skirt," Valentine recalled. "So she's up there playing the records. She's a young girl, so while she's playing 'em, all of a sudden she starts dancing to 'em. It was a dream. It worked." The Go-Go dancer was born. Or, with a nod to Janet Huffsmith back in New York, reborn in a new, fancy package.

The new club was a hit from the day it opened

Brockhurst was such a hit that within two weeks Valentine added two more cages and two more dancing blondes, and began officially calling them Go-Go girls.

Jayne Mansfield and Steve McQueen were regulars. When the Beatles arrived in Los Angeles in August 1964, six months after visiting the two Peppermints, they made sure to hit the Whisky. Valentine was their personal chauffeur. He brought Mansfield along for entertainment. "John was putting Jayne on," Valentine said. "'Jayne, those aren't really your tits, are they?' He got her to show them to him."

Go-Go dancers soon had a uniform to go with their new status. Fringe dresses and shiny white Courrèges boots, named for their French designer, became de rigeur on rock-and-roll dance shows. A year after the Whisky opened, the television show *Hullabaloo* introduced the Go-Go dancer to the rest of America. During the "*Hullabaloo* A Go-Go" segment at the end of the show, the special guests performed in a nightclub setting while the Go-Go dancers spun and twirled in cages above them, not that far, really, from Janet, Ronnie, and the other girls jumping on the rail at the Pep.

About this time, out of nowhere, the spoils from one of the biggest jewel heists in history fell into Johnny and Dick's lap. Hy Gordon, a legendary fence for anything extremely valuable and easily transportable—coins, jewels, art—turned up at Johnny's house very late one night.

Afraid that Johnny's phone was tapped, Hy did not call ahead. He drove up the dark alley behind the house and banged on the garage door. Surprised by the noise, Johnny asked Dick (who was visiting) to accompany him and they warily ventured outside to see who the late-night visitor was. Hy was standing in the darkened alley, looking extremely nervous. "I had to see you right away," he said.

Johnny, puzzled by the late hour, wanted to know what was so important it couldn't wait till morning. "We got a big score," Hy said.

Hy walked into the garage and pulled out what looked like a shiny golf ball. He put it into Johnny's hand. "It's the Star of India," he said.

Johnny hardly glanced at it before dropping it into his son-in-law's palm. Even in the dim light, the stone glowed. Cami couldn't believe what he was seeing. Dick and Johnny had just been watching the news. The lead story that night, October 29, 1964, was the theft of the 563-carat star sapphire and two dozen other irreplaceable gems from the American Museum of Natural History in New York. Valued at

$400,000, the theft was already being called the "jewel heist of the century."

Suddenly dubious, Cami said that if he was indeed holding the Star of India, the thieves must have jumped on the first flight to get down there so fast.

"They drove straight through the night," said Gordon.

"Who pulled it off?" Johnny said.

"Murph the Surf and his boys."

"Murph the Surf?" Dick said, startled.

Johnny looked at Dick. "You know him?"

"Sure. He's always in the Peppermint."

Jack "Murph the Surf" Murphy was a surfing champion, artist, musician, thief, and several other things that on most occasions would qualify him to sit down to Sunday dinner at Johnny's table. But this wasn't the time. Johnny turned back to Hy. "You know this Murph kid good?"

"I get rid of all his swag," Gordon said.

"Then tell him he's got to give it back. Every fucking piece."

Gordon was astonished. This was a monster score. How could they turn their backs on it? Johnny wasn't interested in debating. "What's the matter with you, Hy? The feds will be all over us with this. You don't think we're going to let a punk kid heat up the whole city, do you? If they don't give it back, and I mean all of it, they're going to have more to deal with than the cops."

Hy slumped back to his car. Twenty minutes later, Cami and Futto were on the road. As they drove, Dick tried to put what he knew about Murphy together with the image of an international jewel thief. Murphy seemed a young clubber, nothing more. A bit better-looking than most maybe, in his white chinos and floral shirts, a nice guy, but certainly nothing special. He worked as a beach boy in a nearby hotel, running drinks and towels out to the healthy and the beautiful of South Florida. He and several friends spent most of their time off-duty in the Peppermint's bar, downing tropical drinks and throwing appraising glances at the bikini-clad girls.

Dick and Johnny rolled up to Santo Trafficante's house. Johnny was a powerful man, but Santo was in a whole different orbit. The most powerful American gangster in Batista-era Cuba, Trafficante was a close ally of Sam Giancana, the man who helped put John Kennedy in the White House. He also happened to be the acknowledged top mobster in South Florida.

Johnny went to Santo to make sure he got the right story just in case Hy went off and did something stupid. Johnny liked Hy and trusted him, but something as big as this had to be shared, because anything could happen.

Hy had gone to Johnny hoping his Mafia friends might find a way to sell the jewels. The problem, which Johnny understood immediately, was that the gems were one-of-a-kind, unfenceable stones that would be recognized as soon as they were offered for sale. Trafficante quickly agreed with Johnny's actions and the pair were back home in a short time.

Murphy didn't like what he heard. He and his partners, Alan Kuhn and Roger Clark, had taken the risk, sneaking through a window at the museum and grabbing the jewels. Of course, the museum made it easy for them because the burglar alarms on the fourth floor of Morgan Hall were not functioning. Besides the Star of India, which had been donated by none other than J. Pierpont Morgan, the theft included the sixteen-carat Eagle Diamond, one of the largest stones of its type ever discovered in the continental United States, and the one-hundred-carat DeLong Ruby, the world's most perfect star ruby.

The FBI was on the case in hours and, according to *Time* magazine, quickly learned from "confidential police sources" who was responsible.

When the whole wacky affair was done, after weeks of negotiations conducted through intermediaries, the museum got back its sapphire (found in a Miami bus station locker) and ruby (found in a phone booth), Murphy docilely went to prison and Hy Gordon got a nice payday of $25,000 for his trouble getting the jewels back and serving up Murphy to the law.

The Eagle Diamond was never recovered. It was likely cut up and sold off piecemeal.

The conventional story is that the negotiations for the return of the ruby were conducted through an intermediary, an unidentified female real estate broker. The real story, according to Cami, was that it was Johnny's pal Lee Ratner who brokered the deal. He went to his rich friend, John D. MacArthur, knowing that MacArthur could easily handle the $25,000 payoff to get the stone back to its rightful owners. Though few knew him outside his circle of rich friends and colorful characters like Johnny on the fringes of society, MacArthur was one of only five living billionaires. The fortune he had amassed would fund one of America's great philanthropic foundations, the John D. and Catherine T. MacArthur Foundation. He was also the brother-in-law of Helen Hayes, the beloved leading lady of the stage, whose interest was part of why he got involved in the recovery of the jewels.

It was MacArthur who personally found the DeLong Ruby ten months after the heist at a pay phone in a gas station near the Sunshine State Parkway. The faintly pink star with six spindly arms was about the size of a large grape.

MacArthur took the stone back to room 454 of the Colonnades Hotel, a collection of pale buildings stitched together with arched colonnades, which he owned. After a jeweler authenticated the stone, MacArthur showed the gem to reporters, flipping it in his fingers like it was a silver dollar.

"Here's Ruby," declared the front page headline in the *New York Daily News* the day after its recovery. The following day, Sunday, September 5, 1965, an estimated ten thousand people streamed into the Gothic halls of the museum across the street from Central Park. The Star of India, the DeLong Ruby and the Midnight Star Sapphire were laid out on black velvet inside a bulletproof glass case, safe at last.

MacArthur claimed a $25,000 tax deduction. A friend said MacArthur was "very frugal," not stupid.

MacArthur died in 1978, leaving behind strained relations with his children and a spotty record with the government. But each

March after his death, friends gathered to toast his memory and the genius grants his foundation made every year to keep his name alive.

◎

After giving up the Peppermints in the summer of 1965, Dick and Vinny concentrated on their management business. They quickly got on the trail of one of their biggest successes, a girl group from Brooklyn. Cami wasn't initially interested in representing them. As Vinny liked to say, "If you want to live a long and happy life, avoid managing girl groups."

But the guy who pitched them to Dick said they were killing at this little place under the L in New York called the Club Illusion. Dick sent Vinny to check them out. Vinny reported back that they were raw, but their sound and harmonies were excellent. The lead singer, Barbara Harris, could really sing.

Vinny signed the Toys, nurtured them, coddled them, and finally got them a record deal. He introduced them to songwriters Sandy Linzer and Denny Randell, whom Vinny had allowed to sleep on his couch during their early days. They gave the girls a song called "A Lover's Concerto," a little Motown-esque mid-tempo number based on a melody from Chopin. In a month where the latest smashes by the Beatles, the Rolling Stones, and the Supremes held down the top positions on the charts, the Toys soared all the way to number two.

It was a big score and Vinny and Dick put the group on the road, where they played all the major television rock-and-roll shows, as well as the big hotels in Vegas. They even had a cameo in a surf-and-tits movie called *It's a Bikini World.*

Berry Gordy of Motown Records heard them when they played Detroit's Roostertail club, an expansive entertainment center that sat three thousand patrons in a genial setting adjacent to the Detroit River. After sending the girls a dozen roses each, Berry approached Vinny with an offer to buy their contract. Riding high with big hits by the Miracles, Marvin Gaye, Martha and the Vandellas, the Supremes, and others, Gordy offered $100,000 for the Toys. That was a lot of money then, and now.

Vinny called Dick to ask what he thought. Dick trusted Vinny, who he thought was closer to the situation. Vinny decided to turn down Gordy. "I thought, what are you kidding?" Marchese said. "This is going to be a monster group. They're going to be bigger than the Supremes."

That was aiming high. The Supremes were in the midst of one of the great hit-making streaks in pop music history, five straight number one records: "Where Did Our Love Go," "Baby Love," "Come See About Me," "Stop! In the Name of Love," and "Back in My Arms Again." After "Nothing but Heartaches" reached only number eleven, they hit number one again with "I Hear a Symphony" in 1965.

Vinny didn't have another hit song for the Toys. They put out two more Linzer-Randell numbers as singles, "Attack" and "Toy Soldier." Neither song was another "Lover's Concerto."

Energetic as ever, Vinny tried everything, moving them from one label to the next, trying out different styles. He traveled with them on tours through the South, where he encountered the same spit-in-your-face racism Dick got from the beverage agents at the Peppermint. On the road, he often slept with a chair jammed under the door handle for fear of getting beaten, or robbed. Living in the all-cash world of rhythm and blues nightclubs, Vinny routinely went to bed with as much as $30,000 tucked away in a drawer. Despite all his efforts, nothing worked. The Toys joined the ranks of one-hit wonders, permanently relegated to oldies radio.

Top of the Home

Tommy Maren, the undisclosed owner of Dinty Moore's in Boston, lived in Keystone Point, a development of million-dollar homes near Biscayne Bay, in the winter months. He came by the Peppermint during the day to bullshit with Dick, frequently telling him that his gregarious nature was made for the restaurant business. Maren was considerably older than Cami, but he said that if Dick was interested, maybe they'd open a restaurant together.

Dick *was* interested, particularly now that he was out of the nightclub business. He was thirty years old, with two young children, an unhappy wife, and a father-in-law who was marked for death. It seemed past time to find a little stability and more regular hours.

Dick learned that the owners of the Home Federal Bank building, the tallest structure in Broward County, wanted to put a restaurant on the top floor of their nineteen-story building. He liked the idea. But when his lack of restaurant experience caused the banker that was asked to finance the deal to hesitate, Dick instantly thought of Tommy Maren. "I don't have experience but my partner does. He owns Dinty

Moore's in Boston." Dinty Moore's was a top-drawer establishment with a national reputation. That landed the deal.

At first, Scatsy hated the idea. "Whatta ya, outa ya fuckin' mind?" He couldn't get over the fact that they'd sold off the Peppermints.

Okey was also alarmed. "Can you imagine how much we're going to have to pay for napkins?"

Dick assured them everything would work out, and when they checked out the location they were convinced. Dinty Moore's Top of the Home offered a panoramic view. On one side looking north was downtown Fort Lauderdale. On the other side looking south was downtown Miami, and in between was a fifty-mile panoramic view of the Atlantic Ocean.

The restaurant took off from day one. There were long lines waiting for tables. Within a few months, however, Maren fell ill and Dick bought him out.

Toward the end of the first season, Cami got a call from Joe Baum, the head of Restaurant Associates. One of the most powerful men in the dining industry, Baum had franchised the first chain restaurants in the United States, including the famous Four Seasons in New York. He wanted to buy Dick out.

"You should think about this," Johnny told Dick. "With Maren gone and you with no restaurant experience. You know it's different than a nightclub."

Dick did think about it. Baum kept making offers, each better than the last, but Cami refused each time. Finally Baum got the picture and backed out, but as he did, he gave the young restaurateur the best advice Dick had heard since Morris Levy told him not to mess with the whiskey. He suggested that Dick hire Joe Ezbicki, executive chef of the Boca Raton Hotel and Resort, one of the best convention facilities in the country. Baum said he'd tried, unsuccessfully, to lure Ezbicki to be the executive chef at the Four Seasons in New York.

"Why should I get him?" Dick asked, unconvinced.

"Because he's one of the best chefs in the country, that's why,"

Baum said. He did issue a warning. "He's difficult to work with be-cause he wants everything perfect."

That only cemented Dick's opinion. He had a perfectionist streak himself and knew that the best were always demanding. Cami had to make Ezbicki a partner to get him, but it was worth it. Ezbicki traced his talents to his experience as a child hanging around his Polish mother's kitchen. Whatever the source, his handiwork was extraordi-nary. Chef Joe was inducted into the French Vatel Club, an especially noteworthy honor since he was not French. It helped, too, that Meyer Lansky, a frequent guest at the restaurant, set up Dick with Max Klein, purveyor of the best beef around. Klein always made sure Ezbicki got the best cuts at a fair price. The second season, the restaurant opened as Dick Cami's Top of the Home rooftop restaurant, a landmark on the Miami fine-dining scene for the next twenty-six years.

Lou Clerico, who designed the Playboy Club, laid out the interior, which took up the entire top floor of the Home Savings Bank. When diners got out of the elevators, they walked into another century, the opulent, gaslight era of Diamond Jim Brady and Lillian Russell, with red-flocked wallpaper, dark mahogany woodwork, tables set with crisp white linen, and red velvet chairs.

Paul Vallon manned the piano bar in the lounge, where the wealthy patrons danced and listened to singing bartenders Sonny and Gun-ther do their favorite songs. Rich widows sat on barstools drinking fizzy wine, enjoying the music and view. They were so loaded down with jewelry that Dick once asked Vinny, as a joke, to keep an eye on one of them to see that she didn't fall over.

Cami hired Vallon's extraordinary wife, Virginia , to be the dining-room hostess. In heels, she stood about six-foot-three, and was stun-ning in her custom-fashioned gold and rhinestone evening gown.

Once the restaurant opened and word got around that there was a top-drawer New York–style restaurant in South Florida, the Top of the Home was booked solid for weeks. The Rat Pack ate there, along with famous sports figures such as Mickey Mantle, fight trainer Angelo

Dundee, and ex-heavyweight champ Rocky Marciano, who became a good friend to Cami, as well as being one of the cheapest men Cami ever met. According to Dick, Rocky liked to travel to foreign countries with no luggage, claiming it was stolen on the way. His hosts would invariably rush out to buy the champ both clothing and luggage.

There were plenty of movie stars, politicians, and other dignitaries, ranging from J. Edgar Hoover to Jimmy Hoffa, another good friend of Cami's, and Harold Gibbons, the number two International Teamsters vice president under Hoffa. A fair number of mobsters, who always enjoyed a good meal, also showed up. Johnny stayed out of sight, though, repeating his disclaimer that he didn't want to "stink up the joint."

Every year, in summer, when they closed for the season, Dick traveled to Europe, where he scouted the best restaurants and visited every major winery in France, buying cases of wine direct. Dining in Europe inspired numerous innovations at the restaurant. From Rome, Cami brought back the recipe for fettuccine Alfredo. From Vienna, he got the idea for the made-from-scratch smorgasbord on ice set up at the restaurant entrance. The idea of preparing dishes tableside also came by way of his European sojourns.

Over time, the affable Cami became as much a part of the dining experience as Ezbicki's dishes and elaborate presentations. The famous, not so famous, and infamous were pleased when he stopped by their tables and sat down for a chat.

Meyer Lansky was not only a regular guest, he considered himself a gourmand and was not above asking to watch the chef prepare his meal. Lansky was particularly taken with Chef Ezbicki's matzoh balls. Ezbicki graciously accepted the compliment, adding, "Mr. Lansky, here we call them matzoh dumplings."

"You can call them what you want," Lansky said. "They are even better than what my mother made."

Lansky and his second wife, Teddy, went at it like the Bickersons. Meyer liked to have a cigarette after he ate. When he lit up, she'd snap at him, "So, who told you you could smoke," and snatch the cigarette out of his mouth.

Barney Baker, one of Jimmy Hoffa's boys from Chicago who was known as Hoffa's ambassador of violence, was having dinner one night. Vinny Marchese was sitting in Dick's office when the maitre d' rushed in. Barney wanted to buy a half case of Romanée-Conti, his favorite wine. How much should they charge him?

"Three-fifty," Dick said.

Vinny couldn't believe that Dick was charging only three dollars and fifty cents, and told him so. "What do you mean?" Dick responded. "It's three hundred and fifty dollars. That's what a single bottle costs. They're getting a deal. That's one of the rarest wines in the world. Barney's my buddy—believe me, he knows it. They'll be back, wanting it again next year. It's the same old story."

Alcohol was a curse and curative for the comedian Joe E. Lewis, another frequent patron, often half in the bag. Frank Sinatra, who loved Joe E. and even made a movie about his life called *The Joker Is Wild*, worried about him. He sent his friend, Jilly Rizzo, to see Dick about slowing Joe E. down.

"Frank is thinking, maybe you could hold back on the whiskey," Jilly said.

Cami answered that he tried, but Lewis was hard to control. "He gets mad if the glass isn't filled to the top." Dick added that he made sure Lewis got home safely. "I'm no treatment center," he flared. "And besides, tell Frank that people who live in tin houses shouldn't throw can openers."

Jilly was a friend, so Dick knew he could tell him straight. Rizzo knew Dick was right. Frank commented on his fiftieth birthday, only half-joking, that he would have the body of a twenty-two-year-old man if he hadn't spent all those years drinking with Joe E. Lewis.

Johnny loathed Sinatra but Dick had a more nuanced view after watching Sinatra up close in Miami, where he and his Rat Pack pals were all over the place. They didn't come to the Peppermint; that wasn't their scene. But when Dick opened the Top of the Home, Sinatra came in because, as he often said, they served the best food south of New York. He was always a gentleman, but Dick knew he could be an asshole when he was drinking.

The first time Sinatra came in, Dick assigned his floor captain to attend to him exclusively. The man refused, flatly, and with such vehemence that Dick couldn't understand it. "He once poured a bottle of champagne on my head," the captain explained.

Sinatra invariably regretted his bad behavior the next day and habitually paid up and tipped big for the trouble he'd caused, whether it was ordering five hundred hamburgers from a take-out place or humiliating a server. One time, though, he got himself in a jam that, had it been anyone else, would have landed him in a private hospital room, or worse.

The Dream Bar was one of the hottest hot spots in Miami Beach. It was a popular joint and few knew it was owned by the boys, one of whom was Pasquale "Patsy" Erra, a major South Florida mafioso and another friend of Johnny's. Cami heard the story from Terry Teriaca, another owner, who was there when the incident happened. One night, Sinatra came in with a big party that included Sammy Davis, Jilly Rizzo, Joe Fischetti of Chicago—one of the wiseguys Lucky Luciano assigned to handle Sinatra for the Mob—and a bevy of ladies. Of course, the staff went out of their way to make Frank comfortable.

Sinatra was plowed. They seated him in the balcony over the stage. For some reason, Frank picked up a chair and threw it over the railing. Luckily, it didn't crown anyone. Teriaca rushed up. "Is there a problem, Frank?"

"I didn't like that chair," Sinatra said.

"Fine, let me get you another one," Terry said.

"If I don't like that one, I'm going to throw it, too."

"You throw this one, Frank, and you're going to follow it," Teriaca said.

Just then the waitress approached the table with a tray of drinks. "Take the drinks back," Teriaca said. "Mr. Sinatra is leaving."

Jilly and Fischetti, according to Teriaca, tried to settle the beef, but he wasn't having any of it. Sinatra went wild with rage, getting so mad that he dismissed the limousines waiting out front and forced the whole party to hoof it back to the Fontainebleau, where he was headlining.

Still raging, Sinatra woke up the Fontainebleau's owner, Ben Novack, demanding retribution. Novack was eager to accommodate him until he found out where the incident occurred, and who was involved. Teriaca was no one to trifle with. But Sinatra was in a fighting mood. When Novack put Sinatra together with Patsy Erra, the gangland leader said he'd be willing to have Teriaca meet the singer, but he'd get his ass kicked.

"If Terry threw you out, you had it coming," Erra said.

When Sinatra sobered up, he apologized to Teriaca. "I was out of order," he said. He figured he was off the hook.

That night, however, the crew from the Dream Bar was sitting ringside at the Fontainebleau when the band struck up the *Peter Gunn* theme, Sinatra's entrance music. Spotlights swept the stage dramatically as Sinatra came out of the wings and started to sing. Suddenly, Terry stood, picked up a chair, and tossed it up on the stage. Stepping aside, Sinatra squinted into the lights to see who had hurled the chair. He saw Erra and his boys. They were all standing. "I deserved that," Frank said meekly.

Of course, Sinatra was famous for threatening beatings—and, in some cases, having beatings actually administered. Shecky Greene was Sinatra's opening act. He liked to kid Sinatra, but Frank didn't always find it humorous. One night Shecky opened with a biting one-liner. "I want to tell you folks that Frank is one hell of a guy who looks out for his fellow man," Greene said. "Last night, when two guys were giving me a beating, he put out his hand said, 'That's enough. He's had enough.' What a guy."

One of the many characters who frequented the Top was a mobster known as Donald Duck. His real name was Louis Lamberti and he was a Gambino soldier. Lamberti wore thick, horn-rimmed glasses and never stopped talking. And since he never got embarrassed by any of the slaphappy things he said, why should anyone else?

One time, Donald was eating at the Top and went into a story about his time in the can in North Carolina, where they once gave him a brain scan. "They told me I got a very bizarre mind."

"I'm sorry to hear that," Dick said.

"What do you mean sorry?" Donald said. "That's good, ain't it?"

Donald's friend, a tall, pleasant fellow named Wiggles, interjected. "He thinks it's like a *bazaar*, you know, where people go to have fun and shop."

As this was going on, Judge Alfonso Sepe stopped by the table on his way out of the restaurant. Sepe was widely known for his creative approach to punishment. He once ordered a man accused of shooting into the home of an interracial couple (no one was hit) to attend Saturday breakfasts at a black church and to work for a black charity. Dick stood and shook the judge's hand. Sepe thanked him for a lovely meal and left. As Dick sat back down, Donald Duck said, "Hey, Dick, ain't that guy a judge?"

"That's Judge Sepe."

"I knew it. That son of a bitch gave me three years once."

Another frequent guest was Leo Cahill, a longtime professional football coach in Canada for the Toronto Argonauts. He made headlines when he paid Larry Csonka, Jim Kiick, and Paul Warfield of the famous undefeated Miami Dolphins Super Bowl–winning football team $1 million each to leave Miami and come to Memphis, which had just been given a franchise in the upstart World Football League.

When Leo came into the restaurant, he was wearing a huge gold medallion with a lightning bolt running through the letters TCB. It was the biggest gold chain Cami had ever seen. He immediately recognized it as Elvis Presley's business and personal motto, "Taking Care of Business." Cahill was so conservative, Dick could hardly believe him wearing something like that.

"Where'd you get that?" he asked.

"Presley gave it to me," Leo said.

Elvis was a devoted football fan. When Memphis got its team,

Elvis went to the owners and asked if he could sit on the sidelines with the players. To avoid disrupting the game, he suggested posing as a water boy, wearing a sweat suit, a cap, and sunglasses, with a towel around his neck.

Cahill was delighted and approved the arrangement. Even though the team folded in 1974, after only one season, Elvis was in disguise on the bench for every game and nobody found him out. He gave the gold medallion to Leo as a thank-you. "I have to admit," Cami said. "Every time I hear the rumor that Elvis is alive and hiding out somewhere, I think, well, he did it once."

Dick got a call one day from his old ally Al Miniaci. His nephew, John Juliano, had just bought the old Copacabana nightclub in New York. Seeing what Dick had done with the Top, Miniaci asked if he'd mind going up to New York to help his nephew reopen it.

Dick was glad to help and brought in Vinny to lend a hand. Marchese did some research and discovered it was first owned by Rudy Vallee, who opened the club as the Villa Vallee in 1929. Even to Dick, who loved the old songs and the old singers, Rudy Vallee was a name straight out of the dark ages. But when Vinny checked, he found that, fifty years later, Vallee was still around. They invited him to the grand reopening party, figuring the draw would be irresistible to reporters and nostalgia buffs among New York's party crowd.

Vallee showed up in a Nehru suit, looking like a million bucks, even though he was on the shady side of eighty. He brought his considerably younger wife and a meticulously kept scrapbook filled with articles about the club in his day.

He also showed off pictures of his house in California, a huge mansion perched on a cliff overlooking the Pacific Ocean. "I told my wife that when I go, she should sell the place to an Arab and throw herself in on the deal for nothing," he said.

Dick laughed but couldn't help thinking, with that deadpan delivery, that maybe he meant it.

"When do I go on?" Vallee asked.

This threw them. Vinny and Dick hadn't considered putting the man onstage. His presence was all they expected, to confer a certain cobwebby history to the proceedings. But hell, Dick thought, the crowd will go for it just for the novelty. And somehow, there was something so assured and comfortable about him that Dick doubted there would be a pathetic spectacle.

Vallee had a tape recorder with his music on it, along with a foot pedal he used to stop and start it. He grabbed it while Vinny led the way to the lounge, where a three-piece combo was playing. They made a hasty exit as the aged songster slid up to the mike. He stepped on the foot pedal and off he went, singing "Winchester Cathedral," a recent hit by British songwriter Geoff Stephens, who performed under the name the New Vaudeville Band. He sang in a tinny style to copy the sound of a megaphone like the one Vallee once used. Vallee was singing a song imitating the guy that imitated him. The only one who wasn't confused was Rudy. Everyone was impressed. What a guy.

After the show Dick, Vinny, and Vallee sat around talking with a tableful of notables, including Hollywood film director Otto Preminger. "This place must hold some fond memories for you, Rudy," Preminger said.

"It was at the height of my career," said Vallee. "I'm in the main room performing while my wife was upstairs fucking the plumber."

Jimmy Hoffa was a regular at the Top. The Kennedys made him out to be a crook, but Dick had a soft spot for him. "I knew one thing for sure. No one fought harder for his men than Hoffa did. He knew the names of everyone, and I mean he could name thousands of Teamster delegates." He told Cami that before you go into a room with someone, find out everything you can about them. "Even if you're just having a cigar. You should always be more prepared than the next guy. And another thing: never be on time, always before."

It was advice that Dick heeded. Ironically, the Teamster leader might have violated his own maxim when he went to a meeting with the wrong men. No one knows the real story of Jimmy's disappearance. The FBI figured Hoffa was killed by organized crime elements to prevent him from regaining control of his union, although they never made anybody for the killing.

Jimmy's wife, Josephine, was a strong, beautiful woman, but months went by after his disappearance before she went out in public again. When she did return to Top of the Home, she was in the company of two friends, both wives of Teamster officials. As Dick sat down, he could see Josephine had been crying.

One of the other women explained that someone had told Josephine that Jimmy was cheating on her before he went missing. This was something Dick knew about, so he looked her in the eye and said, "That's a lie, Josephine. Whoever told you that just wants to hurt you. I'm going to tell you a story I've never shared before."

The story was told to Dick by a Teamster vice president who was present at a union convention in Savannah, Georgia. The official had brought his girlfriend along and she brought an attractive friend of hers. The union man approached Hoffa, apparently hoping to advance his career by serving as a pimp for Hoffa. "My girlfriend is here with her girlfriend," he said. "She thinks you're cute. You want to have dinner with us tonight?"

"Excuse me?" Hoffa said.

"My girlfriend's girlfriend—she's a real looker and wants me to ask you to join us for dinner tonight."

Hoffa froze him out. "Are you talking to me?" he said.

The guy retreated. "I guess not," he said.

"I didn't think so," Hoffa replied, glaring at the guy.

Josephine loved the story. "Oh my," she said, turning to her friends, who threw big smiles her way.

"A lot of guys I know would tell you the same thing," Dick said. "The last thing Jimmy had on his mind was other women. There are a lot of jealous people out there who want to hurt you. Don't listen to them."

Chapter 20

Don't You Know
This Is the Life?

Johnny Futto never forgot what he was a part of, or what the
Mob's lack of a retirement plan meant. But even he had blind
spots. Futto believed he could remake himself in the image of the
stand-up businessman he seemed to be. The problem was that keeping his hand in the rackets enough to keep money coming in made
him a target, especially for the greedy wiseguys who'd thrown over
decades of tradition by inducting a younger generation of members
for a fee of fifty thousand dollars. These were the men whom Futto
called the "ice cream mob."

Johnny Futto dodged the bullet many times over the years, but he
could never quite break free from his past. He continued to imagine
that somehow he could get out if he managed his affairs just right, or
kept the right men in his corner. But the Mob didn't work like that.

One afternoon in 1966, Dick and Johnny were leaving Johnny's
house when the FBI agent Peter Clemente came running up. "Johnny,
they're going to kill you," he said. It was Georgie Blair all over again.
Johnny paused at the passenger-side door of his baby-blue Cadillac
and waited for Clemente to catch his breath.

"Why don't you let us help you?" Clemente said.

"Leave me alone, will you," Johnny said. "Don't I have enough trouble with my own people?"

When they were seated in the Caddy, Dick behind the wheel, he started up on a familiar theme of his own. Suddenly aware that Johnny's fate hung in the balance again, he suggested his father-in-law leave the country. "If you're out of the country, you can make a deal," Dick said. "If anybody has the right, it's you."

"Why should I run? I'm not the one who did anything wrong," Johnny said. "If they think they've got me, they better think again. I wasn't made with a finger. Besides, there are things I can do. I'm not out of options yet."

He always carried a snub-nosed pistol. "Don't forget, I'm carrying, too," Johnny told Dick. "They're going to be white as mozzarella when I see them coming."

Seemingly nonchalant to danger, Johnny's calmness in dealing with it made his family, friends, and sycophants almost forget that death was stalking him. Dick, however, was not convinced by Johnny's reassurance. *Assassins do it from behind*, Dick thought.

On March 17, 1967, Johnny had a business meeting with Lee Ratner at his office building in Miami Beach. Normally, Dick would have driven him. But this day he went to pick up St. Patrick's Day decorations for the restaurant. Joe Diamond, a jewel thief and cat burglar, took Dick's place at the wheel of the Cadillac.

Driving along under the bright Florida sun, Dick felt like singing. He remembered the time he gave Jerry Vale a ride to look at an apartment building he'd purchased with comedians Buddy Hackett and Shecky Greene. On the way, Jerry sang along with the radio, harmonizing with Clyde McPhatter, Marvin Gaye, and Freddie Scott. He was so good at capturing the spirit of the rock-and-roll tunes that Dick suggested he try it out for real.

Vale shook his head. "I'm a balladeer and that's where I'll stay," he'd said.

Dick admired the man's self-awareness. Vale knew who he was

and it didn't matter to him that the rest of the world had turned its back to his music.

Dick's reverie was interrupted by a news flash on the radio.

"We've got breaking news that Mob kingpin Johnny 'Futto' Biello was gunned down and killed today in a Miami Beach parking lot."

The newsman went on to recount Joe Valachi's testimony before Congress four years earlier, when he'd named Johnny one of three Mob kingpins living in South Florida. After that, the FBI was all over them. Johnny used to joke that one good thing about it was that nobody would dare to clip him with the FBI watching.

Dick's stomach tightened as he listened in disbelief. Tears flooded his eyes and ran down his face as the big Lincoln careened across three lanes of traffic on I-95. It was a miracle he didn't crash into another car. Along with the weight of grief that knocked the wind out of him, Dick felt a lacerating guilt close in as he turned around and headed for Johnny's house. He should have been with him. He'd felt it that morning. His speed steadily increased, as though he might still do something.

He glanced over and saw the St. Patrick's Day decorations on the seat next to him. Hats, garlands, napkins for Johnny's life. His father-in-law had often counseled him against troubling himself with guilt. "The worst beatings are the ones we give ourselves." But this time Dick couldn't let up. Sure, if he'd been there, maybe he'd have been killed, too. But maybe he could have saved Johnny. The waves of guilt came again and again before he pulled into the driveway behind the Miami Shores house.

Normally, the Biello house was filled with the rich, juicy odors of Italian cooking mixing with the smell of the sea just out the front door. Not that day. The women were crying. Dick's friends were there, Victor Centrella and Carl Cohen, the owner of the Lucerne Hotel. "They finally got him. They finally got him. They finally got him," Victor kept repeating.

Scatsy was in the kitchen, out on his feet. Dick shook Scatsy by the shoulders, finally shouting at him to reveal what he knew. "They shot him six times in the back. He never knew what hit him," Scatsy said.

Joe Diamond was sitting at the wheel when Johnny came out of Ratner's office and walked toward the car. The killer stepped up behind Johnny as he was getting into the car. Just like that, in the middle of the afternoon in a public parking lot in Miami Beach. Usually the driver would be suspect in a hit like that. But nobody believed Joe would turn on Johnny. They were too close. Johnny loved thieves, who he always said took the greatest chances, and Joe Diamond was the best. A regular at the Top, he was sitting at the bar one night sizing up a bejeweled old woman who was a good friend of Dick's, Betty Jarwood, Louis "Lepke" Buchalter's widow. Dick had to scold him, "No, no, no, Joe."

No, Joe was with Johnny up to the hilt. He said that when he heard the shots, he threw open the driver's side door and rolled under the cars parked next to him. It was a miracle they didn't go after him. Only a cat burglar could get away clean. He kept on rolling and rolling under the cars until he was a few rows away; then he jumped up and took off. There was nothing he could have done for Johnny anyway. If he'd stayed, he'd be dead, too. It was a good thing that Scatsy or Dick wasn't driving because they would have most likely gone after the shooter and would have been killed. In the end, it hardly mattered who the shooter was. He was only following orders.

Scatsy, in shock, was too dazed to ID the body, and Millicent was worse. No way was Dick going to put the burden on Joanie. He took it upon himself to go down and see Johnny.

At the morgue, the medical examiner was infuriatingly blasé about the whole thing. "That's the big-shot gangster that was murdered on the beach, right?" he said.

He was a tall and gawky-looking asshole with a wide space between his front teeth. Dick wanted to deck him, but he was afraid if he hit him, he'd collapse in a pile of skin and bones. "We have to wait for someone from the state attorney's office," he said.

Before he could finish, Dave Goodhart walked in. "Cami?" he said. "How are you doing?"

Dick nodded as Goodhart offered his hand. He'd never had a law official show such kindness, excepting perhaps the FBI agent Clemente, who had followed Johnny for years.

"It's nice meeting you," Goodhart said. "I've been in the Top of the Home a few times. My wife, Alice, and I really enjoy the food there. We were in the Peppermint a few times, too, when you had it. She loved the Twist."

Dick smiled weakly, thinking how stupid it was to exchange pleasantries with Johnny lying dead in the next room. "Can we get to it?" he said.

"Sure," Goodhart said. "Sorry." He took out a form. "I have to ask you a couple questions. What's your relationship to the deceased?"

"I'm his son-in-law," he said. Dick took out his driver's license. Goodhart gave it a quick inspection.

"Let's go in," the coroner said.

The three men entered a chilled, bare room with an antiseptic smell mixed with something deeper and more elemental. A lone gurney stood in the middle of the room. On it, a sheet covered the form of a man. With no warning, the coroner ripped it off. Two giant slashes crisscrossed the upper body, where the doctor had cut him open to do the autopsy. Dick knew it would be awful, but he was unprepared for this.

"This him?" the medical examiner said.

Dick continued to stare, saying nothing. It wasn't so much that Johnny was dead. It was that he was undignified. Dick couldn't stand him being laid out like that.

"Is this your father-in-law?" said Goodhart. "You have to answer so we can identify the body."

"Yes. That's him," said Dick.

Johnny was buried at Southern Memorial Park off Dixie Highway in North Miami Beach. The day of the funeral was clear and bright. Scatsy was disappointed. He'd hoped for rain to ruin the day for the

FBI agents who followed the proceedings from a distance with tele-photo lenses. "Look at those guys," said Big Sal. "Where were they when Johnny was shot in the fucking back?"

Dick was more understanding. He recalled that many times when they were being tailed the agents would break off, apparently called away on other business. Knowing Clemente, Dick felt that nothing would have given him greater pleasure than catching someone in the process of committing the murder.

At the funeral parlor, a man in a beige sport coat, who obviously had no idea who Johnny was, came up and asked if Dick was grateful that Johnny was safe with Jesus. "He's safe with six fucking holes in his back," Dick said. "Jesus may have loved him, but everyone else was trying to kill him."

That was uncharacteristic. He took pride in being gracious. "You okay?" Joanie said. Dick nodded and squeezed her hand. She gave Dick a genuine smile; her father's death had brought them closer than they'd been in years.

He remembered how often she'd told him he didn't have time for a wife. It was what he saw in all the marriages where the wives were unhappy. The guys just didn't have time, plain and simple.

Millicent's eyes were hollow and red from crying, but there was the same matronly strength in them that had impressed him from the first. Now he thought the strength he saw was nothing more than resignation, acceptance of a fate already waiting for her husband on the day he took her, fresh from the orphanage, to a big house with a well-stocked kitchen where she presided for more than thirty years.

"I always knew this day would come," she said.

"Me, too," Joanie said. Her profound grief gave Dick a fresh insight to his wife's relationship with her father. From the beginning, she'd told him she didn't want him to have anything to do with her father. Then, when he did the reverse and became as close as the son Johnny never had, she was furious. Dick thought she hated him. Now he saw another side, the pain that was waiting for its time.

Joanie and Johnny had reconciled their differences shortly before his death. The more years that passed following his assassination, the deeper her affection would grow, until she barely remembered the tension and estrangement. "He was so kind-hearted," she said years later. "Right before he died, he was heating food for our dog, Tootsie. I made fun of him. He said, 'You wouldn't want cold food, would you?'"

Dick had his arm around Scatsy. He hadn't liked his mood since Johnny's death and was afraid he was going to do something dangerous and dumb and get himself killed. Dick pointed out that Johnny would have been the first to tell them, if he didn't forget it, they'd be heading for the eight ball.

"You knew this was the life. Stop bullshitting yourself."

That's exactly what Johnny always said, and Scatsy knew it. But Dick wasn't convinced he was ready to let it go.

The priest they hired knew nothing about Johnny, who wasn't a churchgoer. He considered religion a branch of show business. Like Johnny, Dick was an atheist. Neither of them believed any of it, but they always respected others' beliefs. If it did people good, fine. But they should keep their views to themselves. Of course, Dick couldn't care less that God, from his mighty lectern, had made Johnny out to be evil.

"Happy are the dead who die in the face of Christ," the priest said. *Right*, Dick thought. He was betting that it was more likely Johnny was pissed that the rat bastards got him. The whole show was absurd. As the priest droned on, Dick loosened his tie. There wasn't one good thing to come out of this, so far as Dick could see. Even the FBI guys seemed bored.

As the service ended, the funeral director came over. "We have all the pallbearers, but one," he said. "Is there anyone you'd like to choose?"

Dick scanned the funeral parlor, searching out the faces of those close to Johnny. Then he had a brainstorm. "You see that guy with the blue suit and dark tie?" Dick said, pointing to one of the FBI agents. "He was a good friend of Johnny's."

When the funeral director approached him, the guy couldn't hide his disbelief. He wanted to refuse, but Dick knew he wouldn't be able to say no. Seeing the FBI guy hauling Johnny's body to the gravesite brought Scatsy to life. Dick knew Johnny would have loved it.

Like the loss of a child, the subject of Johnny's death was always in the room in subsequent years whenever the family gathered for a holiday. Who did it? Millicent never recovered. She got joy from her grandchildren, but, as the family expected, she would never consider dating or marrying again. It was understood by everyone who knew her that her loyalty to Johnny was as firm as his had been to her and to the code he'd lived by. When Joanie and Dick finally divorced, he poured his attention into his restaurant. It was still important to build something for his boys.

One time, the FBI man Pete Clemente came to the Top and sat down with Dick in his office. "You know Johnny did the same thing, don't you? That was his life." There was no resting place in that. Dick didn't know what he believed; he only understood that he was being told the man he loved and admired like a father had been a bad man.

In an interview, Clemente acknowledged saying that there was only one way to enter the Mafia in Johnny's day and that was by killing. Dick chose to believe that his father-in-law was a flawed but basically good man who did more for the many who depended on him than a lot of people who serve as deacons in their churches. Dick didn't care what other people believed. He had the freedom to go on believing in the man as he imagined him. Still there was no certainty, one way or the other. There never would be.

Clemente did give Dick a gift, however. He said he had a lot of respect for Johnny. He lived by a code and, whatever one thought of it, he never compromised, not even when the government was willing to rescue him and send him off safely and secretly to some small town. All he had to do was cooperate, give up a few names, some dates, a body or two. If anyone had cause to do that it was Johnny, but he wouldn't go for it and the FBI man respected him for it. At least that's what he said. Perhaps it was only another attempt in his never-ending effort to convince Dick to be an informer.

"I was born a man and I'll die a man," Johnny always said.

Still, there was that question. Who killed Johnny? The crime was never officially solved and no criminal was brought to justice.

Clemente believes Fat Tony Salerno ordered the hit.

Supposedly, Fat Tony, a top associate of Vito Genovese, found out Johnny had had a falling-out with Fat Jack Herman, the carpet guy. According to Clemente, Johnny couldn't stand to be around Fat Jack, which Dick knew was true enough. Johnny literally became sick to his stomach being around the abusive tyrant, even though Fat Jack was careful to moderate his behavior around Johnny.

Fat Jack was originally with Fat Tony, but not earning. Once he was with Johnny Futto, he was a good earner and had the potential of being an even bigger one. "Johnny was talking about killing Fat Jack," Clemente said.

But Fat Tony and Genovese supposedly decided to get rid of Johnny first. It was just business, something that Dick knew the sneaky, greedy Fat Tony was capable of doing. According to Clemente, Fat Tony assigned the job to a prolific killer named George Barone, who served with the marines on Iwo Jima in World War II, then returned home and founded the Jets street gang, the one that inspired the musical *West Side Story*. After that, he became one of the most reliable hit men in Mob history. Asked by authorities how many people he'd killed, Barone answered, "I didn't keep score. A lot. Many."

Johnny and Barone were part of the same generation, old boys who held conservative values and looked upon the younger crowd as stupid and needlessly violent. Ironically, while Johnny turned down all appeals from the feds to cooperate, Barone, after killing at least twenty men for the bosses, didn't hesitate to roll over and become an informant when his name showed up on a hit list.

After years of sifting information that came to him from all sorts in the life, including high-ranking mafiosos who liked Johnny, Dick arrived at a different conclusion. According to Cami, the source of the trouble that claimed Johnny was not hostility between him and Fat Jack. But, more likely, it went right to the heart of the modern

Mafia, and to the same lust for power that had sent so many men to early graves.

Cami came to believe that the man behind Johnny's murder was none other than his old Tucson neighbor Joe Bonanno. A thick-necked Sicilian with a youthful face and a politician's easy smile, Bonanno could have been a congressman or a lawyer. Known as Joe Bananas, a name he hated because he thought it made him sound crazy when he wanted to be known as a dedicated family man, Bonanno was a supreme predator with a heart as treacherous as any pirate.

The way Dick heard the story, it was mid-1964, as the Beatles were sweeping the nation. Bonanno, the head of one of the original Five Families, a major force as well as an elder statesman in the Mob, called for a meet with Johnny Futto at a Miami restaurant. Johnny couldn't imagine what his onetime Tucson neighbor wanted but suspected it was something much more serious than advice about Arizona real estate. He wondered: Could Bonanno be planning to be the latest to vie for the top spot, the coveted title of *Capo di Tutti Capi*, or boss of all bosses, the title that had been retired by Lucky Luciano?

It figured that someone would try to fill the power vacuum created by Frank Costello's retirement. Even if that was Bonanno's plan, what could he possibly want from him? Johnny wondered. He was retired—mostly, anyway. He had no soldiers to put into a fight.

Johnny got to the restaurant first and waited alone at the bar. Spotting Bananas, Johnny waved him to a secluded table in the back. In a ceremonial greeting, they shook hands, slapped backs, and had a toast. Johnny suggested the fish. It didn't take Bananas long to come to the point. He leaned in and Johnny did the same. Bonanno's voice dropped to a whisper, "I want you to take out Brown."

The words hung in the air. Besides being an old friend, Tommy "Three-Finger Brown" Lucchese was head of one of New York's five Mafia families. Their closeness, at least within the highly constricted bounds of Mafia alliances, was observed by Cami over lunch several years earlier. Dick wasn't the only one who knew of their relationship; Bonanno was counting on it. This is what the Mafia does when they want someone killed—they go to a close friend, hence the saying: *Keep your friends close but your enemies closer.*

"You would do me honor, Johnny," Bonanno said. "This is something I know you can do. You are close to Brown and he will never suspect anything. This must be done. I have no choice. You know he stands in my way of becoming what we both know I should be."

Johnny was no Brutus. There was no way he was going to kill his friend, especially for a power-hungry egotist like Bonanno. But he showed no reaction, knowing that Bonanno would be scrutinizing every twitching muscle and eye movement.

After dinner, the two men hugged and Bonanno left. Johnny was fairly certain he'd shown enough interest in Bonanno's plan to keep him off his guard.

The next day, Johnny drove his Cadillac over to Naples on the other side of the Gulf. He got a room and spent the day alone, thinking. Only Scatsy knew where he was. The magnitude of Bonanno's plan was breathtaking in its hubris. It was against the code Bonanno had sworn to uphold. It would initiate a bloodbath. After years of peace, Bonanno was threatening to undo everything. Uncounted lives would be lost and all of it would be at Johnny's feet.

He knew only half the story. Bonanno had approached another Mafia *capo* to kill Carlo Gambino. That job was ultimately assigned to Joe Colombo, a former longshoreman whose father had been a *Cosa Nostra* soldier before him and who was found strangled in a car with his mistress.

After thinking things over, Johnny decided to pay a visit to his old mentor. He cautioned Dick not to breathe a word about his trip to New York. At seventy-three, graveled-voiced Frank Costello was still alert and vigorous, something the old don attributed to a lifelong regimen of eating vegetables. He was rarely seen in public anymore outside of flower shows. He still had a big income from legitimate businesses he maintained, but now out of the life, he could really live as he preached: *Make money, not headlines.*

After listening quietly to Johnny's tale, he didn't fool himself into thinking that Johnny's life wasn't on the line. The only thing to do, he finally concluded, was to go public with Bonanno's scheme and expose the traitor for the person he really was. Let him be judged by his own.

One of Luciano's reforms, executed after the demise of the Mustache Pete generation, was to establish a Commission of twelve bosses to rule on interfamily conflicts before they led to war. What Johnny should do, Costello said, was take the matter to the Commission, which would have no choice but to order Bonanno's execution.

Johnny revealed the plot to Lucchese, while Colombo went to Gambino. Everything was now in the open and all that was needed was for the Commission to act. Bonanno was kidnapped in October 1964 and held incommunicado while the Commission debated his fate. (It has been speculated that Bonanno staged his own abduction to avoid appearing before the Commission, but Cami doubts this. If that had occurred, the Commission would have had nothing to rule on. Death would have been the only possible sentence available.)

Unfortunately for Johnny, the Commission decided to show mercy toward one of the Mafia's founding members. They voted not to kill Bonanno, but to banish him to Arizona. Bonanno retreated to Tucson and plotted his revenge.

From that moment, Johnny knew he was living on someone else's clock. On that 1967 St. Patrick's Day, the hour struck.

Dick's account finds support from Vinny Teresa, the Boston mobster turned stool pigeon and author. According to Teresa, Bonanno did indeed approach Johnny to seek his help in getting rid of several bosses so that he could take over the New York families. "Biello was a treacherous bastard," Teresa wrote. That was an ironic comment from a guy who turned informant and took down his oldest friends, while Johnny had refused many times to cooperate with the authorities. It was Johnny Futto, not Vinny Teresa, who upheld the oath he had taken as a young man:

*No man must ever, upon penalty of death, talk about the organiza-
tion or the family of which he was a member, not even within his
own home.*

*Every man must obey, without question, the orders of the leader
above him.*

*No man must ever strike another member, regardless of the provo-
cation.*

*Total harmony must rule both the business and the personal rela-
tionships between the families and the members; no man could
ever covet another's business or another's wife*

Teresa wrote that Biello "was one of those who tipped off the
bosses about what Bonanno was planning to do. When the Mob kidnapped Bonanno and held him while the old dons decided what to do
with him, Biello was one of those who voted to have Bonanno whacked
out. Bonanno never forgave Biello for his treachery."

According to Teresa, this was the Joe Bananas philosophy: "Never
forget—don't let the guy know how you feel. Just keep patting him on
the shoulder. Every time you see him notice what a nice day it is. Pat
him on the back. Tell him he looks good today. Sooner or later this
guy will find a hole in his back when your time is right. The trick is to
make the mark think you're his friend until the right time comes, the
right setup, and then you make your move."

Teresa happened to be in Florida, he wrote, when Bonanno flew
in to make the final arrangements for the hit on Johnny. "I'd met him
twice before and he looked good," Teresa said.

"He got in the backseat and we drove to the Dream Bar. Patsy
(Erra) came in and walked over to our table. Joe Bonanno got up and
the two of them walked over to a corner table, had a couple of drinks
together, and talked in each other's ear."

When Bonanno returned he asked to be driven to the airport, where he caught the 11:00 P.M. return flight to Arizona.

"Now, Biello was a big man," Teresa wrote. "He was the hidden owner of the old Peppermint Lounge in New York and another in Miami that made a bundle out of the Twist craze. He was a millionaire with a lot of influence, but he was still a walking dead man."

According to Teresa, the assassination was set up by Erra, supposedly a good friend of Futto's. The team that carried it out came from Boston, where they worked under Raymond Patriarca.

Patriarca was ostensibly one of Johnny's closest allies. When he needed to drop out of sight for a while he'd always gone to Patriarca. Johnny's oldest daughter and her family lived in Boston, so whenever he went to see them, he dropped in on Raymond. Using these two men was the perfect implementation of the Mafia policy of sending your best friends to put the bullet in your back.

"That shows you what I mean," Teresa wrote. "In the Mob you can't trust anyone. Bonanno was as treacherous as any guy there ever was. He was always looking to get ahead by stepping on someone else."

After Johnny was gunned down, Teresa said he talked to Patriarca about the murder. If the Boston boss had any lingering sympathy for his old friend, it didn't show on his face. "Forget about it, Vinny," he said. "Things will iron themselves out."

Cami is skeptical that Patriarca was involved in the killing. Bonanno and Patriarca were not close, according to Cami. As for Patriarca's advice to forget about it, that's what any mafioso would say about minding one's own business.

A deeper mystery was the disappearance of Johnny's fortune, assuming he had one, which everyone did. Johnny never lacked for money. He owned a lot of property, both in New York and Miami. But after his death, the man Teresa characterized as a millionaire was found to be nearly broke. Johnny preferred not to use banks, knowing the accounts could be subpoenaed by the government. Everything was strictly cash with Johnny, and he always had a big wad.

He had a fondness for the gaming tables. Like Dick, Johnny had even owned a few horses. He learned why it was called the sport of kings; only kings could afford to participate. As Dick often said, "I used to follow the horses. Unfortunately, my horses also followed the horses."

Maybe business troubles were the reason Johnny could never quite retire from the Mob. He simply needed the constant cash infusion that kept all his operations going. It was not an uncommon story, even among the highest of high-living mobsters. People who were supposed to be rich beyond the reach of calculation ended up dying broke. It happened with Meyer Lansky.

"Today, Sandi—Meyer's daughter—and I joke about it," Cami said. "What happened to all the big bucks?"

Millicent didn't have to go begging. Dick and Joanie watched out for her and Connie. He was doing well with the Top, so he could afford to funnel thousands of dollars her way. The Miami Shores house, though mortgage free, was too big and contained too many memories. Dick sold it off for $100,000 and gave the proceeds to Millicent, which she used to buy a small townhome in Hallandale for $17,000. She lived comfortably with Connie until her death, after which Joanie took care of her sister until Connie passed away.

In life, John Biello never succeeded in breaking from his sordid past. There was always something, or someone, tugging him back to the life. In death, however, he finally achieved his dream. He was buried at Southern Memorial Park under the name John J. Biele, the name he'd started using years earlier as part of his effort to present himself to the world as the simple man of business he dearly wanted to become.

Dino's Nose

For years, Johnny repeatedly told Cami to keep his nose out of Mob business. Dick knew he was trying to protect him, and he appreciated it. The FBI nonetheless believed that as close as he was to Johnny, Dick had to be dirty, too. And it wasn't just the government that believed that. His longtime partner, Vinny Marchese, was frequently asked by wiseguys after Johnny was gone whom Dick belonged to.

"He doesn't belong to anybody," Vinny said.

It didn't always sell. It certainly didn't sell with the government. Finally, in 1988, the feds indicted Cami on charges of hiding fugitive Boston mafioso Ralph Lamattina.

Lamattina, who was known as Ralphie Chong because he had a habit of squinting his eyes when he concentrated that his fellow mobsters thought made him look Asian, was one of the Boston crew and very friendly with Johnny. He came to the Peppermint during its heyday and dined at the Top, too. Over the years Dick gave him tickets to shows he was promoting and they took a liking to each other.

When Lamattina showed up looking for a roof and a bed, Dick

helped him find a place. Ralphie's explanation was that he was having trouble with his wife and wanted a place to cool off for a while.
The attorneys were pestering him, he said, so Ralphie asked Dick not
to let on if anyone asked where he was.

Sounded reasonable enough, and Cami was glad to offer a hand.
The truth was different. Lamattina had been caught up in a nasty
feud between his Mob boss, Raymond Patriarca, and James "Whitey"
Bulger. Bulger's Winter Hill Gang was linked to eighteen killings, in-
cluding two women, carried out by Bulger and his vicious associate,
Stephen "the Rifleman" Flemmi.

With the aid of corrupt FBI agents, Bulger decided to take down
Patriarca's Mafia operation, sending the Italian mobsters scurrying
for cover. That's how Ralphie Chong wound up on Cami's doorstep.

Dick didn't realize the serious consequences of his generosity until two years later, when he was indicted by an organized crime
grand jury on six counts of harboring a fugitive.

"I was facing thirty years and, of course, I couldn't believe the
government indicted me for this. My sons Rich and Johnny were in
court with me every day, as well as my sister, Maria, her daughter
Teela, and my partner, chef Joe Ezbicki," Cami said.

He also had the benefit of supporting testimony from character
witnesses and notable friends, including Tom Wohl, Home Federal
and Savings and Loan bank president, Dick Schaap, the well-known
TV sports commentator, and Wilford Brimley, the actor. They all testified that what Dick did for Lamattina was no different from what he
did for lots of people. He was always helping people when they came
to Florida with accommodations or recommendations of where to
stay, with restaurant reservations, or with getting tickets to shows or
events that were happening around town. When his good friend John
Monahan, the vice president for Hyatt International, testified that
FBI director J. Edgar Hoover dined at Dick's restaurant, Cami was
rushed during the court recess by FBI agents anxious for details.

"What am I? A stool pigeon?" Cami said.

Cami was lucky to dodge the most potentially damaging part of the case. The government wanted to bring in a high-ranking mafioso trophy from the Witness Protection Program to testify against him. The guy was going to say that he held meetings at Dick's restaurant with other Mafia men where every crime up to and including murder was discussed.

"People don't realize that once the criminal is in witness protection, they will testify to anything the government wants," Dick said.

The more they testify, the more men they bring down, the more valuable they are to the government and the bigger the rewards they get. Once in witness protection, these men become puppets of the government. They have no more conscience about putting away their former Mafia brethren than they did when they committed crimes.

Dick believed he was indicted because he refused to cooperate with the government, not because of Lamattina. He was no mobster, but he'd spent too many years at Johnny's side to turn informant. So the government forced Dick to take his chances in court.

While Dick was out on bond and preparing for trial, two of the Cami's Seafood restaurants he opened after the Top closed were robbed, one at gunpoint. He decided to give each of the managers a pistol and sent them to get a license to carry so they could protect themselves in the future. Dick's old-time partner, Vinny Marchese, said he had a friend who had a pistol, and that he could buy it for Dick without leaving a paper trail. It was a .38 Smith & Wesson, just the kind of weapon Dick wanted.

Dick was reading the *Fort Lauderdale Sun-Sentinel* a couple weeks later. On the front page was a story about a captured serial killer named Charles Commander, who had chopped up the body of a girl and left the parts floating in the Fort Lauderdale River. The article said the police were looking for a .38 Smith & Wesson that Commander used in another murder he'd committed in New Jersey. The phone rang. It was Vinny.

"Dick, you know that pistol I sold you?" he said. "You're not going to believe this but I got it from Charles Commander."

Fucking Vinny. Dick couldn't believe what he was hearing and could only imagine what the papers would do with the information. He took the pistol down to his lawyer, Dave Goodhart, the former state's attorney who had showed Dick Johnny's body in the morgue. Goodhart turned it in. Luckily, ballistics tests proved the weapon wasn't used in the New Jersey murder. When Goodhart called to give him the good news, he couldn't help posing a question: "How do you get yourself into these situations?"

When the jury came in on Cami's trial for harboring a fugitive, his attorney looked over. "It doesn't look good," he said.

A jury that has found for a defendant will often look at him sympathetically when they come in. If the verdict is guilty they usually avoid his gaze. Nobody was looking at Dick. The jury sat stone-faced. Dick, barely controlling the shiver going through him, started calculating how old he'd be when he got out of prison. Eighty-three. What were the chances of living that long? His mind snapped back to the present as the judge asked the foreman if he had a verdict. The foreman stood and announced it: "Not guilty."

It went like that for all six counts. Something like 2 percent of organized crime cases go to trial. The rest plead out. Of those 2 percent, only 3 percent are found not guilty. Dick was now one of a minute minority of people who actually beat the government in court.

Dick had previously been inducted in London to the Knights of St. Birgitta in recognition of his work on behalf of the Boys' Town of Italy and for other charitable activities. After his trial, he would often remark that he had been both knighted and indicted.

One statistic nobody nosed around was the number of people who beat the government and went on to lead quiet, normal lives. That's because that number is close to zero. The government hates to lose. Only two days after the verdict, a friend in the sheriff's office in Dade County told Cami privately that after his acquittal the FBI put him right back on top of their list of targets.

"I suddenly understood the expression: 'You can beat the rap but you can't beat the ride,'" Cami said.

Dick did have one important ally. Years later, FBI agent Peter

Clemente wrote him a letter stating: "I have never believed you were ever a member of the LCN (La Cosa Nostra) . . . Good luck, Dick, you were a clean-living, honest man."

"That was a nice thing for Peter to do," Dick said. "He didn't have to do it, but he did, largely I guess because he respected Johnny and he knew the truth."

Even after the Peppermint closed, Dick continued promoting concerts and managing artists. Dean Martin was the act that landed him in a well of trouble so deep it didn't appear there was any way for him to climb out. Standing at the top of the well was a gangster named Freddy Franco.

Born Alfredo George Felici, Franco was considered by the FBI to be an important mobster in South Florida. Dick knew something else about him. He was a psychotic maniac. When he went off, there was no reasoning with him. Worse, there was no predicting what would light his fuse.

Franco's association with Dean Martin went back many years. In his youth, Martin held many jobs. He was a blackjack dealer, worked in a steel mill, and tried his hand at boxing, using his family name as Kid Crochet. His nose was broken in a fight. Later on, when he began scuffling around the club circuit as a singer, he was getting nowhere and came to the opinion his crooked schnozz was holding him back. The story was that Freddy Franco loaned Dean the money to get his nose fixed.

According to the story, Freddy Franco lent Dean only $750, but no one in history made more off a loan. Dean repaid Freddy many times over. When Dick was approached to arrange a set of fund-raising concerts featuring Dean, Freddy was in deep trouble once again. He'd been convicted and sentenced to ten years in the slammer. He needed money to fund his appeal and decided to lean on Dean once more.

Freddy was lucky in his choice of associates. Patsy Erra and Terry Teriaca of the Dream Bar were, if not friends, close contacts. It was Teriaca who asked Cami to promote the shows with Dean, who wasn't exactly thrilled about doing Franco this favor but couldn't say no.

To seal the deal, everyone flew out to see Martin at his house in California. Because Franco was out on bond and wasn't supposed to leave the state of Florida, he sneaked out of the state and checked into the Beverly Hills Hotel under the assumed name of Mr. Johnson.

The introduction could have been made over the phone, but Franco wanted to be in L.A. Dick went to the hotel and picked up the house phone. Franco answered in a hoarse whisper, "Are you being tailed?"

When Freddy answered his door, he pointed his finger to the ceiling and whispered, "Be careful what you say, the room might be bugged, the rat bastards."

Franco motioned to Dick to follow him out to the lanai to talk. But he realized he was hungry and asked Dick to order hamburgers. Keeping in mind Franco's concern for privacy, Cami tiptoed to the phone and began to whisper the order. Suddenly, Freddy stepped back in and yelled at the top of his lungs, "Ask them if they got any vinegard peppers."

They didn't have the peppers, but that didn't stop Franco from wolfing down the burgers. Afterward, he phoned Dean and made the appointment for Cami.

At Dean's house, they quickly got down to business. There would be three concerts. Martin wanted to do all three in Texas.

"I know I'll do good there," Dino said. Texans loved his old cowboy roles, even though growing up in the steel town of Steubenville, Ohio, Dean hadn't seen many horses. Looking around the living room, filled with dozens of pictures of Martin in cowboy drag, along with real saddles, ropes, and all kinds of other Western paraphernalia, Dick realized the plan made sense and agreed.

Dean would take $50,000 for each concert. The rest would go to Freddy. The venue was the Tarrant County Auditorium in Fort Worth. The night before the show who should arrive but Freddy Franco? He registered in the same hotel as Dean and Cami under another assumed name. When Dick visited he found him in bed, ill.

Between coughing fits and blowing his nose, Franco outlined a new deal. "What if you don't pay Dean? What the hell, we got expenses, too."

Dick couldn't believe it. Dean agreed to take $50,000 for each concert, which was a bargain considering he was at the time one of the highest-paid stars in the world. He had left behind his role as the foil of Jerry Lewis to star in a string of movies. He had one of the highest-rated television shows of the era, *The Dean Martin Show*, in which he perfected his persona as a randy, easygoing drunk. Though the boozehound bit was, at least partly, an act—one he borrowed from Sinatra's pal Joe E. Lewis—he took pride in it, receiving from the California Department of Motor Vehicles the vanity license plate DRUNKY.

On the other hand, Dick could see Freddy's point of view. If Dean was going to do Freddy a favor, why not let him go all the way with it and work for free? He hardly needed the money.

But Freddy wanted Dick to take the fall for stealing Dean's $150,000. Cami pointed out that if he got a reputation for not paying performers, he wouldn't be a concert promoter very long. "I can't do that, Freddy," Dick said. "But I can ask him to forego his fee for your sake."

Franco hit the roof. His mind took one of the strange leaps for which he was famous. Franco would rather screw Dean Martin than simply ask him to work for free, man to man. It made no sense, but Freddy Franco was a lunatic. Franco's anger increased. He wouldn't listen to reason and the more Dick insisted that he was asking the impossible, the more threatening Franco became.

"I'm going to take you for a ride in a black limo, you son of a bitch," he said. "It's over for you."

Dick realized he had a very serious situation on his hands. In all his years with Johnny he'd never come close to anything like this. He'd gotten so relaxed in the protective cloak Johnny offered that he forgot it was there. Dick scarcely considered that the men he spent time with, who he knew killed without remorse or even much thought, were just as capable of turning their malice on him. Now that it had happened, Johnny wasn't around to bail him out.

As Franco raged, Dick's mind raced wildly. A person can't prepare for a situation like this. When a known killer tells you he's going to kill you, your life flashes before your eyes. A crazy thought crept in. Freddy was sick and weak. Dick was bigger and desperate. What if he grabbed a pillow and smothered him? He was younger and stronger than the aging gangster. He knew he could do it. But murder wasn't his game and, pragmatically, he reminded himself that Franco had friends. He knew too well the law of the Mafia. If Dick killed Freddy, they'd be obligated to come after him.

Dick got out of there as best he could, assuring Freddy that he would think things over. He went straight to Terry Teriaca's room. Teriaca had always been a gentleman. He ran the Dream Bar like any other conscientious businessman, careful with his money and generous to his staff. Dick never believed that he and Erra had helped set up Johnny for a fall. They had always been square with him.

When he laid out the situation, he could see Teriaca was alarmed. This only stoked Dick's fears. "Maybe the pressure of going to the can is getting to him," Teriaca said.

"Terry, you've got to call Patsy Erra and get him out here," Dick said. "He's the only one Freddy will listen to. We both know this guy. He's a fucking wild man. I'll be honest with you. I thought about killing him."

"Don't even say that in jest, Dick," Teriaca said. After mulling it over, he promised to make the call.

Cami went to bed but not to sleep. His alternatives paraded through his head. There weren't many. What if Patsy refused to come? The next choice was Santo Trafficante. *I'll call him tomorrow*, Dick thought, *if Erra doesn't come through.*

At breakfast, Terry informed Cami that Patsy was coming in on the afternoon plane. Dick began to feel that he might survive the day.

Dinner turned into a celebration of Dean's fiftieth birthday. They made a party of it. Someone offered a toast: "Congratulations, Dean, on being middle-aged."

Martin shot back, "Yeah? How many guys you know live to be a hundred?" Martin wasn't to be one of them. He would die on Christmas 1995 at the age of seventy-eight.

When everyone finished laughing, Dick looked over Dean's shoulder and saw Patsy Erra walking into the dining room with Freddy Franco. Dick was pleased but surprised. Franco was a fugitive. What was he doing showing his face in public? He came over to the table and Dean stiffened. Franco put his hand on Dick's shoulder. "Forget about last night, kid," he said. "I wasn't feeling good."

Guy Marks was the comic on the bill for the Dean Martin concerts. He was going with one of the McGuire sisters, Christine, and when in Florida they would frequently dine at Top of the Home. One evening Marks approached Cami. "Dick, I've got some trouble and Patsy Erra told me that if I ever needed his help, I could call on him."

"Well, if Patsy told you that, he's a man of his word," Cami said. "What happened?"

Marks said Christine had won a tennis tournament at the Le Club in Fort Lauderdale. A couple of guys were trying to muscle in on the money she won. Marks said he thought they might be connected. He asked Dick if he'd mind going to Erra for him.

After Cami explained the situation, Patsy said he'd pick him up the following morning and go up to Le Club and see what it was all about. Cami called Guy and told him to expect them. It was crowded when Patsy and Cami made their way to where Guy was sitting outside. "Where are these guys?" Patsy asked.

Guy pointed to two well-dressed men standing by the pool. Patsy said, "Dick, stand behind me and let me do the talking." The men were looking very confident when Patsy and Cami approached them.

"Are you the fucking guys that are bothering Christine?" Erra said.

They seemed surprised by the question. "Who wants to know?" one of them said.

"Now listen to me, assholes," Patsy said. "If I find out that you even speak one more word to her"—Patsy's hand shot out in the direction of the pool—"they'll find both of you in the bottom of that fucking pool."

"Who the fuck are you?"

"That's for you to find out, my friend. Remember what I said. You don't want to see me again."

That was the end of it. The strangers checked out the next day and disappeared. Incidents like this were what made so many people think Cami was connected. For years afterward, Cami told people, "Please don't say I'm a wiseguy. If you keep insisting that I am, you'll end up at the bottom of the fucking pool."

Chapter 22

I Gotta Tell Youse
This Story

Johnny's death hurt everyone around him, but it hurt his brother most. If Johnny was the brains and muscle in the family, Scatsy was its crusty heart. Gruff, profane, irritable, and impatient, he was loved by almost everyone who knew him. He fractured the language in a dozen places, but nobody communicated better.

If a woman was prissy, he called her "satellite," because "she thinks her keister is out of this world."

If a guy was drunk, he'd say, "He's driving because he's too drunk to walk."

About someone who had more money than brains, he'd remark with a sneer, "He may be in Who's Who, but he don't know what's what."

About a bad restaurant, he'd joke, "The food there is so bad they make you pay up front."

If a place had a reputation, "Tough joint? The hatcheck girl's named Vito."

About a dangerous character, "He's so tough he orders broke leg of lamb."

Now that Johnny was gone, the spirit and fun went out of Scatsy, who despaired that only a few of the boys came around. To Scatsy, it was like they were saying Johnny never existed, never earned for them or helped feed their kids when they needed cash.

The love of Scatsy's life was his first wife, who died of cancer not long after his son, Albert, was born. Between the Peppermint and the Top, he got a woman pregnant, married her, and had another kid. Not long after Johnny was killed, the marriage came crashing down. They separated. Scatsy sent money, but that was it.

The older Scatsy got, the more bitter he became. When Joanie and Dick divorced, long after they should have, Dick bought a condo in Hallandale, not far from Millicent.

"I offered Scatsy a room, but he declined," Dick said.

He preferred to stay in a motel in downtown Hollywood, Florida. His son, Albert, a successful computer executive, bought a big condo for him to stay in. It stood empty.

The light went out of his eyes and he became a different person. What he missed almost as much as his brother's presence was the action, the sense of anticipation that something was going to happen any minute. With Johnny around, there were always schemes in the air. Without him, Scatsy tried to lose himself in work, spending endless hours as the service bartender at the Top of the Home, where he'd been since its opening. Refusing to take a day off, as keeper of the back door, he also watched Dick's back.

Dick tried to stay on top of him, but by the early nineties, after selling the Top and opening Cami's Seafood & Pasta restaurants, a chain he ran with his sons, Dick watched helplessly as life drained out of Scatsy. He could never move beyond the past.

One day in 1994, Scatsy threw a rope over the bathroom door in his motel room. When he failed to answer his phone the next day, Dick went over and knocked on the door. Seeing Scatsy's car parked outside, Dick knew something was wrong when no one answered. The manager let Dick in, where he found Scatsy dangling on the rope.

One of Dick's employees said Scatsy had been talking about suicide. As usual in a case like that, the guy thought Scatsy was kidding.

"Sure, I have some guilt thinking back on it," Dick said. "Wondering what could I have done different."

The hardest part for Dick was seeing Scatsy hanging there. "I don't like remembering Scatsy as I found him," Dick said.

The memories he treasures are of the irascible guy whose worst crimes were committed against *Merriam-Webster's*. Scatsy had a saying Dick loved. Maybe because it came to describe his own approach to life after meeting up with him and Johnny.

"I gotta tell youse this story. I can hardly wait to hear it myself."

Chapter 23

The Matty Years

The end of the Twist and Johnny's involvement turned out not to be the end for the cramped club on West 45th Street where all the excitement began. Revived after Matty "the Horse" Ianniello took over in 1965, the Peppermint Lounge, under that name and others, became a part of both the squalor and the ragged rebirth of a new, even rawer kind of music scene that enveloped Times Square in the seventies and eighties. Surrounded by porn theaters and gay bars, the Peppermint Lounge continued to make news on New York's nightlife scene in the next decades.

Under Matty's guidance, the club reopened as a topless bar. Andy Warhol film actress Geri Miller, once a member of the Pep's dance troupe, the Peppermint Twisters, returned as a topless dancer.

Matty, a hulking three hundred pounds of grumpy conviviality, was a fat, golden goose for the New York Mob. As good an earner as Johnny and Fat Jack were, Matty put them both in the shade. Matty controlled dozens of bars and restaurants in Manhattan, and paid for the privilege in the form of tribute to every one of the Mafia families, under an agreement negotiated with members of all New York's Five Families that allowed him to operate in the otherwise neutral territory around Times Square.

"You don't run a bar and grill or sex establishment between 34th and 59th streets, from Fifth Avenue to the Hudson River, without Matty having a piece of the action," said one NYPD detective. Cami's only response when asked to elaborate about Matty was that he always treated him fairly. "Once Matty shook your hand, it stayed shook," he said.

Matthew Ianniello was a war hero who went bad. Born in 1920 in Little Italy and raised on Long Island, he worked as a waiter at his uncle's restaurant and in the Brooklyn shipyards before joining the army in 1943. He was decorated for valor in the South Pacific. After the war, things started to go wrong for Matty. While running a restaurant with his uncle, he was indicted for receiving and selling twenty-two pounds of heroin in 1952. The charges were ultimately dropped for lack of evidence, but the bust left him with the nickname "the Horse." That's one version; another is that they called him that because of his size and bulk.

By the late sixties, he was specializing in gay bars, strip clubs, massage parlors, dirty bookstores, and peep shows. Matty owned the Gilded Grape, a West Village hole-in-the-wall for transsexuals, the hustler bar the Haymarket, the topless Mardi Gras, not to mention many more. In a large sense, Ianniello was the man who made Times Square the tawdry place that it was in the seventies.

When he wasn't trolling his gay bars, chatting up the "girls," he was often found at Umberto's Clam House on Mulberry Street in Little Italy, which his brother Robert owned. Matty was there the morning in 1972 that "Crazy" Joey Gallo and his crew pulled up in front.

The Gallo hit was a particularly brazen dispatch, even for the Mafia. Gallo, who had earned his nickname as a reliable contract killer, chose Umberto's because it was one of the only places still open at five in the morning, when he and his boys got a hankering for some clams, shrimp, and conch. An aspiring Colombo gang member,

Joseph Luparelli, was chatting with Matty outside at the time. Luparelli wanted to be made badly, but couldn't get in. Upon seeing Gallo, whom he knew was wanted by the Colombo gang, Luparelli rushed over to a Colombo storefront and told them Gallo was at Umberto's. Making a phone call, they got the go-ahead to hit Gallo.

Luparelli and three Colombo soldiers drove back to the restaurant. The shooter—not Luparelli—burst in the side door facing Mulberry Street and blasted away with an automatic revolver. One of Gallo's bodyguards was hit in the butt, as was Gallo, who jumped up and sprinted for the front door, facing Hester Street. The shooter fired five shots at him. Besides the one that hit him in the ass, another hit his elbow and a third went into his back and severed an artery. Gallo collapsed outside and died.

Matty was in the kitchen during the shooting and when the bodyguard who was shot in the ass got up, he angrily confronted him. Matty told him truthfully that he had nothing to do with the hit. The bodyguard was easily convinced. He knew Gallo had enemies. Luparelli went into hiding in New Jersey, but the behavior of the Colombo killers so scared him that he lit out for California, where he turned himself in to the FBI and disappeared into witness protection.

Matty's multimillion-dollar operation encompassed more than eighty midtown New York bars and restaurants, as well as the businesses servicing the restaurants such as liquor sales, laundry, and trucking. He also ran a talent agency that supplied his clubs with topless dancers, owned an interior decorating firm, and headed a garbage collection company. He picked out the carpets and drapes, delivered the linen, and took away the trash.

Matty kept track of his money differently from Johnny. He was familiar with Johnny's accounting problems—with so many partnerships, it was difficult to know who was owed what. But Johnny Futto was Dun & Bradstreet compared to Matty. Ianniello didn't keep track of anything. That was impossible when he was already using two sets of books to fool the IRS. He decided on a standard figure to be delivered every week from each club. It was just a guess. He said he didn't know—or care—what the real take was. He got his share and that was all that mattered.

When the Peppermint became a gay bar, Matty changed the name to the Turntable. The Hollywood Club, the little room's next incarnation, featured disc jockey Richie Kaczor, who would a few years later become the star deejay at the famed Studio 54. In 1978, Ianniello remodeled the ground floor of the Peppermint building, turning the former lobby of the Knickerbocker Hotel, which was being converted to condos, into a massive nightclub separated by double doors from the old club. The new room held four hundred comfortably, nearly three times the size of the original Peppermint. In November 1978, Matty opened the club as GG Knickerbocker's P. T. Barnum Room, soon shortened to GG Barnum's. The GG came from his tranny room in the Village, the Gilded Grape.

GG Barnum's introduced a new level of excess and depravity to the Manhattan gay nightlife scene. The place invented male Go-Go dancers, a novelty that unwittingly went straight back to the club's roots in the Twist era. Barnum's featured a "jungle gym in the sky"—young men in swimsuits on trapezes above a net strung across the dance floor. They held cabaret shows featuring guys in drag, many of them hookers. The Wagon Wheel on the corner was another gay hustler bar, where predatory young hawks preyed on wealthy pigeons. There was not the slightest vestige of the heyday of the Twist on the block.

After complaints of pickpockets, johns getting rolled, and, finally, a pair of murders, GG Barnum's shut down. It had been closed a number of months when Jim Fouratt came to look over the place. Fouratt had experience running rock clubs. He managed the dance club Hurrah before forming a partnership with Rudolf Pieper, the thirty-three-year-old son of a German diplomat who went by his first name. The two started a couple of other clubs, including the immensely successful after-hours rock-and-roll dance club Danceteria, where deejays introduced new British rock records.

When Fouratt went downstairs in the basement of the 45th Street club he ran across all the original signs from the Peppermint Lounge,

still carefully stowed away all these years later. He instantly realized
where he was and that he'd stumbled onto a valuable piece of history.

Fouratt pulled out the old signs, restored the club's old logo, and
reopened the club under the old name in November 1980. The Peppermint Lounge was back, not that the name meant much to new
wave kids not yet born when Chubby Checker ruled the charts. Fouratt hired all-new staff and put a female doorperson out front, a brac-
ing change from the time when the door was patrolled by the likes of
the Terrible Turk. An instant success with the rock crowd, the new
Peppermint featured live music every night in the big room that once
served as the hotel's lobby. In the smaller room where Joey Dee and
the Starliters played, a deejay spun records and kids danced to a new
beat.

Fouratt brought in the best of the new rock bands. Fresh new wave
bands from England were turning up from England almost every
week and the American bands weren't far behind. Fouratt's specialty
was eclectic, unexpected bookings such as Latin bandleader Tito Pu-
ente, R&B great Solomon Burke, and avant-gardist Philip Glass. Other
party-throwers and promoters took over on other nights. There was
The Village Voice columnist Michael Musto and Giorgio Gomelsky,
the original manager of the Yardbirds who had relocated to New York
a few years earlier. His "Tropical Hot Dog" nights featured familiar
performers in novel settings, like MC5 guitarist Wayne Kramer playing in front of an eighteen-piece rock-and-roll orchestra.

The new Peppermint may have been the first nightclub in the country to incorporate video into the entertainment. The deejay booth
featured the latest equipment, including broadcast-quality cameras.
The small room that housed the original club was used as a television
studio during the day, where producers shot commercials and other
outside projects. The Pop Network, as the group was called, also produced a syndicated TV show of music video clips, a new wrinkle drift-
ing into the scene from Europe. They played music videos between
set breaks for dancers. Among the habitués in the Peppermint video
lounge was Bob Pittman, a radio programmer who was working at a

fledgling cable TV outlet called the Movie Channel. He was about to take a position as the first programmer of MTV.

Matty wasn't around the club much. He kept his people in the background, but they started to pressure Fouratt for more money. One day, the club manager found himself in a car with a thug assigned to watch the bar, a gentleman named Mario. "I like you, Jimmy," Mario said. "But I'm going to have to kill you." Fouratt opened the passenger door and rolled out of the moving car. His partner didn't believe him until he was beaten up. Then they quit for good.

Frank Roccio had been throwing new wave rock shows with a twenty-four-year-old partner fresh out of NYU business graduate school, Tom Goodkind. They produced shows with bands such as the Talking Heads and the B-52s at Irving Plaza, an old Polish community hall near Union Square. When Fouratt left, they took over the Peppermint Lounge, booking bands six nights a week. Once again, lines of eager patrons snaked down 45th Street.

It might not have been the Twist mania, but it was a great time for music. Early hip-hop pioneers Grandmaster Flash and the Furious Five and Afrika Bambaataa played the club, as did upcoming American rock bands such as Joan Jett, the Go-Go's, the Cramps, X, the Waitresses, Marshall Crenshaw, and British acts like Gang of Four, Duran Duran, and Billy Idol.

Mick Jagger watched from the VIP Lounge while soul greats Sam & Dave made their final New York appearance. In March 1981, Yoko Ono made one of her first public appearances after John Lennon's killing, showing up at the club to promote her new single, "Walking on Thin Ice."

By this time, Times Square was dirty and disgusting, shady and dangerous, the perfect place for rock and roll. Twenty years after Johnny Futto, the Peppermint Lounge was, once again, the hottest rock-and-roll nightclub in New York City.

The rebirth on West 45th Street was aborted when the building was suddenly condemned. There were plans to build a hotel on the site. As a result, the club moved downtown in August 1982 to 100 Fifth Avenue, by 14th Street, where the new location was christened the New Peppermint Lounge. Iggy Pop played a three-night stand the first month and other big names followed into the larger room. Goodkind installed guitarist Lenny Kaye, at loose ends after the Patti Smith Group broke up, as disc jockey in the basement, but it was never the same. The music was more hard rock and punk. The room was never right. Goodkind, who always let his partner deal with the owners, was hearing that they were unsatisfied with the money they were bringing in. When the FBI came around to ask Goodkind about the nature of his partners, he decided to pursue a career as a folk musician. He left the nightclub business and started a trio called the Washington Squares. The Peppermint Lounge closed its doors, once and forever, in 1986.

Matty Ianniello managed to elude the law for many years without spending more than a few months in jail. They busted him in 1975 after undercover cops set up a phony trucking company and caught Matty trying to collect $5,000 to guarantee labor peace. He was indicted on corruption and extortion charges, but he was acquitted on every count.

His luck came to an end in December 1985, when Ianniello and eight of his associates were convicted on charges of skimming more than $2 million from his various clubs and restaurants, including the Peppermint Lounge and the New Peppermint Lounge. The authorities nailed Matty with hidden tape recorders in his plush office. Among more than forty taped conversations played for the jury was a confab where Matty and the others discussed "cutting up" $500,000 annually for four years.

While the Peppermint Lounge was in bankruptcy, according to prosecutors, Matty and his boys even skimmed a workers'-comp check from the club. Matty was sentenced to six years in prison. While serving that sentence, he was tried on corruption charges involving his garbage collection business. Two days after being acquitted on those charges, federal prosecutors announced another indictment against

Ianniello for labor racketeering, gambling, extortion, rigging construction bids, and conspiracy to commit murder. At the conclusion of a thirteen-month trial, he was found guilty and sentenced to thirteen more years in prison.

He served nine and, on his release, went right back to work, at least as he defined it. In 2005, according to the FBI, Ianniello, by then eighty-four years old, had been the acting boss of the Genovese crime family for eight years, after the Chin Gigante went inside. In 2006, Matty faced indictments in both New York and Connecticut and went back to prison. After serving two more years, he walked free at last in April 2009.

One day while he was still in prison, Matty's wife came into the restaurant Dick was running at the time, Cami's Seafood in Miami. Dick expressed his condolences that his old pal had ended up in such a tough spot. "No, it's the best thing that ever happened to him," she said. "You know how big he was. He would have eaten himself to death by now. It's a good thing he's in a place where he can lose all that weight."

Sure enough, when Ianiello emerged from prison, he had trimmed down. He looked so fit that a journalist referred to him as a "spry" eighty-eight-year-old. He might not be the last gangster, but he was a guy who had lived through all the years of violence and was still above ground.

The Thunder Valley Hotel is a behemoth tower sixteen stories tall. The size of two football fields, the entire complex rises like an Emerald City over miles of dusty, flat Valley landscape thirty miles north of Sacramento, just south of nowhere.

Indian casinos are where show business careers go to die. Chubby Checker sits in his modest suite on the top occupied floor, the fourteenth, and readies himself for his evening performance. The seventy-year-old boss of the Twist, the greatest dance sensation in history, doesn't feel the respect he thinks he deserves.

"I have only one regret in my whole life," he says. "It's that my music is not being played and more people aren't seeing Chubby Checker. That's very painful for me. Many nights I have tears in my eyes about that. While I'm praying to God and thanking Him for all the good things, I ask, 'Why don't they play my music? Did I do something wrong?' It's not just any music—the number one song in the world, the only song to be number one twice—why don't they play my music? It's so painful. Why isn't Chubby getting his music played like the rest of the white boys?"

Pano Hall, the showroom at Thunder Valley, is a long way from a big room in Vegas—a boxy meeting room that seats nine hundred with a few lights and a cheesy backdrop behind the stage. Thunder Valley likes the older demographic. An Elvis impersonator is appearing the following night and the surviving member of the Righteous Brothers is coming at the end of the month. A collection of wheelchairs are parked beside the stage (rock-and-rolling, baby!).

Fifty years almost to the day that his record of "The Twist" went number one for an unprecedented second time, the high-water mark of a Twist mania that swept the globe, a moment in time when Chubby Checker was possibly the most famous entertainer on the planet, the man takes the stage at Thunder Valley looking remarkably like his twenty-year-old smiling self, emblazoned in the memories of those who were alive at the time.

He might have slowed his step, but he still has some moves. He entertains a procession of young, athletic women he selects from the audience to dance with him onstage—showing them how to do a dance called the Hucklebuck, which was originally "only done in the privacy of your own room because it was too nasty," he says.

Somehow Chubby makes it more naughty than nasty, which has always been his specialty. Dick Clark knew Chubby Checker could show America how to grind their pelvis on nationwide television and make it seem wholesome. That is Chubby's special gift. "What I bring to the stage is humility," he says. "I don't bring sex. I bring warmth."

On airplane reservations, he is still plain Ernest Evans. He says he is only Chubby Checker onstage. His latest record, in fact, is a bi-lingual gospel number by "Brother Evans." He lives in a remodeled colonial farmhouse on fourteen acres in Paoli, Pennsylvania, that he bought in February 1965 with his wife, the 1962 Miss World, Catha-rina Lodders of the Netherlands. They raised three children and have six grandchildren. "They range in colors from chocolate to gold to blond-haired and blue eyes," he says, "and they all look like me."

In many ways, it doesn't seem that Chubby is doing too badly. Be-tween wax museum shows at Branson, Missouri, and Indian casinos across the country, Checker still keeps up a healthy schedule of per-formances. Still, his Chubby Checker snack line of beef jerky and steaks, he says, is "struggling." He is not represented by a major agency or big-time management. He travels with a five-piece band and the guitarist doubles as road manager. He knows he is no longer top drawer. He dreams of a tour with the Beach Boys, also celebrat-ing a golden anniversary in 2012. He says he left a message for Beach Boys vocalist Mike Love, but hasn't heard back. The injustice of the situation does trouble him.

"Bob Seger, Rolling Stones, Kiss, Mellencamp, Aerosmith—the only difference between them and me is they get their records played," he says. "If my records were played, I would be downtown at the Sacramento Convention Center entertaining fifteen thousand people tonight."

It is a topic he can warm to.

"Alexander Graham Bell brought us the telephone," says Chubby. "He owns the telephones in the buildings. Thomas Edison owns the lightbulb. Whether they took it and did things to improve it, he's the guy. Now, on the dance floor, that belongs to Chubby Checker. Be-cause what Graham Bell did to the phone had been going on for cen-turies, but he did something that made it quite unique. And Edison, there were candlelights for many years, but he brought something else to light that made a difference. And to dance, we brought some-thing to it that made a difference. . . .

"Before Chubby Checker came along, when you went to a dance

and you were a teenager in the fifties and the guy wanted you to see what he looked like, he would stand up in his suit or pants so the girls could see the goods. The girls would also get up and talk to their girlfriends so the guys could check out the goods. Or they went to the bathroom.

"Now the Twist comes along and there's a girl out there—you don't even know who she is—and there's a guy out there and she's wondering what he looks like; he's sitting down. All of a sudden he points to her. She points to him and she nods her head and says, 'Yes, I will dance with you.' He gets up. She gets up. They're walking toward each other. He's now looking at everything's she's got and she's looking at him.

"All of a sudden they start dancing the Twist. Now he gets to see the front, the back, the side, the top, the bottom, all the moves. By the time the song is over, he's seen everything. She's seen everything and they're both having a heart attack."

The Twist was the biggest thing to happen in music between Elvis and the Beatles. Chubby Checker was the undisputed king of the Twist. He is the brand. That he has not been inducted into the Rock and Roll Hall of Fame doesn't seem right and he has not been shy about that, either.

"I told them that because of the importance of what we have given to the music industry and the music industry and the entertainers are still enjoying the great things Chubby Checker brought here, I should like for you to erect a statue of me in the courtyard of the Rock and Roll Hall of Fame inviting everybody in to rock and roll. Who is the best spokesman? Elvis? I don't think so."

Checker never exactly disappeared, but after "The Twist" went number one the second time in 1962, his days in the Top Ten ended later that same year with "Limbo Rock."

Until he was able to rehabilitate the brand, culminating in a return to the hit parade with rap stars the Fat Boys on a new version of "The Twist" in 1988, Checker suffered a long cultural exile, living in the irrelevance of county fairs and oldies-but-goodies shows. From where Chubby Checker has been for most of the past fifty years, Indian casinos look great. He stayed true to his code and has lived long enough to become a classic.

Onstage at Thunder Valley in jeans jacket and red T-shirt, he expertly coaxes the crowd into singing the "la-la-la" chorus of "Limbo Rock," bringing the place to the brink of, if not pandemonium, at least immodest enthusiasm, before unleashing the cathartic release of his concert performance of "The Twist." He has saved his secret weapon—the men in the audience.

After teasing women into shaking and squirming onstage with him all through the show, he finally brings out the males in the house ("Where are all the men?"), who prove to be somewhat less inhibited. The Twist is an opportunity for any exhibitionist. Chubby presides over the resulting mayhem like a satisfied ringmaster, running all three rings at once. After the show, he spends more than an hour signing photos and CDs at the merchandise table outside the hall in the casino.

In his suite that afternoon, he happily goes through his grievances. He makes his case without a trace of bitterness, his singsong voice barely above a whisper. Even arguing for his own redemption against lifelong injustices, Chubby Checker does it with a smile. That's how he sold the Twist to America.

The Peppermint Lounge? "I was there for twenty minutes one night," he says. "Everybody still says they met me there."

When it comes to the Twist, he is the king, the boss, the sine qua non, the one, true Twister. He is dismissive of pretenders ("Joey Dee played Chubby Checker music," he said, "because there wasn't any other Twist music but Chubby Checker music at that point.") and he is confident of his own contribution and his lack of recognition.

"*Billboard* named 'The Twist' the number one song from 1958 to 2008, on September 11, 2008. 'The Twist' was named the number one song of the last fifty years. The next time this event will take place will be September 11, 2058. 'The Twist' is the number one song of the sixties decade. The biggest song of the sixties began around the summer of 1960. That was Chubby Checker.

"We were the only people who had five LPs all in the top twelve at the same time," he says. "The only people who had anything close to that was the Beatles. They had the top five singles. They had number one, number two, number three, number four, and number five. What was the number one song that they had? 'Twist and Shout.' At their best, they were doing the Twist.

"Did you know that 'Let's Twist Again' was the first record to ever receive platinum? It became official in 1986. Do you know the first rock-and-roll record ever to receive a Grammy? It was 'Let's Twist Again.' How about that?"

Chubby traces his interest in singing to the time his mother took him to the Georgetown County Fair in South Carolina, where his father had a farm. He saw country star Ernest Tubb. "When I saw Ernest Tubb, I went, 'Yeah, this is what I want to do.' Fourteen years later, my dream had come true and I wasn't even out of high school. This was a blessing from God. The things I am talking about here, these are things that never happened to another singer who ever sang on the planet. They are God given and I know I am not being treated properly in the music industry. Can you understand this? Anyone who made a song that had a beat with it since Chubby made 'The Twist'—the dance floor is like the lightbulb and there's Chubby on the dance floor."

Chubby is right about one thing. The sun will never set on the Twist. It was a slight bend in the road in the history of Western civilization that altered the direction of everything that followed—a new angle on the sun. Centuries from now, as historians comb the detritus of a lost culture trying to understand the point where all hell started to break loose, they're going to find an old phonograph record with an orange label and a big hole in the center, the Rosetta stone of an entire civilization. And when they drop the needle, the voice of Chubby Checker is going to echo through the ages, making the naughty seem nice.

Acknowledgments

If a book is a journey from concept to completion, this has been a particularly tangled one, consuming many years and too many miles to tabulate.

The idea of telling the story of the Peppermint Lounge grew out of the lifelong friendship between nightclub owner Dick Cami and record-industry executive Dick Kline.

Kline had already been turned away at the door of New York's famous Peppermint Lounge when he moved to Miami in 1962 to take a job as regional promotion manager for London Records. His apartment on Harbor Island was just down the road from the Miami Peppermint, which Dick Cami had just opened with his father-in-law, Johnny "Futto" Biello.

"I'd blow in there whenever I was in town," Kline said. "Which was usually three or four times a week."

The two men grew close. Cami was naturally gregarious and, even if he wasn't, it paid to stay on good terms with record-industry types like Kline, who would eventually rise to senior vice president of Atlantic Records. Over the years, Cami and Kline became best friends.

Dick went to stay with Cami for a few days in 1984, by which time the Peppermint Lounges had become a part of history. As the days stretched into weeks, they began tossing around the idea of telling Cami's story of how the Mob secretly shaped sixties culture.

For years, the idea percolated. It was going to be a movie. In 1996, they signed with a producer. A top scriptwriter was hired, but things stalled, as they will. Stuck in turnaround purgatory at Jersey Films/Columbia Pictures, the two decided in 2001 to look for a book deal.

With Kline still very active in the record business and Cami running a restaurant in Arizona, the project lingered until Kline's friend, Dave Marsh, the Springsteen biographer and rock critic, referred him to Joel Selvin, the longtime pop music writer for the *San Francisco Chronicle*. Marsh knew that Selvin had done a lot of research into the Mob's influence in the music industry for a biography of songwriter Bert Berns ("Twist and Shout," "My Girl Sloopy").

Selvin was busy with other projects, so he told Kline that, as much as he liked the story, he couldn't take on the book. Once more, the project stalled, and this time it looked like it might be a permanent hiatus.

But Dick Kline is a very determined man. Five years later, with interest in the sixties soaring as a result of shows such as *Mad Men* and the fifty-year anniversary of the Twist looming, Kline called Selvin back.

As it happened, Selvin had recently retired from the *Chronicle*. This time, he was ready to participate and believed he had just the person to pitch in with the detailed research required of a story about the intersection of the Mob and the music business. He reached out to his old friend John Johnson Jr., who coincidentally had just left his position as a writer at the *Los Angeles Times*. Among his credits, Johnson had covered the Menendez murders for the paper and written a book about the killings in Beverly Hills.

The two friends had begun their journalism careers on the same college newspaper and had always thought about writing a book together.

Thus, this book is, with apologies to Dickens, a tale of two friendships, and of the persistence of an idea.

The authors must thank, first and foremost, the other pair of friends. Without Dick Cami, there would be no story. Without Dick (Dickie) Kline, there would be no book.

Sincere gratitude, too, is due for the help and assistance of the FBI's Records Management Division in Washington, D.C., especially Section Chief David M. Hardy and able researcher Bart Kenworthy. Bart went out of his way, and beyond the call of duty, to comb through Johnny Biello's 4,259-page FBI file to compile a detailed dossier of Biello's life and activities over the decades. Thanks also to retired FBI agent Peter Clemente, who personally trailed Biello, both in New York and Miami, developing a grudging respect for a man who, whatever one thought of it, lived and died by a strict code of honor that many of his Mafia brethren cast aside.

A number of fellow journalists helped in the process, starting with Marsh, who put Kline and Selvin together and continued to cheer from the sidelines. Domenic Priore, of course, knew all about the Peppermints in Hollywood. Deborah Schoch and Jim Ricci were attentive readers and kind, but rigorous, critics. Caryn Rose opened the door to the Peppermint's second coming (and the club's Facebook group, which also proved very helpful). Peter Guralnick seems always to be available to parse some detail of Sam Cooke's life and career. Kenny Laguna, as always, was extremely valuable.

Thanks to Barbara Anders, Ernest Evans, Ronnie Spector, Sarah Dash, Janet Huffsmith, and the many other people who shared their stories. Thanks, too, goes to Jonathan Greenfield. Also thanks to Tom Goodkind, Jim Fouratt, and Stefan Gosiewski for the story of the club in the eighties.

The services of our literary agent, Frank Weimann of the Literary Group, are deeply appreciated. Thanks also to Elyse Tanzillo at the agency.

The San Francisco Public Library deserves all the support and thanks it can get. Also thanks to the library of the *San Francisco*

Chronicle (Hi, Bill) and the excellent librarian at the *Los Angeles Times*, Scott Wilson, who, among other things, helped track down one of the world's first Go-Go dancers. Accommodations for this project were provided by Art Fein of Hollywood.

The authors also wish to thank one another for more than forty years of friendship.

Finally, thanks to Dylan Johnson and Carla Selvin for their love and support.

—John Johnson Jr. and Joel Selvin

My sincerest thanks to John Johnson Jr., former *Los Angeles Times* investigative crime reporter, for the two years he put in writing this book, fusing my experience with his diligent and detailed research of the organized crime stories in the book, some of which even I knew nothing about, including my father-in-law's 4,000-page FBI file. I am especially grateful for his dedicated expertise and professional persistence in bringing this book to completion.

Equal thanks to co-writer Joel Selvin, music critic and journalist for the *San Francisco Chronicle*, for all his writing and rewriting and, specifically, his invaluable help verifying all of my music stories included here.

This book would have never come about without the tenacious efforts of Dick Kline, my longtime friend and the former record executive and promotion man extraordinaire of King and Atlantic Records.

I acknowledge all the people who have helped me, directly or indirectly, as I have worked on this project. To my family and my two sons, John and Rich, I owe a long-term debt for their constant support and for putting up with me. A nod, too, to my former partner, Vinny Marchese, with whom it's always good to sit down, look back, and catch up. My very special thanks to Cindy Aumann, who has been by my side with love, encouragement, and editorial support during the process of writing stories for the book over the years.

As my father used to say, "'Tain't easy, McGee." It's not easy collaboratively writing a book, and many times those involved have been brought to the brink. I'm fortunate enough not to have gone over, and the fact that a couple of restaurants I opened were respectively named Crabby and Grumpy Dick's had nothing to do with anything . . . You know what I mean?

—Dick Cami

Bibliography

BOOKS

Betrock, Alan. *Girl Groups: The Story of a Sound*. New York: Delilah Books/ Putnam Publishing, 1982.

Bradford, Sarah. *America's Queen: The Life of Jacqueline Kennedy Onassis*. New York: Penguin Books, 2000.

Bradley, Lloyd. *This Is Reggae Music: The Story of Jamaica's Music*. New York: Grove Press, 2000.

Brewster, Bill, and Frank Broughton. *Last Night a DJ Saved My Life: The History of the Disc Jockey*. New York: Grove Press, 2000.

Bronson, Fred. *The Billboard Book of Number One Hits*. New York Billboard Books, 1992.

Carpozi, George. *Let's Twist*. New York: Pyramid Books, 1962.

Clark, Dick, and Richard Robinson. *Rock, Roll & Remember*. New York: Thomas Y. Crowell Company, 1976.

Cole, Clay. *Sh-Boom!: The Explosion of Rock 'N' Roll 1953–1968*. Garden City, N.Y.: Morgan James Publishing, 2009.

Collins, R. Thomas. *NewsWalker—A Story for Sweeney*. Vienna, Va.: RavensYard Publishing, 2001.

Davis, John H. *Mafia Dynasty: The Rise and Fall of the Gambino Crime Family*. New York: HarperCollins, 1993.

Dawson, Jim. *The Twist: The Story of the Song and Dance That Changed the World*. Boston: Faber and Faber, 1995.

Douglas, Susan J. *Where the Girls Are: Growing Up Female with the Mass Media*. New York: Three Rivers Press, 1994.

Ertegun, Ahmet, and others. *"What'd I Say": The Atlantic Story: 50 Years of Music*. New York: Welcome Rain, 2001.

Foster, Chuck. *Roots, Rock, Reggae: An Oral History of Reggae Music From Ska to Dancehall*. New York: Billboard Books, 1999.

Fox, Jon Hartley. *King of the Queen City: The Story of King Records*. Champaign: University of Illinois Press, 2009.

Goldman, Albert. *Disco*. New York: Hawthorn Books, 1978.

Guralnick, Peter. *Dream Boogie: The Triumph of Sam Cooke*. New York: Little, Brown and Company, 2005.

Haden-Guest, Anthony. *The Last Party: Studio 54, Disco, and the Culture of the Night*. New York: William Morrow, 1997.

Jackson, John A. *American Bandstand: Dick Clark and the Making of a Rock 'n' Roll Empire*. New York: Oxford, 1997.

James, Etta, and David Ritz. *Rage to Survive: The Etla James Story*. New York: Villard Books, 1995.

Joe, Radcliffe A. *This Business of Disco*. New York: Billboard Books, 1980.

Jones, Alan, and Jussi Kantonen. *Saturday Night Forever: The Story of Disco*. Chicago: A Cappella Books, 1999.

Katz, David. *Solid Foundation: An Oral History of Reggae*. London: Bloomsbury, 2003.

Kriplen, Nancy. *The Eccentric Billionaire: John D. MacArthur*. New York: AMACOM, 2008.

Lacey, Robert. *Little Man: Meyer Lansky and the Gangster Life*. New York: Little, Brown and Company, 1991.

Lawrence, Tim. *Love Saves the Day: A History of Dance Music Culture, 1970–1979*. Durham, N.C.: Duke University Press, 2003.

Lucchese, John A. *Joey Dee and the Story of the Twist*. New York: MacFadden Books, 1962.

Maas, Peter. *The Valachi Papers*. New York: Putnam, 1968.

Moore, Sam, and Dave Marsh. *Sam and Dave: An Oral History*. New York: Avon Books, 1998.

Nash, Jay Robert. *World Encyclopedia of Organized Crime*. Cambridge, Mass.: Da Capo Press, 1993.

Raab, Selwyn. *Five Families: The Rise, Decline, and Resurgence of America's Most Powerful Mafia Empires*. New York: Thomas Dunne Books/St. Martin's Press, 2005.

Rickles, Don, with David Ritz. *Rickles' Book: A Memoir*. New York: Simon and Schuster, 2007.

Schultheiss, Tom, ed. and comp. *A Day in the Life: The Beatles Day-By-Day 1960–1970*. Ann Arbor, Mich.: Pierian Press, 1980.

Shore, Michael, with Dick Clark. *The History of American Bandstand*. New York: Ballantine Books, 1985.

Spector, Ronnie, with Vince Waldron. *Be My Baby: How I Survived Mascara, Miniskirts and Madness, or My Life as a Fabulous Ronette*. New York: Harmony Books, 1990.

Teresa, Vincent, with Thomas C. Renner. *My Life in the Mafia*. New York: Doubleday, 1973.

Whitburn, Joel. *Top Pop Records 1955–1972*. Menomonee Falls, Wis.: Record Research, 1973.

———. *Top Rhythm and Blues Records 1949–1971*. Menomonee Falls, Wis.: Record Research, 1973.

Wolfe, Tom. *The Kandy-Kolored Tangerine-Flake Streamline Baby*. New York: Quality Paperback Book Club, 1999.

Wolff, Daniel, with S. R. Crain, Clifton White, and G. David Tenebaum. *You Send Me: The Life and Times of Sam Cooke*. New York: William Morrow, 1995.

ARTICLES, ETC.

"And now everybody is doing it." *Life*, November 24, 1961.

"Anybody for the Wobble?" *The New York Times Magazine*, November 11, 1962.

"Atlantic's Ahmet Ertegun Says the Public Will Keep Twistin'." *Billboard*, February 24, 1962.

"Café Society Rediscovers Harlem." *Ebony*, June 1962.

Checker, Chubby, and Geoffrey Holder. "To Twist or Not to Twist?" *The New York Times Magazine*, January 14, 1962.

"Chubby Checker—Singer Sparks 'Twist Craze.'" *Ebony*, January 1961.

"Crime Group Leader Said to Rule Many Businesses in Midtown." *The New York Times*, August 1, 1977.

"Der Liszt Twist." *Newsweek*, February 16, 1962.

"Ex-Mafia Man Slain in Miami Beach." *Miami Herald*, March 18, 1967.

"Five Hundred Greatest Songs of All Time." *Rolling Stone*, December 9, 2004.

"Has the Twist Had It?" *Billboard*, May 26, 1962.

"Instant Fad." *Time*, October 20, 1961.

"Jury Hears About Skimming." *The New York Times*, November 27, 1985.

Kamp, David. "Live at the Whisky." *Vanity Fair*, September 2006.

Kolanjian, Steve, with David Brigati and Kate Blacklock. "Hey Let's Twist: The Best of Joey Dee and the Starliters." Liner notes, Rhino Records, 1990.

"Lehigh Acres: Florida's Lesson in Unregulated Growth." *Tampa Bay Times*, August 9, 2009.

"Let's Twist Again: Chubby Checker on the dance and song he took to No. 1 50 years ago." *San Francisco Chronicle Sunday Datebook*, January 29, 2012.

"The Museum Jewel Robbery." *Time*, November 6, 1964.

"Nine of Ten Found Guilty in Skimming Trial." *The New York Times*, December 31, 1985.

"Peppermint Lounge Goes Dark." *The New York Times*, December 28, 1965.

"The Sacroili-act." *Newsweek*, December 4, 1961.

"So What Is the Attitude at the Beach." *The Miami Herald*, February 15, 1964.

Stone, Henry. "Heart of Stone: The Henry Stone Story." Liner notes, Henstone Music, 2002.

Talese, Gay. "Harlem for Fun." *Esquire*, September 1962.

"Teens Go Buggy Over Beatles; They Let Their Hair Down." *Miami News*, February 14, 1964.

"Turkey Trot to Twist." *The New York Times Magazine*, January 14, 1962.

"Twist: New Dance Step at Peppermint Lounge." *The New Yorker*, October 21, 1961.

"'Twist' Wiggles into Big Time." *Business Week*, December 2, 1961.

United States Senate. Select Committee on Improper Activities in the Labor Field. Sen. John L. McClellan, chairman. April 29, 1957.

Wolcott, James. "A Twist in Time." *Vanity Fair*, November 2007.

Index